Aspects of Colonial Tanzania History

Lawrence E. Y. Mbogoni

D1519685

MKUKI NA NYOTA
DAR – ES – SALAAM

PUBLISHED BY
Mkuki na Nyota Publishers Ltd
P. O. Box 4246
Dar es Salaam, Tanzania
www.mkukinanyota.com

© Lawrence E. Y. Mbogoni, 2013

ISBN 978-9987-08-300-8

Visit www.mkukinanyota.com to read more about and to purchase any of Mkuki na Nyota books. You will also find featured authors, interviews and news about other publisher/author events. Sign up for our e-newsletters for updates on new releases and other announcements.

Distributed world wide outside Africa by African Books Collective.
www.africanbookscollective.com

Contents

Acknowledgements

Research for this collection of essays spanned a number of years and involved numerous visits to research libraries and archives in the United States of America, the United Kingdom and Tanzania. In due course I have accumulated a mountain of scholarly debt to many people that I cannot all mention by name. To begin with, I would like to thank Judy Matthew, Jeneen Artis and Urooj Khan from the Interlibrary Loan Section of the Cheng Library at William Paterson University for their diligent assistance. During the 1990s while at Luther College, Iowa, I received financial support which enabled me to travel to Caversham, England, where I worked on the BBC archives for the essay on radio broadcasting in Tanganyika as well as to make several trips to the Public Record Office, London, for research on the essays on the trial of Oldus Elishira and the case of Chief Makongoro. Last but not least, many thanks to my family without whose moral support it would have been near impossible to accomplish this book project.

PART ONE

Economy and Politics in Tanganyika

1

Colonialism as a "Civilizing Mission"

I have tried in this collection of essays to examine the impact of colonialism and colonial rule upon the lives and experiences of the colonizers and the colonized in what is today known as Tanzania. Modern day Tanzania comprises of the mainland, which was from 1919 until 1963 known as Tanganyika, and the Islands of Unguja and Pemba which historically have been known under the name Zanzibar. Before 1919 Tanganyika was a German colony and was known as German East Africa. The British took over its administration after the defeat of Germany in World War I. Until 1890 when Zanzibar became a British protectorate it was a sovereign state under the rule of Oman Arabs. Tanganyika received its independence in December 1961 whereas Zanzibar became independent in December 1963. Tanganyika and Zanzibar united in April 1964 to form the United Republic of Tanzania.

It is commonly understood that nineteenth century British imperialism was driven by the needs and demands of industrialization such as (a) the need to secure new sources of raw materials, (b) to open new markets for manufactured goods, and (c) to create global outlets for capital investments. However, it was the presumption of British racial, cultural and moral superiority that bolstered Britain's justification for colonial rule. Like other Europeans, nineteenth century Britons believed they had a "mission to civilize" their African colonial subjects.

The *Oxford English Dictionary* (*OED*) defines the verb "to civilize" as follows: "to make civil; to bring out of a state of barbarism; to instruct in the arts of life; to enlighten; to refine and polish." The *OED* also defines civilization as "the action or process of civilizing or of being civilized; a developed or advanced state of human society." These definitions seem to refer to the behavioral and material aspects of human cultures as well as to different stages of advancement. Used in either sense, the British labeled themselves "civilized" to set themselves apart from the Africans whom they considered barbarians, savages, and primitive people.

The standard bearers of the British "mission to civilize" were, first and foremost, the officers of the Colonial Service. They were expected to live exemplary lives according to British mores. More importantly, they were not supposed to behave in ways that brought disrepute to the Colonial Service. Besides the officers of the Colonial Service any white person was also expected to live and behave in ways that did not undermine European racial superiority in the eyes of the colonized. These expectations reveal the anxieties of the British ruling class which deeply undercut its pride in the British sense of self-worth. One of the anxieties was whether or not Britons abroad would "go native" and be tempted to behave in un-British ways. This concern was not without merit.

Many junior officers of the Colonial Service not only lived in isolated stations but also led lonely lives. One of the terms of their employment was that for a number of years they were not expected to marry. For some the effects of isolation and loneliness were devastating. Col. R. Meinertzhagen, a district officer in neighboring Kenya from 1902 to 1906, published his *Kenya Diary* in 1957 in which he recounts the effects of his isolation and loneliness. The entry dated September 15, 1905 is worth quoting at length and goes as follows:

> *The feeling of slowly becoming a prey to one's own mind has taken possession of me, and I have been experiencing much difficulty in constantly finding some distracting work. In daylight I can usually find sufficient to occupy my mind, but in the evenings time hangs heavily on my hands, and except when I write or endeavour to use my paint box, needs must I brood and worry over things which will not leave my mind. I think it is a family inherited from the Potters. But climatic influences have a good deal to do with mental depression and tend to accentuate any feelings of morbid dissatisfaction with life in general. I have tried to analyse my mind and find that what worries me most is disappointment and bitterness that my own family seems to regard me as a black sheep.*

> *Local conditions in Nandi only accentuate these feelings. Living isolated in a savage country, rarely speaking my own language, and surrounded by a population whose civilization is on a much lower plane than my own are conditions to which I have indeed grown accustomed, but which do not improve on acquaintance unless one lowers one's own plane to that of the savage, when perhaps one might be contented.*

> *Normally I am healthy-minded, but the worries and conditions of the past few months have been too much for me. All men are not affected in the same way. Others with greater strength of character than myself might suffer little from moral and intellectual starvation. To others, natural history or some object of unceasing pursuit is an effective barrier against complete isolation. But my experience shows me that it is but a small percentage of white men whose characters do not in one way or another undergo a subtle process of deterioration when they are compelled to live for any length of time among*

savage races and under such conditions as exist in tropical climates. It is hard to resist the savagery of Africa when one falls under its spell. One soon reverts to one's ancestral character, both mind and temperament becoming brutalised. I have so much of it out here and I have myself felt the magnetic power of the African climate drawing me lower and lower to the level of the savage. This is a condition that is accentuated by worry or mental depression, and which has to be combated with all the force in one's power. My love of home and family, the dread of being eventually overcome by savage Africa, the horror of losing one's veneer of western civilization and cutting adrift from all one holds good – these are the forces which help me to fight the temptation to drift down to the temporary luxury of the civilisation of the savage.[1]

The overriding fear about Britons abroad "going native" was that they would engage in sexual intercourse with native women. This fear was also not without merit. For instance, Judd has shown that the British Empire offered opportunities to engage in forms of sexual behavior that would have been difficult, if not downright impossible, at home.[2] As Chapter 2 will make clear, after 1909 the British Colonial Office deemed it necessary to issue a Circular that condemned interracial concubinage as an "injurious and dangerous" evil.[3] Chapter 2 examines the claims by J. R. Cresswell-George that some Europeans in Tanganyika lacked self-respect, molested African women and engaged in excessive consumption of alcohol. He complained to the Colonial Office that such behavior lowered the dignity and prestige of the British which was essential if they were to succeed in their "mission to civilize" their African subjects.

Tanganyika was a place where fortunes could be made by those whose opportunities were limited by their circumstances in Britain. Cresswell-George would not have made his complaints about licentiousness and alcoholism in Tanganyika had he not followed his brother to try his luck on the Lupa gold fields. Others sought their fortunes in other ways such as hunting. Unlike neighboring Kenya and Uganda, Tanganyika's wildlife offered more opportunities for big game hunting. It was the chance to earn a fortune from ivory hunting that attracted George Gilman Rushby to Tanganyika. His career as a poacher and game ranger in Tanganyika is the subject of Chapter 3.

In Tanganyika, the distinctions between the colonizers and the colonized took many different forms. The distinction of race resulted in racial discrimination. For instance, European government servants were accorded rights and privileges that were denied to African government servants. Every European government employee, however humble, had a right of appeal to the Secretary of State for the Colonies if he had a grievance. This is clearly demonstrated by the case of Chief Makongoro of Ikizu, Musoma District, examined in Chapter 4. On the one hand, unlike George Gilman Rushby Chief Makongoro was accused of poaching, tried, found guilty, and deposed. On the other hand, as chief of Ikizu he was a salaried servant of the colonial government. However, because he was African he

---

1   Meinertzhagen, R. *Kenya Diary: 1902 – 1906* (Edinburgh: Tweeddale Court; London: Oliver and Boyd, 1957): 217 – 219.

2   Judd, Denis, *Empire: The British Imperial Experience from 1765 to the Present* (London: Phoenix Press, 1996): 172.

3   Hyam, Ronald, "Concubinage and the Colonial Service: The Crewe Circular (1909)," *Journal of Imperial and Commonwealth History*, Vol. XIV (1986): 170 - 186: 171.

did not have the right that European colonial officials had to appeal his case to the Secretary of State for Colonies.

Tanganyika was not a settler colony like Kenya. However, by the 1950s it had attracted a small white settler community of about 25,000. The settlers acquired land ownership rights (in the form of leaseholds) in different parts of Tanganyika; many were especially attracted to the Southern Highlands and the Northern Province which included Arusha and Kilimanjaro Districts. Relations between the settlers and local African communities varied from relative harmony in the Southern Highlands to latent hostility in the Northern Province. In the latter settler concerns about personal safety and the safety of property created a "siege mentality" which motivated the settlers to arm themselves and to acts of vigilantism.

The settlers' sense of insecurity in the Northern Province was exacerbated by lack of effective policing of the region[4] and an increase in offenses against the person and against property. A territory-wide picture of the crime rates against the person and against property is reflected in Graphs 1 and 2 below. Table I indicates the number of cases and amount of stock stolen in the Northern Province from 1954 to 1959.

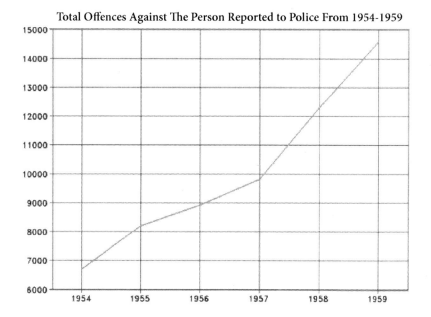

Total Offences Against The Person Reported to Police From 1954-1959

---

4   The Police Department Annual Report for 1954 shows a territory-wide police force numbering 4,196 in a country with an estimated population of 9 million spread over more than 360,000 square miles. These statistics give a ratio of 1:1,733 or 1:72 square miles.

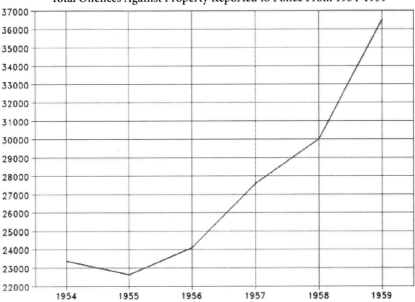

Total Offences Against Property Reported to Police From 1954-1959

Table I: Number of Theft Cases and Stock Stolen in Northern Province

Year	Cases Reported	Number of Stock Stolen	Number of Stock Recovered
1954	341	2,811	1,357
1955	307	2,519	916
1956	367	1,952	981
1957	365	2,910	1,606
1958	300	N/A	N/A
1959	468	N/A	N/A

In the Northern Province individual settler farmers took it upon themselves to protect themselves and their property by employing guards and by doing their own "policing" such as "arresting" trespassers. As Chapter 5 will make clear, those "arrested" by the settlers did not take kindly to such treatment. Harold M. Stuchbery was murdered as he attempted to "arrest" Oldus Elishira for trespassing.

The colonial authorities in Tanganyika required more than the police to maintain law and order as well as to actualize the claims of empire as a civilizing mission. Although chiefs acted as conduits of information from the government to the people the government still considered it necessary to create mass means of communication. Newspapers were the earliest to be introduced although their effectiveness in disseminating information was limited by the illiteracy of the majority of Africans. Unlike newspapers, film and other forms of electronic communication like radio were regarded as especially useful media for reaching the primarily illiterate audiences that were the targets of community development.[5] Thus between 1920 and 1940 agents of the British government produced dozens of films whose objectives were to teach colonial audiences agricultural and medical techniques while others were designed to raise awareness about issues of hygiene and public health.[6] Besides being used for instructional purposes films served as instruments of propaganda and became a staple of imperial governance in British territories in Africa, Asia and the Caribbean.

Chapter 6 examines the origins of colonial film production in Tanganyika and the endeavor to "civilize" the colonized with film shot on location in recognizable village sites. All of the films that were made in Tanganyika were didactic short films on topics of health and hygiene, animal husbandry and cooperative economics. Others advertized the institutions (i.e. the Police, the Post Office), the infrastructures and the personnel of colonial rule. The producers wanted the films to be both instructive and entertaining.[7] They also strove to make the films understandable to the illiterate peasant.[8] The mobile-cinema-display teams covered great distances and aimed at as broad an audience as possible.

Whereas instructional/educational cinema was intended to speak to the Tanganyikan's mind by visible demonstration radio was intended to influence him by word of mouth. By the early 1920s Britain and other countries with imperial interests focused attention on the power of radio, in particular of shortwave, for communications, albeit for the benefit of the military and both radio amateur and commercial sectors.[9] In Britain commercial radio broadcasting began in 1922. In East Africa, the first transmission station was built in Kenya, Tanganyika's neighbor to the north, in 1928. Initially the station, owned by British East African Broadcasting Company, simply served as a relay station for the BBC Empire Service broadcasts which were in English and were intended to provide European settlers and administrators with a touch of "home away from home."[10]

Radio broadcasting in Tanganyika began in 1951 when the construction of a modest transmitter at Dar-es-Salaam was completed. At first listenership was restricted to Dar-es-Salaam, Tanganyika's capital located on the shore of the Indian Ocean. However, with the installation of a more powerful transmitter the station was able to be heard upcountry. Soon the "magic" of listening to a voice coming from far away Dar-es-Salaam not only popularized listening to the radio but contributed to a tremendous growth in radio ownership. Chapter 7 examines the history of radio broadcasting in colonial Tanganyika focusing on its broadcasting as a propaganda and educational tool.

✳   ✳   ✳

---

5   Windel, Aaron, "The Bantu Educational Kinema Experiment and the Political Economy of Community Development," in Lee Grieveson and Colin MacCabe, eds. *Empire and Film* (London: Palgrave Macmillan, 2011): 207.

6   Burns, James, "American Philanthropy and Colonial Film-Making: The Rockefeller Foundation, the Carnegie Corporation and the Birth of Colonial Cinema," in Lee Grieveson and Colin MacCabe, eds. *Empire and Film* (London: Palgrave Macmillan, 2011): 55.

7   Windel, "The Bantu Educational Kinema Experiment," 212.

8   For Tanganyika audiences explanations of the films were given in Kiswahili.

9   Anduaga, Aitor, *Wireless and Empire: Geopolitics, Radio Industry, and Ionosphere in the British Empire, 1918 – 1939* (Oxford: Oxford University Press, 2009): xvii.

10 Browne, Donald R. "International Broadcasts to African Audiences," in Sydney W. Head, ed. *Broadcasting in Africa: A Continental Survey of Radio and Television* (Philadelphia: Temple University Press, 1972): 176.

Nineteenth century Zanzibar was a destination for peoples from the Gulf States, India, Europe and America. Zanzibar's fame was the result of Seyyid Said bin Sultan al-Busaid's endeavor to turn it into an emporium of Eastern Africa. When he died in 1856 Zanzibar already enjoyed consular and commercial relations with Britain, France and the United States of America as well as the Hanseatic States. Every company that conducted business in Zanzibar had an agent stationed there. When Zanzibar became a British Protectorate in 1890 its European community included British civil servants under a British Resident.

Zanzibar was deemed to be an unhealthy place for Europeans as pertaining to sanitation, disease, and climate. Capt. Richard F. Burton, who arrived at Zanzibar in December 1856, described Zanzibar's shore as a cess-pool in which corpses floated at times upon the heavy water.[11] Zanzibar's killer diseases mentioned by Burton included dysentery, yellow fever, and inflammation of the neck of the vesica, cholera, and malaria. Burton identified the source of these fatal diseases to be lack of drainage.[12] However, according to Burton even if Zanzibar could be drained into comparative healthiness its double seasons and its uniformly heated and humid atmosphere would still accord ill with the irritable temperament of northern races.[13]

The scramble and partition of Africa toward the end of the nineteenth century brought to the fore disease and health concerns about tropical areas such as Zanzibar that Burton and others raised earlier. Could European colonization and settlement of the tropics be undertaken without negative consequences? On the one hand, there were those like Dr. Luigi (Louis) Westenra Sambon who believed that Europeans could easily adapt to tropical climates. On the other hand, there were those who believed that European acclimatization to tropical climates was impossible. In the words of Ernest G. Ravenstein, "To render tropical countries fit places of residence for European colonists it will be necessary either to change the constitution of Europeans or to bring about a change in the climate."[14]

For Europeans who ventured to tropical regions such as Zanzibar their major concern was how to live there: "To survive in the tropics, the physical body needed to observe a rigid routine of hygienic habit, including the wearing of such special tropical apparel as the flannel binder, the solar topi and the 'solaro'. At the same time, a no less rigorous regimen of moral hygiene had to be followed if degeneration was to be avoided."[15] As Chapter 8 will show, Dr. Pitchford not only contravened medical regulations against engaging in a sexual liaison with a patient but blamed his infatuation with Miss Gool Talati on Zanzibar's climate. He attributed his infatuation with Miss Talati to a condition that was then known as neurasthenia – a condition associated at the time with decline in reasoning which could be recovered only by the bracing influence of a northern winter.

Europeans and Americans who travelled and resided in Zanzibar did so for commercial and other reasons. Whatever their reasons for traveling to Zanzibar, in the Western imagination the name Zanzibar was not only associated with "exotic"

---

11 Burton, Richard F. *Zanzibar; City, Island, and Coast*, 2 Volumes, Vol. I (London: Tinsley Brothers, 1872): 80.

12 Ibid. 102.

13 Ibid. 177.

14 Quoted by David N. Livingstone, "Tropical Climate and Moral Hygiene: The Anatomy of a Victorian Debate," *The British Journal for the History of Science*, Vol. 32, No. 1 (Mar., 1999): 93 – 110: 99.

15 Ibid. 109.

treasures such as sandal-wood boxes inlaid with mother-of-pearl; cashmere shawls, heavy brocades, camphor wood chests and ivory but also conjured images of "exotic" women locked up in harems. The latter was the reason why George A. Cheney, an American merchant aboard the *Sacramento* which dropped anchor at Zanzibar on July 11, 1850, wanted to spy on the Sultan's harem which was directly opposite the harbor. From his diary we read: "The harem is not a magnificent edifice. There are some much handsomer buildings in the city. This is a large, square, black-looking old stone building, more like a prison than anything else. In fact, it is a prison for the women there. They cannot get out. The windows are barred and guards are stationed outside."[16]

Cheney's imagination of harem life and his desire to spy on its "inmates" had caused him to bring along a telescope the use of which, according to his diary, enabled him to become somewhat acquainted with one of the daughters of the Sultan, whom he calls Lady Bebe Holy.[17] After the description of the Sultan's harem above, his diary entry continues:

> *I became somewhat acquainted with one of the daughters of the Sultan, Lady Bebe Holy. It happened in this way. After we came to anchor, I was looking at the Harem through the glass and at one of the windows I saw a lady doing likewise. I lifted my cap to her; she returned the salute. The next day a slave came on board with some nick nack or other. I sent something back. Well, something used to come off nearly every day and I used to hold a sort of conversation with her through the glass. . . Sometimes there would be a young lady with her without a mask. I found out from the slave who brought off the things that the one with the mask was Sayyid Said's daughter and the other was his wife, a Persian girl, daughter of the King of Persia[18]. . . She came to Zanzibar some four years ago; she was then but fifteen. . . Her skin is very white, her eyes piercing black, her hair jet black. (I have a sample of it). . . Lady Bebe's dress I cannot describe. She was dark-complexioned, with large, almond-shaped eyes and jet black hair. Her eyes were her handsomest feature. They were certainly very beautiful.[19]*

From Cheney's diary we learn that he developed a closer relationship with Sehesade than with Khole. Cheney and Sehesade would sometimes chat by some window of the palace by means of signs, some few words of English, and Cheney's halting Swahili. During one of these chats Cheney showed Sehesade his fiancée Sarah's picture: "She wanted to take it into her hand and sent a slave to fetch it. I was foolish enough to let it go. I never saw it again."[20] Years later Cheney was to learn that Seyyid Said had found out about these encounters and, the day after he sailed,[21] had removed her to a more secluded house and soon thereafter had sent her back to Persia.

16 Downing, Harriet C. "Tales of Zanzibar," mimeograph dated January 5, 1942, Ivoryton Library, Connecticut.

17 This was none other than Khole. According to the memoir of her half-sister Salme aka Emily Ruete she was a girl of rare beauty. See Emily Ruete, *Memoirs of an Arabian Princess from Zanzibar* (New York: Markus Wiener Publishing, 1989): 27.

18 Her name was Sehesade. This is the spelling given by Ruete, *Memoirs*, 44.

19 Downing, "Tales of Zanzibar," 8.

20 Cheney's diary entry of the date of his departure is September 1, 1850.

21 Ruete, *Memoirs*, 44.

However, there is probably more to Cheney's encounters with Sehesade than he admits in his diary. According to Ruete, Sehesade occasionally left the palace. Could she and Cheney have physically met? Were they in love? Ruete hints that Sehesade had only married her father for his high station and his wealth, "and had loved some one else all the time. He was about to protest her conduct one day on her return from one of her excursions, and it was on this occasion that faithful old Nubi had saved him from committing a great crime."[22]

The story about Cheney's spying and acquaintance with Khole and Sehesade indicates that the women of the Sultan's harem found ways to circumvent their seclusion. As Chapter 9 will show, where there is a will there is a way. Chapter 9 examines the love affair between Seyyida (princess) Salme and Heinrich Ruete, a German merchant. The couple did not only find a way of getting acquainted with one another but were able to meet physically. Eventually they eloped and got married in Aden. The chapter also examines the consequences of this inter-racial marriage of a couple who subscribed to different religious faiths, namely Christianity and Islam.

During the nineteenth and early twentieth century inter-racial sexual liaisons between Europeans and Africans/Arabs in Zanzibar were the exception rather than the norm. What was the norm were inter-racial sexual liaisons between Arab men and African women. According to Villiers, sailors from Arabia eagerly looked forward to their arrival in Zanzibar where they could carouse with the local women who were supposed to be the best in the Indian Ocean.[23] Villiers quotes a sailor, one Yusuf, who disapproved of such women as being too free to take in marriage: "By the age of twelve the women had acquired an insatiable taste for variety which made them poor spouses for any man, most of all for a sailor."[24] For Yusuf, since a prostitute was there for the taking it was of no use marrying one. This attitude applied to the eager maidens of the Gulf of Arabia who were available on a casual basis. They served as prostitutes but not as mothers for a respectable man's sons.

In nineteenth and early twentieth century Zanzibar sexual exploitation of African women and men was greatly facilitated by slavery. Slavery provided Arab men the opportunity to abuse their female and male African slaves. However, besides sexual exploitation other adverse consequences of slavery in Zanzibar have not been explicitly examined by students of Zanzibar history. Chapter 10 examines an exchange between two Makerere University students from Zanzibar during the 1930s who disagreed about the nature of slavery in Zanzibar; the essay highlights the most nefarious consequences of the slave trade and slavery in Zanzibar.

Lastly, the legacy of slavery and British inability to steer Zanzibar toward majority rule polarized the society along racial lines, the Arabs on the one hand and the Africans on the other. Failure to move beyond racial politics created hostilities that led to bloodshed in the elections of June 1961. Chapter 11 examines the issue of race and racial identity in Zanzibar during the crucial transitional period to self-government and provides an account of events during and after the June elections.

---

22 Villiers, Alan, *Sons of Sinbad; an account of sailing with the Arabs in their dhows, in the Red Sea, around the coasts of Arabia, and to Zanzibar and Tanganyika; pearling in the Persian Gulf; and the life of the shipmasters, the mariners, and merchants of Kuwait* (New York: Scribner, 1969): 185.

23 Ibid. 200.

24 Ibid. 200.

2

The Lupa Gold Rush of the 1930s

Introduction

On March 9, 1938, J. R. Cresswell-George wrote to the editor of *East Africa & Rhodesia* about what he perceived at the time to be an increasing tendency to have little regard for self-respect, and still less thought to the maintenance of the dignity and prestige of the British especially in the outlying districts of colonial Tanganyika. He noted that there appeared to be "a blatant disregard of morals, excessive indulgence in alcohol, and unfortunately, quite a few women are the worse for the mal-influence of alcohol, all of which is having a damaging effect on the minds of the natives and lowering British prestige."[25] Even more alarming to George were cases "of white men (so called) who think fit to molest native women, (or keeping native wives as they call it) – can there be anything more degrading! . . . With all this sort of thing going on, can we, as a white race justify our claims to superiority with our higher standards of civilization?"[26] The editor declined to publish George's letter on the excuse that it might be used for propaganda by the Germans.

Undeterred, on March 14, Cresswell-George wrote to E. A. Boyd at the Colonial Office to reiterate his concerns about "the very serious offence of white

25.   Public Record Office (PRO), CO 691/165/4 Allegations by J. R. Cresswell George of the immorality amongst Government officials in Tanganyika, letter dated March 9, 1938.

26.   Ibid.

men molesting native women."[27] Although he had no concrete evidence of any Government officials (such as PC, DO, and ADOs) being implicated, he had very good reason to believe that there were officials who were not above reproach in such offences. He suggested that medical records at the Dar es Salaam Hospital could be checked for cases of Government officials being admitted for venereal disease treatment or skin diseases. Cresswell-George also requested an audience with Boyd to further discuss this issue.

However, Boyd was not inclined to meet with Cresswell-George; instead he arranged a meeting between George and D. M. Kennedy, Tanganyika's Chief Secretary, who was then in London on leave. Following their meeting, Kennedy briefed Boyd about his conversation with Cresswell-George. According to Kennedy, George was "an honest, teetotal, crusader", who left his job in England to join his brother, E.V.H. Cresswell-George, who was already established in the Lupa goldfields. He returned to England in August 1937 because he "did not fit in."[28] According to Kennedy life in the Lupa goldfields had shocked Cresswell-George given that "gold miners do not, as a rule, live according to the conventions of a London suburb in the eighties!"[29]

Although Kennedy respected Cresswell-George's "prejudices", he told Boyd he felt that Cresswell-George had allowed himself to be led into making wholesale and general charges by picking up rumors and gossip on the field.[30] Apparently, a Government medical officer had told George that he would be surprised at the number of cases of V.D. amongst officials and that a retired official had mentioned a certain administrative officer whose wife had left him because of his extra conjugal habits.

Kennedy told Boyd that he was able to convince Cresswell-George that complaining to members of parliament and writing letters to newspapers were not the correct media for the transmission of his views in "a matter in which his information was palpably sketchy and that local government was quite competent to maintain discipline." Boyd was thankful to Kennedy for persuading Cresswell-George not to make public vague charges of immorality in Tanganyika that could have given everyone around a lot of trouble.[31]

However, Cresswell-George's concerns about interracial sexual liaisons and alcoholism in the margins of the British Empire were not a figment of his imagination. Besides reflecting the moral rhetoric of late Victorian and Edwardian England, their validity is ascertained by government efforts to address these problems by means of legislation. British government officials in the colonies and mandated territories were officially prohibited by Circular B of 1909[32] from cohabiting with native women. Lord Crewe, the Secretary of State for the Colonies, noted why this was unacceptable:

> *The moral objections to such conduct are so generally recognised that it is unnecessary to dwell on them. There is, however, another aspect of*

27.   PRO CO 691/165/4 Cresswell George to E. A. Boyd, letter dated March 14th.
28.   PRO CO 691/165/4 Kennedy to Boyd, letter dated June 28, 1938.
29.   Ibid.
30.   Ibid.
31.   PRO CO 691/165/4, Boyd to Kennedy, letter dated June 6, 1938.
32.   Lord Crewe was the Secretary of State for the Colonies.

this question on which I must lay stress, namely, the grave injury to good administration which must inevitably result from such ill conduct between Government officials and native women.

Gravely improper conduct of this nature has at times been the cause of serious trouble among native populations, and must be strenuously condemned on that account; but an objection even more serious from the standpoint of the Government lies in the fact that it is not possible for any member of the administration to countenance such practices without lowering himself in the eyes of the natives, and diminishing his authority to an extent which will seriously impair his capacity for useful work in the Service in which it is his duty to strive to set an honourable example to all with whom he comes in contact.

I am anxious to make it clear that this circular is not intended to cast any reflection upon those who are about to be admitted into the ranks of an honourable profession. Its object is simply to advise those who enter the service of a danger in their path, and to warn them of the disgrace and official ruin which will certainly follow from any dereliction of duty in this respect.[33]

Unlike the French, the British were not cognizant of the sexual needs of their colonial personnel to make allowance of even "temporary" unions with local women. In colonial Tanganyika, the colonial civil service and commercial staff was not only male oriented but very few of the junior officials, who constituted the majority, were accompanied by wives. This was reflected by the type of housing provided both by Government and commercial firms for their expatriate staff.[34] Many of the single Europeans or those whose wives were on home leave were members of the Dar-es-Salaam Club and used its facilities for lunch and dinner, etc.[35]

The Colonial Office was also very much concerned about alcohol and drunkenness in the colonies. In England itself, strong feelings against alcohol and attempts to encourage temperance, if not abstinence, date back to the beginning of the nineteenth century.[36] During the period from the late 1850s to the mid 1870s attention was focused on experiments to inhibit the sale of alcohol through legislative action.[37] Although the experiments in England failed, the use of legislation was pursued in the colonies where legislation was especially intended to control African access to European alcoholic beverages.

In colonial Tanganyika, *Government Notice, dated May 24, 1920,* prohibited the import of (1) Trade spirits of every kind and beverages mixed with these spirits; (2) Distilled beverages containing injurious substances. *Government Notice No. 212, dated October 13, 1921,* prohibited the import of all spirits (other than gin, geneva, hollands, schnapps or liqueurs) for human consumption, unless these spirits had been matured in wood for not less than two years. *Government Notice No. 172, of November 6, 1928,* prohibited the import of distilling apparatus and machinery except under a permit issued by the Chief Secretary to the Government.

33.   PRO CO 850/4714, "The Crewe Circular of 1909."

34.   Crow, Richard D. "Tanganyika in the 1940/50's," (n.d.): 1.

35.   Ibid. 4.

36.   Harrison, Brian H. *Drink and the Victorians: the temperance question in England, 1815-1872* (Pittsburgh: University of Pittsburgh Press, 1971).

37.   Shiman, Lilian L. *Crusade against Drink in Victorian England* (New York: St. Martin's Press, 1988): 4.

Moreover, Article 48, of the *Intoxicating Liquor Ordinance, 1923,* prohibited any person from supplying any intoxicating liquor to Africans and no African could consume or have in their possession any intoxicating liquor. However, Africans could be employed as messengers or servants to carry or serve intoxicating liquor. Any such employees were not supposed to be under the age of 16 years.

The Native Liquor Ordinance, 1923, regulated the manufacture, sale and consumption of African intoxicating liquors. This Ordinance was in force in townships only, but could be extended by regulation to any part of the territory.[38] The term *"native liquor",* employed in the Ordinance, meant pombe,[39] fermented asali,[40] tembo,[41] and all liquors prepared by Africans or of a kind usually prepared by Africans which contained more than one per cent by weight of absolute alcohol, and any liquor which could be declared by regulation to be an African liquor. Article 18 of the Ordinance stipulated that African liquor could not be sold to Africans in Government employ during their hours of work, or, as a general rule, to any African members of the military or police forces. The licensing officer could order that African liquor not be supplied to Africans who by excessive drinking of such liquor were injuring their health or were unable to support themselves or their families.

Whereas colonial legislation aimed at preventing African access to liquor, wine, beer and other European-type beverages, the Colonial Office was also concerned about European drunkenness among government civil servants. Its policies toward alcohol use in the colonies, especially in Africa, was outlined in its 1897 publication titled *Hints on the Outfit and Preservation of Health on the West Coast of Africa,* in which abstention and moderation were encouraged.[42] Candidates for the British Colonial Service were subject to medical examinations for evidence of alcoholism. From 1898-1904,[43] 3846 medical examinations were conducted in which physical symptomology was used for purposes of identification. Although only 79 candidates (2%), who were all male, exhibited evidence of alcoholism,[44] there was no guarantee that once in Africa those who were teetotalers or moderate drinkers would not engage in excessive drinking.

In Tanganyika, European lifestyles before the Great Depression came close to being outlandish. A firsthand account written by Eric Reid, MBE, is worth quoting at length:

> *In the years preceding the depression of 1930 most of the white inhabitants of Tanganyika admittedly lost all sense of proportion both in public expenditure and in their private scales of living. A period of unprecedented prosperity upset the sense of values of most of the world. The "boom" in Tanganyika and the high prices obtained for produce resulted in a large increase both in the numbers and salaries of Government officials and Native employees.*

---

38.   Government Notice No. 145, of September 29, 1928 (Supplement to the *Tanganyika Territory Gazette,* Volume IX, No. 45, dated October 5, 1928, page 160), extended the Ordinance to the Lupa goldfields.

39.   An alcoholic beverage made of fermented millet or corn flour.

40.   An alcoholic beverage made of fermented honey mixed with millet.

41.   Palm wine.

42.   Knowlton, Richard and Berridge, Virginia, "Constructive imperialism and sobriety: Evidence of alcoholism among candidates for the British Colonial Service from 1898-1904," *Drug: education, prevention and policy* vol. 15, no. 5 (October 2008): 439-450: 441.

43.   According to Knowlton and Berridge from 1898-1919 nearly 12,000 such examinations were conducted by the medical adviser to the Colonial Office.

44.   Knowlton and Berridge, "Constructive imperialism," 439.

*Ostentation in entertaining, protracted "sundowner" parties, "treating" in
clubs, and rushing around in motor-cars, all these things contributed. . .*

*The practice by shops and stores of giving long credit[45] to European customers,
especially for liquor and groceries, and the insidious "chit" system, tended
to insolvency in the average household budget. The same pernicious system
of extended credit applied in all trading transactions. Anyone who did not
follow was dubbed a curmudgeonly fellow and ostracized. . .*

*In a country like Tanganyika, where the Staff List shows the salary of every
Government official, the temptation to live up to one's income was seldom
evaded. . . . Settlers were able to raise mortgages on their land, advances on
their crops, or loans for development of their farms which bore no proportion
to common sense. "Overdraft" came to be looked upon as the technical term
for a bank balance. Numerous firms were trading on an insecure basis of long
credits and heavy stocks in hand. Land changed hands at unheard-of prices.
Thus the country became a fool's paradise.[46]*

The slump of 1930 was a wake-up call; in Government and private expenditure
many folk quickly came to their senses. A jettisoning of the former indiscriminate
hospitality, a decrease in the consumption of spirits and the number and frequency
of luxuries and entertainments once considered essential to existence followed.[47]
According to Reid, club life, at any rate, "reached sensible levels": "As was the case
with the former extravagance, the standard of this new mode of life has been set
from the top."[48]

Although after the depression European residents in Tanganyika came to their
senses, as Reid puts it, they still could not quite readily do away with some of the
"essential" comforts of home. Before the depression, the chief item in the average
European's expenditure used to be drink: "A computation done by a Treasury
official, based on Customs import duties, revealed that one-third of the average
man's income went on drink! The silly habit grew and grew."[49] After the depression,
the sale of drink on credit was forbidden by law.

It is difficult to determine the extent to which heavy drinking declined after
the depression. Indeed, it may well be that the good sense of the majority now
frowned upon indiscriminate treating. However, drinking itself remained in favor;
wine and beer, taken at diner, were believed to aid digestion and promote health
and wellbeing. Household budgetary calculations in the Armitage-Smith Report
of 1933 included expenditure on 2 oz. of whisky per day! While moderate drinking
may have been exercised at home, as we shall see, at sundowner parties, wedding
receptions and other occasions people continued to indulge in heavy drinking.

---

45.   These were credits extended over 90 days or three month-periods.

46.   Reid, Eric, *Tanganyika Without Prejudice: A Balanced, Critical Review of the Territory and her Peoples*
      (London: East Africa, A Weekly Journal, 1934): 66-68.

47.   Ibid. 70.

48.   Ibid. 70.

49.   Ibid. 70.

Drunkard and licentious settlers and government officials

When Michael J. Macoun arrived in Dar-es-Salaam, the capital of colonial Tanganyika, in 1939 to begin his duties as police officer he had little or no idea what to expect. Onboard the *SS Mantola* which carried him from Marseilles he had had conversations with other passengers among who were colonial service officers and their wives, businessmen and settlers from East and central Africa. Some of these old hands told him that he was about to enter a world where heavy drinking among Europeans was the norm.[50]

Macoun arrived on a Sunday morning. He says he was met at the Dar-es-Salaam harbor by a staff officer who was suffering from a "monumental hangover".[51] When he got to his assigned quarters the superintendent in charge of police training with whom he was to be billeted with was still in bed "recovering from a hangover".[52] On this account the impression one gets is that in Dar-es-Salaam Saturdays were spent carousing and Sundays were spent recovering from "monumental hangovers."

On the day Macoun and his fellow cadets arrived in Dar-es-Salaam they were invited to dinner at Government House.[53] Dinners at Government House were preceded by "sundowners" and followed by further drinking. In the course of drinking there was a customary moment when the Governor asked his male guests if they wanted to go out and "see Africa". This was a cue for anyone who wanted to go out and pee. Needless to say, Macoun was very pleased with the "generous hospitality" of the Governor which enabled him to spend his first night sleeping under the stars at New Africa Hotel oblivious to the heat and the incessant call of "bush babies."

In 1946, while stationed at Mbeya Macoun was invited to a "Caledonia diner party"[54] at which the master of ceremony turned up drunk and passed out at the dinner table. After diner, Macoun says, drinking went on into the wee hours of the morning. However, being officer in charge he excused himself and went home early. His slumber was later interrupted; he writes: "I was woken with some difficulty in the early hours, suffering from a monumental hangover, by a call from the police station to the effect that a police patrol had found the body of a large European in a ditch. . . I hurried out in some disarray to find the provincial veterinary officer unconscious in the ditch."[55] Apparently after the party he had been involved in a heated argument with a junior officer and they had slugged it out, "black ties and all, until he was felled and then dumped by his opponent in the ditch."[56] According to Macoun, the provincial commissioner chastened both for their misbehavior. He notes that in both cases their careers in the colonial

---

50.   Macoun, Michael J. *Wrong place, right time: Policing the end of Empire* (London . New York: The Radcliffe Press, 1996): 15.

51.   Ibid. 15.

52.   Ibid. 15. Macoun arrived on a Sunday which means the officers had been out on a drinking spree Saturday night.

53.   This was the residence and office of the Governor. An imposing building of Moorish architecture, it comprised of a ballroom and musicians' gallery, as well as a billiard room and a squash rackets court.

54.   The Celts formed a large proportion of the British community in colonial Tanganyika. To keep their "national spirit" alive they socialized under the banner of their Caledonian Societies. In Dar-es-Salaam there was also a St. Patrick's Society.

55.   Macoun, *Wrong place, right time*, 141.

56.   Ibid. 141.

service came to a premature end a few years later.

Tanganyika's reputation as part of a world where heavy drinking among Europeans was the norm is supported by data on alcoholic liquors imported into the territory; only Europeans had access to and permission to drink wine, beer, gin, brandy and whisky. In 1928, the adult European population of 4,785 was availed with enormous quantities of imported alcoholic beverages. That year imported liquors included wines (28,690 gallons), beer (114,458 gallons), brandy (5,135 gallons), gin and geneva (3,445 gallons), and whisky (26,622 gallons).[57]

In colonial Tanganyika, hard drinking was associated with virile masculine behavior and the drink of choice was whisky, preferably taken nit. Whisky came in several brands. There was the ubiquitous *Johnnie Walker* and its competitors, namely Queen Anne Scotch whisky, White Horse Scotch whisky, Black and White Scotch whisky, and Vat 69. Brand competition was reflected in the ads even though some brands were sold by the same agent. Thus the African Mercantile Co. Ltd., the agents for the Queen Anne and Vat 69 brands, advertized them as "rare and exquisite" and "Sanderson's luxury blend" respectively. Twentsche Overseas Trading Co. Ltd., the agents for *Johnnie Walker*, ran ads that simply said, "There is no finer Scotch whisky than 'Jonnie Walker" or "*Johnnie Walker* is Scotch Whisky at its best."

Whereas whisky was given the allure of virile masculinity, wine and beer taken in moderation were said to be good for one's health. Wincarnis, a wine brand, was touted as the answer if one was worried and overworked. Its ad ran as follows: "When you're feeling worried and run-down-tired and perhaps depressed, Wincarnis is what you need to put new life and energy into you – quickly! Wincarnis is nourishment itself! Rich, full-bodied wine with which special extracts have been blended. It's a tonic that makes you healthy and *keeps* you healthy! Many thousands of recommendations from medical men testify to its value. WINCARNIS, THE *QUICK ACTION* TONIC."[58]

At any sundowner one could expect to be served with beer, wine, brandy, gin and whisky. It must be noted that sundowners from early on became part of European colonial culture. The venues ranged from private homes, clubs and hotels and, in Dar-es-Salaam, the Governor frequently had sundowners at Government House.

After World War II the New Palace and New Africa Hotels in Dar-es-Salaam were popular venues for sundowner receptions and sendoff dinners. The size of these gatherings must have brought a cheer to the hoteliers. For instance, in August 1946 Messrs. A. G. Abdulhusein and members of the Diamond Jubilee Celebrations Committee entertained about 120 people at the New Palace Hotel to say farewell to Dr. W. J. Aitken (Medical Officer of Health and Acting Municipal Secretary) on his retirement. J. E. S. Lamb, His Excellency the Governor's Deputy and several senior officials were present.[59] The same month Mr. and Mrs. P. J. Bharwani entertained a similar number also to a sundowner and dinner at the New Palace Hotel, to meet Mr. and Mrs. N. W. Gellatly, Alijah Abdulla Sumar, president of the Bombay Ismailia Provincial Council, Vazir Gulamhusein

---

57. *Report by His Britannic Majesty's Government to the Council of the League of Nations on the Administration of Tanganyika Territory, 1928*: 56.

58. As advertized in the *Tanganyika Standard*, January 11, 1947.

59. *Tanganyika Standard*, August 30, 1946: 3.

Moledina, also of Bombay, and Mr. Ibrahim Nathoo, who was private secretary to H.H. The Aga Khan during his recent visit to Tanganyika. Gellatly was well known in Dar-es-Salaam as a former manager of Barclays Bank.[60]

Besides drinking, Macoun notes that in upcountry stations "shipboard" affairs were common. While stationed at Iringa he became aware of no less than five illegitimate European births. People did not just sleep with other people's wives but some women eloped with their lovers. Often these were women much younger than their husbands and eloped with much younger, likeable and virile bachelors.[61] Such sexual escapades were exacerbated by inverse sex ratios. For instance, in 1928 the territorial European population was 5,778, of which 3,250 were men, 1,535 women and 993 children.[62]

However, although extra-marital affairs in the European community were frowned upon, Cresswell-George and others of a similar mindset deplored sexual liaisons between white men and African women the most. At the time Cresswell-George made his allegations there had been one case of interracial concubinage that attracted the attention of the territorial administration. It involved an official named C. E. Anderson and an unnamed African woman.

C. E. Anderson first arrived in Tanganyika in 1911 as a lay teacher in the service of the Universities Mission to Central Africa (hereafter UMCA). It is not clear under what circumstances he quit his employment with the UMCA. Subsequently, he joined the colonial administration. In November 1916, Anderson was appointed Assistant District Officer, Mwanza, where he remained until November 1919. It was while he was stationed in Mwanza that Anderson began his liaison with an unnamed African girl. She was at the time living with her parents. She was from Ukerewe where Anderson met her during one of official visits to the island. In acknowledgement of their liaison Anderson gave the father's girl a "present".[63]

Anderson was transferred from Mwanza to Moshi in September 1920 where he was stationed until April 1923. In the meantime, Anderson got married to a white woman in July 1920. However, his wife died at Moshi in December of that year. After his wife's death the African woman followed him to Moshi. He was transferred from Moshi to Lindi in April 1923. In December 1923, the woman followed him to Lindi and stayed with him for a period of nine to twelve months. Other officials and the police knew Anderson was cohabiting with the woman.[64] Anderson was transferred to Kilwa in 1927. At Kilwa Anderson cohabited with this woman in his Government house from October 15, 1927, to early January 1928, during which period he went on a safari with her from October 29 to November 17. Thereafter she moved to a house in town and visited him by night.[65]

The circumstances under which their liaison was reported to higher authorities remain unclear. It appears that there was intense friction between Anderson and certain officials at Kilwa; according to the Governor Sir Donald Cameron this

---

60.   Ibid. 3.

61.   Ibid. 146.

62.   *Report by His Britannic Majesty's Government to the Council of the League of Nations on the Administration of Tanganyika Territory, 1928*: 77.

63.   Public Record Office (PRO), CO 323/1018/1

64.   Ibid.

65   Ibid.

had brought great discredit on the public service.[66] According to Anderson, the matter was reported to the Provincial Commissioner, Mr. Turnbull, by a European member of the police force when the Provincial Commissioner visited Kilwa at the end of January and the beginning of February 1928. When the Provincial Commissioner asked Anderson about it he admitted culpability but pointed out that the "informant had not reported this to him in his zeal for service, but from personal reasons only."[67] Anderson further told the Provincial Commissioner that his concubinage with the African woman "had in no way influenced my work or my relations with the community, official or non-official, native or non-native, that the matter was not generally known, that I had taken every reasonable precaution to guard against pubilicity (sic), and that were the general public questioned on this matter, few, if any, would truthfully be able to say that they had any knowledge of the matter."[68]

In his conversation with the Provincial Commissioner Anderson promised that he would strictly adhere to the principle laid down in Circular B (see below), and whilst in the service of the Government he would not co-habit with any native woman. The Provincial Commissioner did not report the matter to the Governor and it came to the ears of the Chief Secretary through the Commissioner of Police and Prisons. The Governor then directed the Provincial Commissioner to make a full enquiry and to report to him. As a result, charges were made against Anderson who was later summoned to Dar-es-Salaam where he pleaded his case before a Committee of the Executive Council.

The Committee of the Executive Council, "after a most painstaking enquiry", was of the opinion that nothing else could truthfully be alleged against Anderson except that he kept an African woman as his mistress; an act which he confessed when first questioned on the subject by his Provincial Commissioner. The Committee considered Anderson to be "a quiet well spoken person". Governor Cameron, who had met Anderson but once, was extremely surprised when he learnt that "he had been guilty of such foolish and disgraceful conduct".[69] Nevertheless, Cameron formed the view, shared by the members of his Executive Council, "that the present incident would serve to fortify his character and that in the course of time he would be able to live down the past if he were allowed to remain in the service."[70] For this reason the Council recommended that he should remain on his then current salary of 630 pounds sterling a year for four years; his punishment being the loss of annual increments totaling 180 pounds. This recommendation was duly submitted to the Colonial Office in London for approval.

Reaction in the Colonial Office about the case varied. G. E. L. Gent noted that what first struck him about this case was that an unnecessary and unfortunate fuss had been made: "I should have thought that after Mr. Anderson had frankly confessed his conduct when first questioned on the subject by his Provincial Commissioner, and had give a solemn undertaking in writing that he would have nothing more to do with the woman...Mr. Anderson might very well have

---

66   PRO, CO 323/1018/1, Governor to Amery, dated 16 July, 1928.

67   PRO, CO 323/1018/1, Anderson's reply to his charges, dated 20 May, 1928.

68   Ibid.

69   PRO, CO 323/1018/1, Cameron to Avery, dated 16 July, 1928.

70   Ibid.

been transferred to a station in another part of the territory and the matter might have been hushed up."[71] Gent also appears not to have been amused by the fact that both the enquiry held by the Provincial Commissioner and that held by the Committee of the Executive Council "necessitated the calling of a number of native witnesses to bear evidence in a case in which allegations were made against a white official."[72] He thought the involvement of African witnesses should have been avoided. Otherwise, "These proceedings themselves would appear to have been quite as likely to have injured the good name and repute of the Service as Mr. Anderson's foolish conduct."[73]

On the moral aspects of this case, Gent said he did not feel qualified to express any views. Yet, he considered the liaison to be a "somewhat crude" and an "unfortunate" union. Gent could not contain his outrage against Anderson for engaging in such behavior: "How any white man of taste and discrimination could even contemplate the possibility of union with a black woman without suffering literally a physical nausea, passes my comprehension . . ."[74] Finally, Gent opined that he would have excused Anderson's erring were he to have been young and lacking of local experience, and if the concubinage had occurred over a short period.

A. Fiddian considered Anderson's case to be "an exceptionally difficult case" and felt obliged to say that Governor Cameron had not made it easier for the Colonial Office by sending a dispatch in which he endorsed the findings of the Executive Council, and accompanied it with a private letter in which he virtually invited the Secretary of State to take a more severe view. Fiddian also noted how Governor Cameron's predecessor, Sir Horace Byatt, dealt with a case which was much more serious. Fiddian pointed out that Sir Horace was content with a censure and never notified the Secretary of State about it. He stated: "I do not understand how Sir Horace Byatt can have regarded it as consistent with his duties as a Governor not to report the case."[75] Fiddian also wondered why a good many of Anderson's senior officers must have been engaged in something approaching to a conspiracy.

C. Davis agreed with Fiddian's conclusions. In his opinion the case was one of extremely undisguised cohabitation and ought to have come to light long ago: "The fact that it did not do so is itself an indication that to adopt the most severe methods would do no good – the local atmosphere is likely to tend to concealment if the result of revelation is dismissal."[76]

Subsequently, the top guns at the Colonial Office concurred with the recommendation made by the Governor and his Executive Council that Anderson should lose his annual increments for three years. In his dispatch to Governor Cameron, Amery noted: "While I have accepted the recommendation made in this case, I request that you impress upon Mr. Anderson, that it was only after considerable hesitation, that I consented to approve so lenient a punishment.

---

71   PRO, CO 323/1018/1, Gent's memo dated 23 August, 1928.

72   Ibid.

73   Ibid.

74   Ibid.

75   PRO, CO 323/1018/1, Fiddian's memo dated 5 September, 1928.

76   PRO, CO 323/1018/1, Davis' memo dated 7 September, 1928.

It must not be assumed that in any future case of a similar kind, I would be prepared to such mitigation of the usual penalty."[77]

In order to understand the moral concerns raised by Gent and others at the Colonial Office about the Anderson reference must be made of Circular B, issued by Lord Crewe, cited above. The Circular's objective was to dissuade colonial civil servants from engaging in concubinage with native women. Lord Crewe noted that it had been brought to his notice that officers in the service of some of the Crown Colonies and Protectorates had in some instances entered into arrangements of concubinage with local girls or women belonging to the native populations. Why was this unacceptable to Lord Crewe? Because such conduct could lower the prestige of the administration and cause the dereliction of European personnel.

Lord Crewe was 51-years old when he wrote Circular B. The host of colonial problems which engaged his attention during his tenure included the liquor traffic in Southern Nigeria and the danger posed by interracial sexual liaisons in many parts of the Empire. The way he handled these and other colonial problems was to some extent influenced by his religious beliefs. Of the latter, Pope-Hennessy writes: "Crewe belonged, indeed, like his grandfather before him, to that large majority of Englishmen whose religious preconceptions remain those of 1689 and who regard with no enthusiasm a direct descendant's marriage with a Roman Catholic."[78] In matters sexual, Lord Crewe espoused the morals of the Victorian era.

In The Making of Victorian Sexual Attitudes Michael Mason identifies what he calls "anti- sensualism" as the dominant motif of Victorian private sexual behavior and public attitudes. Mason views Victorian prudery not as a pathological but as a popular and progressive characteristic of Victorian society. The Victorian emphasis on the control of the body does not suggest that Victorians did not engage in licentiousness, however. As Steven Marcus notes, "amid and underneath the world of Victorian England as we know it – and as it tended to represent itself to itself – a real, secret social life was being conducted, the secret life of sexuality. Every day, everywhere, people were meeting, encountering one another, coming together, and moving on. And although it is true that the Victorians could not help but know of this, almost no one was reporting on it; the social history of their own sexual experiences was not part of the Victorians' official consciousness of themselves or of their society."[79]

The moral objections against European concubinage with native women which Lord Crewe says were so generally recognized at the time that the circular was disseminated were based on the Victorians values about "respectability" and "cleanliness." These and other Victorian values were not only considered important for the good life of individuals but also for the well-being of society. Moreover, although these values were time and place-bound they were also gender, class as well as race-bound.

Gent's memo cited above about Anderson's case indirectly touched on the Victorian value of cleanliness. Gent noted how any white man of taste and discrimination could be intimate with a black woman without being physically nauseated. Apparently Gent considered black women to be very disagreeable and

---

77   PRO, CO 323/1018/1, Amery to Governor Cameron, dated 18 September, 1928.

78   Pope-Hennessy, p. 90.

79   Marcus, (1985): 100-101.

therefore nauseating. Gent's sense of smell tells us something about Victorian olfactory symbolism which Gent used to express not only his disgust with interracial unions but to express white identity and sexual preferences. As Corbin notes, descriptions of Africans by early European anthropologists included purported "foul odor" of Africans.[80]

However, just as beauty is in the eye of the beholder, so is sweet smell in the nose of the smeller. While men like Gent were nauseated by black women others were supposedly attracted by their smell. The French anthropologist, Dr. Jacobus, suggested at the beginning of the twentieth century that the "depraved lust of the White for the Negress" had something to do with the latter's odor: "The White man to whom the strong smell of the Negress is rather attractive than repellant, is already physiologically depraved. I have known many such, – officers and officials – who have returned to France and married charming young women, but who long for the black skin and woolly hair of the daughter of Ham."[81]

To allude that African women smelled bad, as Gent did, betrays ignorance of their sense of hygiene. The Rev. John Lindsay's observations in Senegal in the 1750s led him to believe that Senegalese women were cleaner than white women, if only because they bathed twice a day! Be that as it may, Gent describes Anderson's concubinage as "crude" and "unfortunate." To Gent, there was something un-European about it. In his view, white civilized men like Anderson had no business sleeping with smelly uncivilized African women. By cohabiting with an African woman Anderson had shown no self-respect and his "foolish" behavior was bound, Lord Crewe, Gent and others believed, to cause disrespect to Europeans.

Paradoxically, Gent and others at the Colonial Office wished that the whole affair was hushed up in the first place. Secrecy was a cherished Victorian value. We are told that Lord Crewe, the author of the circular against concubinage, carried discretion almost to excess: "His axiom was that one must never divulge a secret, and even when it became public property, better never admit you had ever known it" (Pope-Hennessy, 1955: x). The problem, however, is that even if it was possible to keep such interracial sexual liaisons secret, the progeny from these "clandestine" encounters could not be hidden from the public. Thus, those at higher levels of the imperial administration must have realized that the children resulting from such liaisons would ultimately complicate the social dynamics of colonial societies, especially if they sought to claim social, political and economic privileges for themselves.

Besides being looked at as moral pollutants, in some circles African women posed a medical danger as alleged sources of sexually transmitted diseases. This was indeed Cresswell-George's claim. But Cresswell-George was not the first to make such allegations about African women as carriers of sexually transmitted diseases. Marius Fortie arrived in Tanga in 1901 when preparations were underway for the construction of the Tanga-Usambara railway. He described the European construction workers as a bunch of individuals of all nationalities who "led improvident lives of pioneer hardships which they called freedom." They consorted with African girls who were "idle, lazy, overdressed town beauties

---

80   Quoted by Classen, (1992): 134.

81   Jacobus, (1937): 242.

who changed masters in a sort of rotation." As a result, they "scattered dreadful diseases among the Arabs, Hindus and whites of Tanga."[82]

Fortie shunned their company and got himself a more faithful African girl of fifteen called Mirembe, whom he bought from an Arab man. According to Fortie, besides her young age Mirembe had other very good attributes. Fortie notes that she was well proportioned and of good height: "Her smooth skin had the satin luster of a rifle barrel. Rather than black, it was of a deep warm bronze that attracted me forever, that made the white skin of my race seem sickly and cold."[83] After Mirembe, Fortie had numerous other African women wherever business took him into the interior. None supposedly exposed him to sexually transmitted diseases.

Be that as it may, according to Cresswell-George, the proof that government officials were among those infected with sexually transmitted diseases could easily be found in the records of the Medical Laboratory in Dar-es-Salaam. A closer examination of such records shows some very interesting data about European specimens tested for sexually transmitted diseases such as gonorrhea. Before we examine the data, some historical background regarding sexually transmitted diseases in colonial Tanzania is necessary.

As a Briton, Cresswell-George would have been familiar with Victorian concerns about venereal disease. By the 1890s, English brides and their parents were advised to require a certificate of health from a prospective bridegroom to show that he was free of disease.[84] British feminist Christabel Pankhurst used male exposure to venereal disease to champion the rights of British women: "Never again must young women enter into marriage blindfolded. From now onwards they must be warned of the fact that marriage is intensely dangerous, until such time as men's moral standards are completely changed and they become as chaste and clean-living as women."[85]

Cresswell-George's disquiet about the prevalence of venereal disease among government officials in colonial Tanzania was not shared by the Colonial Office in London and the colonial administration in Tanzania. Instead, both the Colonial Office and the colonial administration were concerned about its prevalence among the African population. The medical scientific research endeavors of the 1920s and 1930s in part focused on identifying and determining the prevalence of sexually transmitted diseases among Africans in colonial Tanzania. Government sociologists, Arthur Culwick in the 1930s and Hans Cory in the 1950s, singled out prostitution, sexual promiscuity and alcoholism as the most crucial factors in the spread of syphilis, gonorrhea and yaws in colonial Tanzania.

It is not clear when or how syphilis and gonorrhea were introduced into Tanzania. It is said that syphilis appeared prominently in Europe at the end of the fourteenth century, and by 1500 syphilis had spread everywhere in the continent. Later, it was supposedly carried to Calcutta by Vasco da Gama's crew, and by 1520 syphilis had reached Africa and China. By the nineteenth century syphilis was one of the most sexually transmitted diseases throughout Europe, Asia, the Americas and Africa.

---

82   Fortie, Marius, *Black and Beautiful: A life in Safari land* (Indianapolis & New York: The Dobbs-Merrill Co. Publishers, 1938): 13.

83   Ibid. 9.

84   Savage, Gail, "The willful communication of a loathsome disease: Marital conflict and venereal disease in Victorian England," *Victorian Studies* (Autumn 1990): 35-54: 36.

85   Quoted by Savage, ibid. 35.

In colonial Tanzania, syphilis and gonorrhea were known by their Swahili names, *Kaswende* and *Kisonono*. In Europe, their treatment was notably improved by the discovery of the micro organisms that caused them; those for gonorrhea were found in 1879 and those for syphilis in 1905. The development of sulpha drugs and antibiotics provided a wider range of effective treatment against these diseases. The author is not aware of African pharmacopeia that was used to treat syphilis and gonorrhea. This ignorance does not preclude the existence of such local remedies and means of treatment.

Be that as it may, those infected with venereal disease came from the full range of the racial spectrum, namely European, Asian and African. However, it is the infection of the former which caused the most concern for Cresswell-George. The question is: how serious was the rate of infection in terms of numbers? An examination of medical annuals reports up to 1939 is instructive.[86] The Main Laboratory's annual report for 1936 shows that urine, urethral and vaginal smear specimens of 10 European patients tested positive for gonococci compared with 3 and 2 positive results for Asian and African patients respectively. The Clinical Laboratory at Sewa Haji Hospital in Dar-es-Salaam determined that out of 143 specimens submitted for testing, 69 had gonococci bacteria.[87]

In 1937, the Main Laboratory tested sixty-four urethral and vaginal specimens; 16 European specimens tested positive for gonococci compared with 12 and 5 for Asian and African patients respectively. The total tested for each group was 25 European, 19 Asian and 20 African specimens.[88] The Clinical Laboratory at Sewa Haji Hospital returned positive results for gonococci in 3 urine specimens and 35 urethral smears.[89] A newly opened laboratory in Tanga tested two hundred and thirty three urethral smears. Gonococci were found in 51.5 per cent of the specimens.[90]

In 1938, the Main Laboratory tested two hundred and thirty three urethral and vaginal smears: 22 European, 9 Asian and 202 African. Gonococci were present in 2 European specimens, 9 Asian specimens and 50 African specimens. Also, scrapings from penile sores were tested; seventeen by dark-ground illumination. Two were European specimens of which one tested positive for gonococci. The rest, one Asian and fourteen African specimens were negative.[91] At the same time one hundred and five specimens were examined under the category "medico-legal." Of these, twenty six were urethral (10), vaginal (10) and anal (6) smears. Two urethral and two vaginal smears tested positive for gonococci but all six anal smears were negative.[92] The Clinical Laboratory at Sewa Haji Hospital returned four positive urine specimens. However, out of the two hundred and fifty eight urethral specimens tested gonococci were found in sixty nine specimens; two out of twenty eye smears were also gonococci positive.[93] At the Tanga laboratory, two hundred and forty urethral smears were tested and one hundred and thirty three contained gonococci bacteria.[94]

---

86   After 1939, medical and laboratory annual reports did not disaggregate data of infected specimens by racial   groups.

87   Tanganyika. Medical Department, *Annual Report, 1936* (Dar-es-Salaam: Government Printer, 1937): 103. Sewa Haji was the African main hospital in Dar-es-Salaam. The Europeans were treated at Ocean Road Hospital.

88   Tanganyika. Medical Department, *Annual Report, 1937* (Dar-es-Salaam: Government Printer, 1938):77.

89   Ibid. 77.

90   Ibid. 80.

91   Tanganyika. Medical Department, *Annual Report, 1938* (Dar-es-Salaam: Government Printer, 1939): 89.

92   Ibid. 91.

93   Ibid. 96-97.

94   Ibid. 100.

The 1939 Medical Department's annual report was an abridged one with an Appendix that recorded 248,533 cases of infectious and parasitic diseases. Of this total of cases of infectious diseases, 10,842 were of gonorrhea and 22,245 were cases of syphilis.[95] Subsequent annual reports up to 1944 were equally abridged. The 1944 Medical Department's annual report had this to say about venereal diseases in the territory:

> The prevalence of these conditions, which has been more forcefully brought to notice as a result of cases occurring in the Army, led to the enactment of regulations for compulsory treatment; and some attempt was made to deal with the difficult problem of prostitutes found to be infected.[96]

According to the Director of Medical Services, R. R. Scott, the worst cases of infected prostitutes were in Dodoma town and Bukoba. Of 207 prostitutes in the town of Dodoma twenty four showed clinical signs of syphilis, and urethral smears taken from ninety three of them were positive for gonorrhea in forty two cases on a single examination. In Bukoba, large increases both of genital sores and gonorrhea were reported. Bukoba had nearly half (1,864) the out-patient gonorrhea cases in the Lake Province (4,094).[97]

Drunkenness and licentiousness in the Lupa goldfields

The discovery of alluvial gold in the Lupa area in 1922 attracted a lot of small scale European diggers and African laborers. It is estimated that in 1931 alone some two hundred Europeans arrived from the Belgian Congo and Northern Rhodesia as well as East Africa; "hundreds more followed in the next few years."[98] Under international law Britain could not prohibit immigration into Tanganyika of nationals of members of the League of Nations. This open-door policy facilitated the increase in numbers of the European community in the territory. At the end of 1935, the total European community was estimated to be 8,455, which included 2,665 Germans.

Besides the Europeans prospectors, thousands of Africans from neighboring Northern Rhodesia, Nyasaland, and Tanganyika also flocked to the Lupa area. It is estimated that there were probably 10,000 African laborers by 1933, 17,000 in 1935 and 12,000 in 1938.[99] Since Africans were not allowed to hold prospecting licenses they were there to only to work for the European prospectors.

The Lupa gold rush took place in a remote, arid and sparsely populated area, and it was not easily susceptible to government regulation.[100] Conditions in Lupa goldfields soon raised concerns to warrant official investigation by teams from Nyasaland and Northern Rhodesia in 1935 and 1936 respectively. Later even the League of Nations got involved. A Permanent Mandates Commission of Inquiry (hereafter PMC) was sent to Tanganyika to investigate. Its report was damning. Among its criticisms was that European employers either did not pay their laborers regularly or not at all.

---

95   Tanganyika. Medical Department, *Annual Report, 1939* (Dar-es-Salaam: Government Printer, 1940): 5.

96   Tanganyika. Medical Department, *Annual Report, 1944* (Dar-es-Salaam: Government Printer, 1945) 23.

97   Ibid. 23.

98   Roberts, A. D. "The Gold Boom of the 1930s in Eastern Africa," *African Affairs*, vol. 85, no. 341 (Oct., 1986): 545- 562: 556.

99   Ibid. 558.

100   Ibid. 558.

In response, E.V.H. Cresswell George, a member of the Lupa Control Board (whose members were appointed by the Tanganyika Government), wrote a long letter to the editor of *East Africa and Rhodesia* and lambasted the Chairman of the PMC for his ignorance of the "truth about the Lupa." He pointed out that in 1937 unpaid wages amounted to less than ½% of the wage bill of the field. He also noted that employers deemed undesirable by the Board were immediately expelled from Tanganyika. By and large, he did not think the PMC appreciated the role of the European diggers as pioneers whose initiative and enterprise had developed an industry in a barren piece of country in which thousands of Africans were now gainfully employed; that any profits the diggers made were spent in Tanganyika. E.V.H. Cresswell George castigated the PMC's view that Europeans in the Lupa goldfields had lost all sense of justice and decency. He particularly seemed annoyed by a PMC member's presumption that Europeans in the Lupa area were all there because they had failed elsewhere.[101]

The concerns of the PMC were addressed by British members of parliament. In the House of Commons debate of November 16, 1938, Mr. Leslie asked the Secretary of State for the Colonies whether, as the result of the anxieties expressed at the last Session of the PMC, any steps had been taken to deal with the health conditions of the Lupa goldfield in Tanganyika.[102] Mr. MacDonald drew Leslie's attention the House of Commons Debate of July 13, 1938, at which time he explained that during the past two years conditions had much improved on the Lupa goldfields; that the Government had provided a large staff of administrative, medical, labor and other officers; labor camps had been set up; and a hospital and three dispensaries had been established.[103]

In 1938, Dr. Donald Latham was transferred to the hospital at Chunya, the main town in the Lupa goldfields. His wife Gwynneth published her reminiscences in 1995 in which she offers very fascinating details about life there during the gold rush. She compares the Lupa gold rush conditions to those of America portrayed in the old silent films in which there were tragedies and comedies: "khaki-clad, unshaven men living in hovels and furiously panning for gold in the rivers; beautiful women, mostly bottle-blonde barmaids; poverty; riches; greed; hate; love; excessive drinking; fisticuffs and some wild shooting."[104]

Gwynneth Latham describes the hotel they stayed at in Chunya when they first arrived: "It was surrounded by cars of every vintage, right back to the T-Ford model; mules were tied to the verandah posts and the dining room and bar were packed to capacity."[105] There was also a club whose membership, to the amusement of Gwynneth, "was for men and 'women of their household' – i.e. there was so much living in sin that the term husbands and wives could not be used."[106]

The Lathams heard many tales of the early days from the old "characters" who had rushed there when the discovery of gold was announced. These are stories of "contrasts in wealth and poverty, of men from English public schools working cheek by jowl with the riffraff, of the curse of drink, the hospitality, the furious

---

101   E.V.H. Cresswell George, "The Truth About the Lupa: Reply to Geneva Criticisms," *East Africa and Rhodesia*, October 7, 1937: 122.

102   *Hansard*, 16 November, 1938, vol. 341 cc 852-4.

103   *Hansard*, 13 July, 1938, vol. 338 cc 1305-7.

104   Latham, Gwynneth and Latham, Michael, *Kilimanjaro Tales: The Saga of a Medical Family in Africa* (London. New York: The Radcliffe Press, 1995): 186.

105   Ibid. 187.

106   Ibid. 188.

fights, the Christian acts; of the pathos and bathos, the lucky gold strikes and the disappointments; of the births and marriages and of course sickness and death."[107]

According to Gwynneth, during their sojourn in Chunya at least three men died of drink, literally of drink: "Most of the alluvial diggers were elderly and hard drinking. They lived in squalor in leaking mud-and-wattle huts, which could be abandoned without much financial loss when they moved to a new claim. Some had white wives, some had black wives, and others had mistresses of either color. Some lived alone, with a native boy to cook and clean, and often to dig as well."[108]

Alcoholism was one of the major concerns in the Lupa goldfields. Drinking not only squandered hard earned money but in some cases drove men mad. One of the tragic cases narrated by Gwynneth is worth quoting at length:

> *"One young man was brought in raving with delirium tremens, known colloquially as the DTs. This is a state of severe disorientation, often violent, in alcoholics following withdrawal from alcohol. It is frequently fatal. The African staff were (sic) quite incapable of coping; they were terrified and would runaway if the patient shouted or jumped out of bed. Don was not keen on an African using force on a European and in such circumstances force was usually necessary. On this occasion he called for volunteers from the male (European) community and as ever found many willing to help. The hospital beds had poles at each corner to support mosquito nets and, after his night on duty, one young volunteer told of how the patient had climbed up the poles and adjusted the knobs, listening intently and talking as though he were receiving and sending out radio messages to his girlfriend. His language during this period was neither gentle nor genteel and quite obviously his girlfriend had done him wrong."[109]*

Why was drinking so heavily indulged in by diggers in the Lupa goldfields? To begin with, alcohol was readily available. The *Goldfields Hotel* with a bar was one of the first businesses to set shop in Chunya. Whereas previously diggers had had to travel several miles to Mbeya for a weekend of drinking, the opening of the hotel and bar in Chunya permitted habitual drinkers to imbibe on a daily basis.

The nature of mining work encouraged drinking. Alcohol can relieve psychological as well as physiological strain.[110] For the diggers on the Lupa goldfields drink moderated the harshness of physical isolation and lack of recreation activities. There were no TVs and videos in those days; the old fashioned battery-operated wireless, or radio, provided the only contact with the outside world. One could tune in to BBC (London) or KBC (Nairobi) for news and entertainment programs.[111] Often reception was not reliable or clear.[112] Be that as it may, the bar was a place to meet, socialize and share news and gossip.

There were other pernicious influences that encouraged drinking. Life in the Lupa goldfields involved more than a mere struggle against the environment. The

---

107   Ibid. 191.

108   Ibid. 192.

109   Ibid. 193.

110   Harrison, *Drink and the Victorians*, 41.

111   The British Broadcasting Corporation started broadcasting in 1922 and the Kenya Broadcasting Corporation was established in 1928. Tanzania did not have a local station until 1951.

112   Mbogoni, Lawrence E. Y. "Radio broadcasting and Government information management in colonial Tanganyika, 1951-1961," *Proceedings of the International Mass Communications Symposium*, vol. 1, Spring 1999, Sponsored by CNN World Report Television Archive and School of Mass Communications, Texas Tech University.

European diggers also struggled against their own weaknesses. They were fortune-hunters driven by a desire for quick riches. Yet when their returns were good instead of saving they went on a drinking spree. Others on hard times resorted to drinking "firewater" distilled from such ingredients as rotten pineapples, bamboo, papaws, bananas, and sundry wild fruits of the bush.[113]

In the Lupa goldfields drinking released inhibitions and incited more amorous behavior.[114] The physical isolation of the Lupa encouraged licentiousness. In her memoir Gwynneth Latham notes that in the Lupa goldfields there was a preponderance of males, in the lives of whom alcohol and women played a big part:

> *"At one time the barmaid, known endearingly as Lupa Lil, was the cause of many fisticuffs. Outside the hotel it was not uncommon to see even women tearing out each other's hair, or wildly clawing and scratching in a rough and tumble. One man, on seeing his woman sitting in a car with his rival, madly hit at him with his fist, completely forgetting in his drunken jealousy that the windscreen separated them; the result was shattered glass and a badly cut hand. Another couple, an elderly wealthy miner and his young and beautiful wife, decided to spend the night in town after a dance. They had separate rooms at the hotel. Late in the night the husband, glass of whisky in hand, went along to bid his wife goodnight. He found her younger lover foolishly sheltering behind the door; the husband threw the liquid in his face, broke the glass and, in true Irish fashion, stuck the jugged remains in his rival's mouth – and a nasty mess he made. The victim, who was quite a 'somebody' in town, was ashamed to show himself at the hospital and, as a result, bore a nasty scar for the rest of his life. Another jealous man had the habit of taking every stitch of his woman's clothing to town when he left her, so that she was bed-bound for the day."[115]*

The manner in which Lupa gold diggers engaged in licentiousness with an ardor heedless of consequences calls for an explanation. We must begin with the physical setting of the Lupa goldfields. First, the Lupa area was a frontier in the sense that as a place it was characterized by a low ratio of people to inhabitable space. The alluvial diggings stretched out for miles in all directions like the spokes of a wheel with Chunya as the hub.[116] Therefore many staked claims were isolated and far apart. This meant that the loneliness of a miner's existence would have been unbearable unless ameliorated by companionship especially of the opposite sex. Besides the obvious sexual advantages, such unions served other purposes; the women cooked, washed and provided other comforts of home which made frontier life bearable.

Marriage, cohabitation and other sexual relations between European men and women, between European men and African women, were based on either shared cultural values or fraught with cultural miscommunications. In the Lupa goldfields European women did not cohabit with African men but European men had African "wives" and mistresses. This is indicative of a double standard of sexual morality that discouraged interracial sex or sex outside of marriage for European women but not for European men.

---

113   Bulpin, T. V. *The Hunter is Death* (Long Beach, CA: Safari Press, 1987): 214.

114   For a general analysis of the relationship between liquor and sex see, Morris Chafetz, *Liquor: the servant of Man* (Boston, Toronto: Little, Brown and Co., 1965): chapter 4.

115   Latham, *Kilimanjaro Tales*, 197.

116   Ibid. 187.

We have no information whether African women who were "married" or cohabited with European men accompanied them to the Lupa or arrived separately. More importantly, what understanding did each bring to their relationship? The case of Joe Battersea and Kalega is instructive about expectations and cultural miscommunication in these relationships. Joe had some money when he arrived but squandered it on drinking and gambling, and he was gradually pauperized. The pretty English girl he had been living with went off with another man. Kalega, a sultry African girl with a golden body, was attracted to the pauperized Joe but Joe would not even look at her. When they eventually began cohabiting Joe was physically abused. According to Alastair Cobin, Kalega mistook the abuse for love:

> As is the way with women, Kalega threw herself rather hard at Joey's head; he threw her out of his camp, rather harder, with the toe of his boot to encourage her. This, to her primitive mind, could be nothing less than a demonstration of affection, for what man ever noticed a woman sufficiently to kick her if he was not madly in love with her?

Although Kalega hung round Joe she eventually tired of being kicked out and disappeared for a while. In the meantime Joe hit rock bottom when he assaulted the manager of the mine he was working at and was sent to jail. On his release he met Kalega in Chunya. Being African Kalega was not permitted to buy alcohol; she therefore gave Joey money and asked him to buy them a drink. Subsequently, they got "married" and settled down on a farm Joey bought with money from a sizable nugget that Kalega had Joey steal from her former Indian "half-caste" boyfriend.

T. v. Bulpin tells a similar story about another interracial couple.[117] These were Asha Lusinde and Lambert Lock. While Lambert worked his claim Asha ran a popular pub. A regular customer, an African named John Tusakarege, inadvertently diverged information about the presence of gold on a small stream which ran into what was known as Bayliss Creek. She told Lambert who went to investigate only to find the area was already claimed. Instead he pegged an adjacent area with an ironstone hill which did not look promising. As it turned out it was on this hill that found the reef that came to be known as Lock's Luck, one of the most lucrative finds on the Lupa. In February 1939 Lock's laborers unearthed a 127 pound nugget, the biggest ever found on the Lupa goldfields; it yielded 1,025 ounces of smelted gold.

However, to the majority of diggers the Lupa was a phrenetic world without much to celebrate about. Yet there were many boisterous occasions on the Lupa. According to Bulpin, the first "all-Tanganyika" heavyweight boxing tournament took place in the square outside the Goldfields Hotel in Chunya. One-time amateur heavyweight boxer of Sweden, Thorsten "Swede" Pierson, took on Piet van Dyk: "The whole diggings had seemed to be there that day, in swirling mass of half-frenzied punters, drunks, and individuals whose inflamed feelings made them less intent on watching the contest than on settling personal scores in a series of free fights on the fringe of the crowd. Fupi [Shorty] Jordan, an ex-bantamweight professional boxer, refereed the main bout, with the men boxing for a 50 pound purse together with side-bets and the championship. The end was a draw, after a rattling good ten-round fight."[118]

As the prospects and returns from claims dwindled the mass of European diggers eventually vanished leaving nothing behind save holes in the ground and

117   Bulpin, *The Hunter*, 214-216.
118   Ibid. 220.

heaps of rubble along the streams. The carelessness that attended the exploitation of the Lupa goldfields represented one of the worst modes of capitalist exploitation of Tanganyika. As has been observed by A.M.M. Hoogvelt and A.M. Tinker with regard to iron mining in Sierra Leone:

> *Colonial exploitation was not interested in spreading or perpetuating reproductive capitalist relations in the colonies themselves – it was not, therefore, just exploitative, but super-exploitative. It was rapacious rather than reproductive, bent on quick returns rather than long-term exchange. It was destructive of the soil and resources, yet failing to provide for alternative forms of livelihood. It was content to work in makeshift technological and capitalist enclaves, allowing itself to be supported by the surrounding social formation, rather than attempting to change or improve it. For the character of super-exploitation included a failure to fully reproduce the factors of production within the enclave itself . . .*[119]

Many of the ex-Lupa gold diggers remained in Tanganyika and ventured into other careers including settler farming and professional hunting. The next chapter examines the hunting career of one of them, George Gilman Rushby.

---

119   Quoted by B. Swai, "Synthesising the Modern History of Tanganyika: A Review of J. Iliffe: *A Modern History of Tanganyika*," *Utafiti*, vol. 5, no. 2 (2 December, 1980): 184-274: 263.

3

George Gilman Rushby:
From Ivory Poacher to Game Ranger

Introduction

George Gilman Rushby is the subject of three biographies,[120] one TV documentary and numerous newspaper articles. In 1920, at the age of twenty, Rushby was able to buy a steerage passage to Africa. Although he had an apprenticeship as an electrician he found his calling in the vast landscapes of central and eastern Africa as an ivory poacher, gold prospector, settler farmer, forestry officer and game ranger. He evidently "earned his fame" because he is mentioned in most books about white hunters in Africa and those by other white hunters about their exploits in Africa.

Rushby's pride as a hunter in Africa is vividly illustrated in the poem *The Ring Fence* with which he chose to begin his autobiography.[121] The poem, "in memory of a dead elephant hunter," is worth quoting at length:

> *At first – in other worlds, it seemed – the wilderness was free,*
> *A man might go where'er he dreamed nor pause to pay the fee,*
> *Out of the herd might take his toll earned at the risk of death,*
> *Wander afar beyond control caressed by Nature's breath _*
> *The world was wide – the herds were strong, and killing was no sin,*
> *No law but sportsmanship he knew – no Ring Fence hemmed him in.*

120   Bulpin, T. V. *The Hunter is Death* (Long Beach, CA: Safari Press, 1987); Capstick, P. H. *Man eaters* (Los Angeles, CA: Petersen Publishing Co., 1981); Capstick, P. H. *Death in the Long Grass* (Long Beach, CA: safari Press,).

121   Rushby, George G. *No More the Tusker* (London: W. H. Allen, 1965).

And so, he trod the wider ways far from the city crowd
And threaded Nature's tropic maze, thinking his thoughts aloud,
Followed the herd from dawn to dusk and slept from dusk to dawn,
Pillowed upon a gleaming tusk in tangled wastes of thorn.
But those who frame the Laws of Men were plotting in his track Till,
east and west and south and north the Ring Fence turned him back.

Now, though the world is just as wide, though herds are still the same,
Though seas of grasses still divide before the rush of game,
From 'British East' to 'German West' from Congo to Karoo,
There is no gap to fail the test and let the hunter through,
'Thou shalt not kill the Elephant' – so runs the Law today
– Hang up thy battered bandolier, the Ring-Fence bars the way.

Hang up thy battered bandolier and let the rifle rust,
For now the dreams of yesteryear and all they held in trust
Must take the place of strenuous days and starlit nights of old,
Of morning mists and noontide blaze and weariness and cold ... No more
the Tusker of those dreams shall charge, with trunk encurled, No more,
at dawn, thou'lt pace the paths with dancing dew empearled ... No more
crouch low and test the wind ... the Ring-Fence hems the world.[122]

Hunting in general and elephant hunting in particular predated the advent of European colonialism in Tanganyika. Archaeological evidence (including rock paintings at Kolo, Kondoa Irangi) indicate that prehistoric communities in Tanganyika were hunters; not by choice but rather by necessity. Hunting for commercial purposes emerged much later. J. Desmond Clark notes in his book *The Prehistory of Africa* (1970) that a site in the Olduvai Gorge has a semblance of a butchery; a large number of stone tools have been found in conjunction with the bones of an extinct "elephant" (*Elphus reckii*) believed to be more than 500,000 years old.[123] As Doran H. Ross notes, whether such creatures were actually hunted at this time is not clear, but they were nevertheless exploited as a source of food, since many of the bones were smashed to gain access to the marrow.[124]

With the rise of agriculture the elephant became a threat to crops; it was therefore hunted as much to protect the fields as for the meat. Such hunting methods as existed and the use of spears, arrows, or various trap devices, did not threaten the survival of the elephant. However, the introduction of firearms changed all that and subsistence hunting was transformed into what ultimately became a species-endangering massacre.[125]

External demand for ivory reached its apogee during the nineteenth century. Beachey notes that in this period "ivory over-topped all rivals, even slaves, in export value, and it retained this position right up until the end of the century."[126] Thousands of ivory tusks were exported each year. The missionary David Livingstone estimated that 44,000 elephants were killed annually to supply the ivory imported into England alone in 1870.[127] Even if Livingstone's figure is an

---

122   Rushby, *Tusker*, 9-10.

123   Clark, J. Desmond, Quoted by Doran H. Ross, "Elephant the Animal and its ivory in African culture," *African Arts*, vol. 25, no. 4 (Oct., 1992): 65-108: 66.

124   Ibid. 66.

125   Ibid. 67.

126   Beachey, R.W. "The East African ivory trade in the nineteenth-century," *Journal of African History*, vol. VIII, 2 (1967): 269-290: 269-270.

127   Ibid. 287.

exaggeration, to export thousands of tusks required the slaughter of thousands of elephants. It is for this reason that the nineteenth century, and especially the second half, came to be known as the "Golden Age" of elephant hunting in East Africa in general and in colonial Tanganyika in particular.

What made hunting in colonial Tanganyika a bonanza to professional hunters in the nineteenth century was the absence of restrictions or regulations. As Beachey notes: "In 1898 exclusive rights to elephant hunting in German territory were entrusted to elephant hunters who were required to deliver one tusk of every pair to the district station. These privileged hunters were induced by their own interest to report unlawful killing, and they learned also to hunt in sportsmanlike manner."[128]

The 1896 Wildlife Decree introduced by the German colonial administration was essentially intended to regulate the acquisition of hunting permits and to monitor access to hunting grounds. Subsequent amendments to the 1896 Decree in 1900, 1903, 1905, 1907 and 1911 did little to change European hunting habits in Tanganyika. The only exception was perhaps the 1907 amendment which limited hunting in the Serengeti and Ngorongoro sanctuary areas.

When the British took over from the Germans in 1918 they endeavored to have to a closer control of hunting in the territory. In 1921 the Game Preservation Ordinance established a Game Department which was specifically charged with controlling and regulating the hunting activities of European professional and sportsmen hunters as well as of Africans who hunted for the pot. Restrictions on African hunting would result in the famous case against Chief Makongoro of Ikizu who was accused and found guilty of poaching.

The 1921 Game Ordinance was amended in 1940 and eventually repealed and replaced by the Fauna Conservation Ordinance of 1957. In 1946 the British administration introduced sport hunting on a formal basis. Any administrative officer of the Game department or the Governor in Council could issue hunting permits to tourists. Needless to say, the demand for hunting permits in the 1940s and 1950s was considerably high.

In colonial Tanganyika, as was the case in neighboring Kenya (aka British East Africa), big game hunting provided a hidden subsidy, and in the case of ivory a massive underwriting, of the colonial enterprise.[129] We have noted that the German administration required that hunters deliver one tusk of every pair to the district office. Moreover, government officials could and did take out hunting licenses especially to collect trophies and to provide meat for their porters, servants and local allies. However, it was the poacher and professional hunter who derived the most profit from Tanganyika's wild game. One professional hunter whose name stands out in the annals of pre-World War I hunting was Frederick Courtney Selous. Selous was born in London on 31 December, 1851. He was a British army officer, hunter and conservationist. From an early age, Selous is said to have been influenced by stories of the adventurers and explorers of the time. Although he studied medicine, his love for the natural sciences led him to study the behavior of animals and their natural habitats. His curiosity to understand wild animals took him to the wilds of Africa in 1871 where besides studying wildlife his goal was to earn a living as a professional elephant hunter. Between 1874 and 1876 Selous is said to have killed 78 elephants and countless lions.

In Africa, Selous mostly travelled in southern, central and eastern Africa. A marksman, he preferred the .450 Nitro Express to anything else for hunting elephants. Other hunters, such as Harry Manners and Wally Johnson who began

128   Ibid. 285.

129   Steinhart, E. I. "Hunters, Poachers and Gamekeepers: Towards a Social History of Hunting in Colonial Kenya," *The Journal of African History*, vol. 30, no. 2 (1989): 247-264: 251.

their elephant hunting in partnership in Mozambique in 1937, used off-the-shelf Winchesters with Kynoch 300-grain .375 solid bullets.[130] Years after his death, Selous' preferred .470 Nitro Express bullet was superseded by the .500 Nitro Express which, however, had the same velocity at 2150fsp.

In the 1940s and 1950s, the portrayals of Tanganyika as an exotic and unique landscape teeming with wondrous wildlife in literature and films like *Mogambo* and *Hatari!* not only glamorized the white hunter in Africa but portrayed professional hunting as the ultimate measure of white masculinity. The hunting scene in Tanganyika after World War I was dominated by George Gilman Rushby. His career as poacher, settler farmer, prospector, forest officer and game ranger are examined below.

George Gilman Rushby, ca. 1900 – 1968.

George Gilman Rushby was born in February 1900, the son of Police Constable John Henry Payling Rushby of Eastwood and Catherine Rushby (nee Purdy). After his marriage Constable Rushby retired from the police and ran the Three Tuns Public House in Eastwood. In 1901 when George was only one year old, his father died. His mother took over the running of the pub and later married James Gregory-Simpson, who managed the Queen's Head Hotel at Riddings. The couple then bought the Portland Arms in Jacksdale.

It is said that as a boy Rushby had been very much impressed by two game keepers from the estate of the Duke of Portland, who had frequented the Three Tuns pub and had taken George on hunting trips with them. Little is known about George's schooling but he is reported to have taken up employment at James Oakes and Company at Pye Bridge as an electrical engineer. At the age of nineteen or twenty he left for South Africa. According to Bulpin, from Cape Town he worked his way north, first to Durban and then to Mozambique where he was employed as a shift engineer for the Delagoa Bay Development Corporation (hereafter DBDC) which owned a power plant that supplied electricity to Lourenco Marquis, the capital of Portuguese Mozambique.[131]

Rushby's hunting career started in Mozambique. At the end of July 1921, Rushby quit his job with the DBDC and sailed for Beira. At Beira he met a group of white employees of Messrs Pauling & Co who were constructing the new railway line to Nyasaland (now Malawi). They told him there were vacancies if he wanted a job. He hitched a ride with the men to the railhead and was employed on the spot. However he could not get along very well with Italian supervisor. He quit and took to hunting game whose meat he sold to the gangs of African laborers building earth embankments and cutting drains for the new railway. He moved further north as the railway construction extended toward the Zambezi River.

It was close to the banks of the Zambezi that Rushby encountered his first elephants. However, it was further north at Karonga, which he reached 1921, that he engaged in his first serious hunting of elephants. The place was being ravaged by rogue elephants and he was asked to help. Although Rushby obliged it soon occurred to him that hunting "altruistically as a defender of raided African villages might provide some reason for shooting, but it was hardly economic to a private individual of some limited means."[132]Early in 1922, Rushby left Karonga and entered colonial Tanganyika for what would turn out to be quite an adventurous life for him as a poacher, farmer, gold digger and game ranger.

---

130   Marsh, Brian, "The .375 on Elephant," *African Hunter*, vol. 5, no. 2 (n.d.): 32-34.

131   Bulpin, *Hunter*, 11.

132   Bulpin, *Hunter*, 31.

At Tukuyu Rushby met Vivian Lumb, a trader with a store at Ruiwa on the Usangu plains. Lumb told him that there were plenty of elephants in Tanganyika; the problem for Rushby was that there was at the time a limit of three elephants per license per year. In his view, unless he became a poacher it would not be possible to make a living from such a "restricted bag."[133] Then he heard that in neighboring Belgian Congo there were not only plenty of elephants but the Belgians allowed a hunter four elephants per license per year in each of the territory's numerous districts. Moreover, it was said that local officials there were amenable to bribery. So to Congo he went.

However, once in Congo Rushby soon got himself in trouble with an official at Basongo. He had exceeded his license limit and forgot to bribe the official. He was tried for poaching. Rushby was not only fined a thousand francs but was forced to surrender all his guns. He also forfeited the twelve tusks that were over the permitted limit for his license. From Basongo he found his way to Boma where he became a bar tender. After a while he got a letter from Lumb telling him that gold had been discovered on the Lupa. Rushby immediately left Boma for London where he spent a few weeks with relatives at Jacksdale. Then he sailed for Dar-es-Salaam where he arrived at the end of May 1923.

When Rushby arrived at the Lupa there were just eight European prospectors, namely Mickey King (ex-King's African Rifles), Charles B. Bird (an elephant hunter), Vivian Lumb, Danny Maher (an Australian), J. F. McDonald, Charles Breasley, H. G. Jones (a former district officer from Northern Rhodesia) and Bill Cumming (credited with discovering the gold).[134] No sooner had Rushby staked his claim when he came down with black water fever which nearly took his life. On doctor's advice he left for Tukuyu to recuperate.

While he recuperated Rushby heard that the Tanganyika government was concerned about the elephant population in the territory and wanted the herds culled. To do so the administration was issuing what were dubbed as "Governor's Licenses" which permitted a licensee to shoot twenty-five elephants on two conditions: "One tusk of every elephant shot was to be the property of the government. All elephants shot had to carry tusks of between 50 and 70 pounds. If the hunter shot an elephant with tusks of a lesser or greater weight, he had to surrender both tusks to the government."[135] Rushby applied forthwith for one of these special licenses and was granted one.

With a handful of porters he made his way in September 1923 into the Kilombero River valley where, "roaming around in a wilderness of bush covered plain, there was reputed to be an immense concentration of tuskers."[136] Within a month he had accounted for all twenty-five elephants his license permitted him. He sold his share of the tusks at Kilosa for a good profit. C. F. W. Swynnerton, the game warden stationed at Kilosa granted him a second license. By the time Rushby went back a second time to Kilosa he had shot a total of fifty-three elephants whose tusks averaged between 50 and 90 pounds.

When the administration ended the culling process Rushby made the decision to become a poacher. That was in 1924. However, he chose to do his poaching along the Northern Rhodesia and Congo border, especially in the vicinity of Lake Mweru. On his way there he passed through the Lupa where he noticed that twenty new European prospectors had arrived since he was last there. Among the new arrivals was Estcourt Vernon Herbert Cresswell-George, formerly of

133   Ibid. 38.

134   Bulpin, *Hunter*, 54.

135   Ibid. 57.

136   Ibid. 58.

Pietermaritzburg and later a Nyasaland tobacco farmer who came to the Lupa to escape the Depression.[137] Another new arrival was John Park who was married to Cresswell-George's sister, Doreen, the first European woman to live on the Lupa.

While it lasted Rushby's poaching in the Mweru Lake area earned him a small fortune of about five thousand pounds sterling; his fortune cost the lives of seventy-five Northern Rhodesian bull elephants. Eventually British officials in Northern Rhodesia complained to the Belgian administration in Congo. When the heat was on Rushby decided it was time to take decamp. Rushby booked into Spiro's Hotel du Lac at Albertville on Lake Tanganyika. At Albertville Rushby took a license that allowed him to hunt four elephants. He chose to hunt in the Kamba hills to the north-east of Albertville populated by the Mbuti (derogatorily referred to as a mongrel pygmy tribe). It was there that he collected his heaviest tusker weighing 165 pounds. To Rushby's disappointment the elephant he shot carried only this one tusker. Thereafter he went to Dar-es-Salaam for a vacation.

Early in 1926, after a vacation in Dar-es-Salaam, Rushby went to try his "luck" in Equatorial Central Africa. For the next two and a half years Rushby poached in Equatorial Central Africa. By January 1929, he had sold ivory worth about fifteen thousand pounds sterling.[138] Later that year he took another vacation; this time he traveled to England to visit his mother and to have his nose which he had broken while tending bar at Boma fixed. However, he did not stay long in England whose atmosphere and climate no longer appealed to him. He booked a passage to Cape Town. While waiting for departure he stayed at the Overseas Club in London where he met Eileen Graham. She was from Cape Town. When Rushby told her he was going to Cape Town she insisted on giving him an introductory note to a friend of hers there whom she also wrote to. The friend was Eleanor Dunbar Leslie.

When Rushby disembarked at Cape Town on June 16, 1930, Eleanor was waiting on the quay. It was love at first sight. She insisted he stay with her family. However, his future father-in-law, a magistrate, was not impressed when he was told Rushby was a hunter and intended to marry his daughter. Mr. Leslie thought hunting was a very destructive way of making money and certainly was inadequate to support a family. Rushby countered that it was no more destructive than, say, mining gold. In any case, he reassured him that that part of his life was over. He was going to become a settler farmer once he got back to Tanganyika. His future father-in-law was not impressed by this alternative career either.

Rushby had absolutely no idea about farming, and about coffee farming in particular. Needless to say, six years after he got married to Eleanor his Mchewe farm near Mbeya was still not doing well. Faced with an infestation of beetles all he did was lament: "There was no technical guidance available, no chemicals completely suited to local conditions, and his neighbours were all just as inexperienced as himself."[139] Their farms were wrecks. The same dismal picture applied to other settler farms in the Southern Highlands whether it was the Mbozi and Mbeya area, or Sao Hill near Iringa.

Thus settler farming looked to the Rushbys like what the Swahili call *kazi bure* (wasted effort).[140] Eleanor almost bought into current local lore that the place was cursed: "Perhaps it's because everybody has tried to do something against the natural grain of the place. . . I suppose that is why many settlers in new lands do go broke. They try to fight nature and lose. They break their hearts wondering what went wrong, and all the time the real key is not to struggle against such self-

137   Ibid. 64.
138   Bulpin, *Hunter*, 120.
139   Bulpin, *Hunter*, 183.
140   Ibid. 198.

appointed odds... Perhaps its (sic) because we try to graft new crops and livestock on an unnatural base that we all make the same mistake."[141]

In February 1936, Rushby went back to the Lupa to try again digging for gold. The year 1936 was a bountiful one on the Lupa goldfields and digging made the place appear like a madhouse. Thousands of Europeans, Asians and African laborers were busily engaged digging the gold-bearing earth. The cloud of dust they raised from the dry blowers "would have been enough to give miners' phthisis to the angels."[142] Needless to say, Rushby had no luck on the Lupa. Soon his financial position was such that he deemed it necessary to look for some regular source of income. He applied for jobs in the forestry and game departments. He got the forestry job and was posted to Mbulu in the Northern Province.

The Rushbys left their Mchewe farm at the beginning of March 1938. Their stay at Mbulu was short lived. In October 1938, the thirty-eight year old Rushby was offered the permanent post of a ranger, largely to be employed on elephant control in the Eastern Province.[143] For a short while before the outbreak of World War II the Rushbys resided at Nzasa, the then headquarters of the Game Department of the Eastern Province. However, when war began the headquarters were transferred to Morogoro where the Rushbys stayed until March 1944 when Rushby was transferred to Lyamungu, the headquarters of the territorial Game Department.

For a few months from October 1945 Rushby's expertise and experience as a hunter were put to the test, not by unruly elephant herds but by a scourge of man-eating lions in Njombe district. The problem seems to have started way back in 1932 although W. Wenban-Smith, the district commissioner, had no idea how the killings had started. He informed Rushby that the lions seemed to confine most of their activities within three sub-chiefdoms namely, Mtwango, Rujewa and Wanging'ombe. The area affected was about 1,500 square miles. From the information that Rushby was able to gather from the chiefs of the affected areas he was able to estimate that since 1941 the lions had killed approximately 1,500 people!

According to local lore these were not ordinary lions. Capt. Monty Moore, the district game warden, intimated to Rushby that there could be some similarities with the "lion-men" known as *mbojo* that were at the time killing people in Singida District, Central Province.[144] In Singida, the colonial government hypothesized two scenarios. On the one hand the government felt that the killings were at least in part due to the depredation of real lions; and on the other hand it felt that the lion men were murderers dressed in lions' skins, and the motive for the killing was thought to be political.[145] Working on the former scenario the government sent professional hunters to Singida to shoot the man-eaters.

However, the Nyaturu people in Singida believed that *mbojo* were either men dressed in lions' skin, or men who may have been transmorphized into lions, or (c) real lions that were under the control of a human being.[146] In Njombe, according to James L. Giblin, the Bena people as late as the 1990s believed that the man-eaters were either real lions acting on their own or at the command of

---

141   Ibid. 199.

142   Ibid. 205.

143   Ibid. 246-7.

144   In 1920 these "lion-men" were reportedly responsible for the deaths of two hundred people in the Usure area adjacent to Singida.

145   Schneider, Harold K. "Male-Female Conflict and Lion Men of Singida," in *African Religious Groups and Beliefs: Papers in Honor of William R. Bascom*, ed. Simon Ottenberg (Meerut, India: Archana Publications for Folklore Institute, 1982): 96.

146   Ibid. 97.

some human being.[147] Informants interviewed by Giblin believed that the lions were under the command of one Matamula Mwangela who was aggrieved by missed Native Authority appointments. Mwangela is believed to have acquired the medicine from the Bemba in Northern Rhodesia (modern day Zambia) that enabled him to conjure up the lions and set them prowling in the three sub-chiefdoms for human prey.[148] His informants told Giblin that the lion attacks ceased after the British appeased Mwangela by appointing someone to the sub-chieftainship whom he was known to be able to manipulate.[149]

However, according to Rushby it was he together with a select number of African scouts who against all odds were able by July 1947 to wipe out the elusive pride of man-eaters. Taking on the man-eaters of Njombe enhanced Rushby's celebrity status in England. His success in eliminating the man-eaters was noted in the Guinness Book of Records. In 2005 the Natural History Unit of the British Broadcasting Corporation (BBC) aired a series of adventure documentaries; one of the documentaries was about the man-eaters of Njombe starring Adrian Rawlings (Harry Potter's father) as Rushby.

Besides "disciplining" unruly elephants in the Rufiji River valley and hunting down man-eating lions in Njombe, Rushby was like other game rangers in Tanganyika called upon to check and stop "illegal" hunting especially in areas adjacent to game reserves. Throughout the colonial period the administrations expressed concern about the "illegal" hunting of game for meat. Given the paucity of data it is impossible to assess the patterns and reasons for the demand for wild meat in colonial Tanganyika. Anecdotal evidence indicates that consumption was regular especially by inhabitants of areas adjoining game reserves and those in tsetse-infested areas where domestic livestock could not be kept. For these communities and others wild meat provided a secure protein source as well as a supplemental source of income.

Africans were the main culprits of "illegal" hunting of game for meat. But what constituted as "illegal" hunting in their case? On the one hand, hunting legally meant taking out a hunting license and reporting game killed on a license. On the other hand, it was "illegal" either to hunt without taking out a hunting license or to not record the game one had killed on a license. Illegal hunting was also blamed for the use of "bad and cruel" methods such as snaring and trapping.

However, the "illegality" of game hunting in colonial Tanganyika was also a cultural construct. More specifically, it was a relic of British aristocratic culture. From the Middle Ages to the end of the Victorian era wildlife in the English countryside was the property of the aristocracy with big estates. The Enclosure Movement created communities of poor and starving folk who lived on the fringes of such estates. Inevitably these poor and starving folk helped themselves to the game population of these estates. Laws were enacted to stop such "encroachments" and the culprits were labeled "poachers." The estate owners employed gamekeepers to keep the "poachers" out, and if they were caught, the local sheriff put them in jail.

In colonial Tanganyika all "unoccupied" land was designated "Crown land" and, by default, all wildlife on such land belonged to the colonial state. If one wanted to hunt on "Crown land" one had to take out a hunting license and was obligated to record all animals killed on the license. In this regard, colonial legislation alienated African communities from wildlife which most depended on

---

147   Giblin, James L. *A history of the excluded: making family a refuge from state* (Oxford: James Currey; Dar- es-Salaam: Mkuki na Nyota; Athens, OH: Ohio University Press, 2005): 76.

148   Ibid. 77.

149   Ibid. 77.

as a source of protein. Almost any game rich territory was converted into what came to be commonly known as "Shamba la Bibi", a Kiswahili term for animal preserve. The origin of the term remains a mystery. One explanation is that it was the nickname of the Selous game reserve after Kaiser Wilhelm II gave it to his wife as a birthday present. Another explanation is that it arose out of local lore and referred to the activities that were permissible on such restricted areas namely collecting firewood and other forest products, all women's (*bibi*) work, not men's.

Rushby was one of very few professional hunters in colonial Africa who turned from hunting into game rangers. This transition from professional hunter to ranger begs the question: did they do so because they were, to use Beinart's term, "penitent butchers"?[150] According to Rushby, the reason he stopped being a professional elephant hunter was economic and had to do with the world wide slump during 1929 and 1930. He notes that "the price of ivory fell so low that it was no longer possible to make a living at elephant hunting."[151] Also, he found the idea of a pensionable job appealing.

For Rushby, the irony of his transition is that as a ranger he was intent on impressing upon African poachers that "their pursuits were unprofitable"[152] when not so long ago he himself had very well profited from doing it. Besides, as game ranger he continued to kill enormous amounts of elephants only now the excuse was to prevent them from damaging African crops. In his own estimation an average of one thousand elephants were killed each year in the Eastern Province where he was in charge.[153]

For the Game Department, the irony of condemning African "poaching" as "unprofitable" is the fact that it was the conduit for the collection of handsome sums of money from selling trophies and hunting licenses as well as charging Safari fees and selling of permits to export live animals to zoological institutions all over the world for display and scientific study. From 1947 to 1956, the Game Department collected revenue in the amount of 506,437 pounds sterling from ivory; 26,369 pounds sterling from rhino horns; 5,483 pounds sterling from hippo teeth; 9,092 pounds sterling from leopard skins; 210 pounds sterling from lion skins; 1,284 pounds sterling from other game trophies; 15,060 pounds sterling from export of live animals; 239,833 pounds sterling from sale of game licenses; and 1,507 pounds sterling from sale of trout licenses. Total revenue collected amounted to 805,275 pounds sterling.[154] From 1957 to 1961, total revenue collected from the sale of Government trophies and fees paid in respect of capture of wild animals, game licenses, trophy dealer's licenses, Governor's licenses and Controlled Area fees amounted to 768,063 pounds sterling.[155]

For the local communities, prohibitions to hunt without a permit and being labeled "poachers" if they did appeared senseless if not unjust. They endeavored not only to find ways to circumvent the prohibitions but also increased their "poaching" efficiency.[156] In 1958, as an indication of the extent of "illegal" hunting

150 einart, William, "Empire, Hunting and Ecological Change in Southern and Central Africa," *Past & Present*, No. 128 (Aug., 1990): 162-186: 175.

151 Rushby, *Tusker*, 11.

152 Bulpin, *Hunter*, 267.

153 Rushby, *Hunter*, 11.

154 Tanganyika. Game Department, *Annual Report, 1955-56* (Dar-es-Salaam: Government Printer, 1957): 44, Appendix III.

155 Tanganyika. Game Division, *Annual Report, 1961* (Dar-es-Salaam: Government Printer, 1963): 18, Appendix I.

156 Tanganyika. Game Department, *Annual Report, 1958* (Dar-es-Salaam: Government Printer, 1959): 5.

a lorry-load of wire snares was removed from the Luganzo controlled area, and, on a number of occasions, game rangers had been compelled, after loading their vehicles to the full, to abandon large quantities of snares in the bush.[157] In the Kimali area a large hunting party was encountered consisting of not less than 300 people. It was estimated that 200 animals had been killed by this party.[158]

The District Commissioner, Musoma, reported that "poaching" continued unabated and the slaughter of game by local hunters using such "illegal" methods as traps, snares and nets had reached alarming proportions. He estimated that in Musoma district alone it was probable that 10,000 head of game were killed annually by "illegal" hunting methods, even though many of the hunters may have possessed Native Authority hunting permits.[159]

Besides commercialized meat hunting, African hunters made money from selling valuable trophies, such as ivory, rhino horn and leopard skins; these were sold to private dealers. Other trophies, such as wildebeest tails, zebra tails, eland tails, giraffe tail hairs, lion fat and lion claws were in demand by a largely African clientele. Eland tails were the most highly prized at Shs. 60/- or 1 cow or 1 bullock, followed by wildebeest tails (Shs. 30/- to Shs. 35/-) and zebra tails (Shs. 15/- each). Lion fat cost Shs. 5/- per beer bottle and lion claws cost Shs. 5/- each.[160]

Rushby and his colleagues did all they could to apprehend those they believed were guilty of breaching the law. In 1955 and 1956, the numbers of convictions obtained in district courts for offences against the Fauna Conservation Ordinance were 394 and 496 respectively. In 1957 the number was 632 convictions. The numbers reached a peak in 1958 with 859 convictions.[161] 1958 was the year that Chief Makongoro Matutu of Ikizu, Musoma district, was accused of "poaching" and his case was widely publicized. This case is the subject of chapter four.

In the meantime, while officials complained about the increase in African "poaching", they did not complain about the increase in the number of white hunters, both professional and sportsmen, from abroad. The increase was reflected in the revenue obtained from game licenses which continued to rise especially from 1946 onwards. A total of 185 visitors' licenses were issued in 1955, and approximately 320 in 1956, the highest in the history of the Game Department.[162]

The Game Department's annual report for 1955-56 notes that hunters came from many parts of the world, including England, Germany, France, Italy, Holland, Switzerland, Persia, India, Egypt, South Africa, Brazil and the United States of America. Four parties of foreign royalty visited in 1955. In February, H.H. the Maharajah of Baroda, accompanied by his son, hunted for a short period in the Northern Province and obtained a number of trophies. In July, H.H. the Maharajah of Mysore visited the territory and hunted in the Western and Northern Provinces. Finally, in November, H.R.H. Prince Bernhard of the Netherlands paid his third visit to the country in as many years. He again visited the territory in September, 1956. Rushby had the honor of accompanying Prince Bernhard and the experience crowned his career in the Game Department. Rushby retired from government service in 1956.

---

157   Ibid. 5.

158   Ibid. 5.

159   Tanganyika. Game Department, *Annual Report, 1955-56* (Dar-es-Salaam: Government Printer, 1957): 33.

160   Tanganyika. Game Department, *Annual Report, 1958* (Dar-es-Salaam: Government Printer, 1959): 5.

161   Tanganyika. Game Department, *Annual Report, 1959* (Dar-es-Salaam: Government Printer, 1960): 16, Appendix IV.

162   Tanganyika. Game Department, *Annual Report, 1955-56* (Dar-es-Salaam: Government Printer, 1957): 30.

4

Chief Makongoro of Ikizu: Beneficiary and Victim of Indirect Rule

Introduction

Questions about the nature of British colonial administration in sub-Saharan Africa continue to be raised by historians.[163] Recently focus has been on how Indirect Rule functioned and whether or not it was effective or even indirect.[164] Until recently the historical origins of this policy were traced to Sir Frederick (later Lord) Lugard's administration of Northern Nigeria.[165] However, this has been questioned by Mahmood Mamdani who has argued that the lessons of Indirect Rule were first learnt in South Africa and then applied to the rest of Africa.[166] What made Indirect Rule attractive was the administrative expediency of co-opting traditional rulers into the colonial bureaucracy. However, what dictated its adoption was "the failure of the assimilationist or direct administration policy,

163 Ranger, T. and O. Vaughan (eds.) *Legitimacy and the Twentieth-Century Africa: Essays in honor of A.H.M. Kirk-Greene* (The Macmillan Press Ltd., 1993).

164 Chipungu, S.N. (ed.) *Guardians in Their Time: Experiences of Zambians under colonial rule* (Macmillan, 1992).

165 It was Sir George Goldie who suggested to Frederick (later Lord) Lugard the need to use traditional rulers as surrogates of the Royal Niger Company. Later, Lugard applied the idea in the administration of Northern Nigeria.

166 Mamdani, M. *Citizen and Subject: Contemporary Africa and the Legacy of late Colonialism* (Princeton, NJ: Princeton University Press, 1996).

which was in vogue in the nineteenth century".[167] In any case, the British could not have governed people who did not understand English and had no tradition of English law without engaging in the expensive educational operation of training thousands of local administrators to govern in that language and with that law.

The cornerstone of Indirect Rule was the Native Authority whose promulgation differed from colony to colony. In colonial Tanzania, Native Authorities came into existence upon the enactment of the Native Authority (establishment) Ordinance of 1926. The ordinance empowered the Governor to appoint persons to be Native Authorities or members thereof. For the appointment of chiefs three principles applied: personal ability, hereditary or traditional right and custom, and the will of the people.[168] These principles reflect the hegemonic objectives of the policy of Indirect Rule. By capitalizing on the existing respect for traditional authority, the colonial Government could protect itself against anti-colonial agitators and "against the disruptive behavior which would be a consequence of the breakdown of the old habits and traditions".[169]

The Native Authority Ordinance of 1926, which repealed that of 1923, stipulated the duties and powers of Native Authorities (Sections 4, 8, 9 and 15); the manner by which they could cease to be recognized as native authorities (Section 3, iv), and the penalties to which they were liable (Section 14). Chiefs became salaried functionaries of the colonial administration. This however did not make them mere puppets of the colonial administration[170] or "ndiyo" (yes) men as some historians have suggested.[171] Some chiefs, such as Mohammed Makongoro Matutu of Ikizu, Musoma District, performed "official" duties and reinvented traditional authority for personal benefits.

Chiefs had quite some leeway to do as they pleased because of limited supervision by their British overlords. Furthermore, because the Native Authority Ordinance (1926) said nothing about the raising of revenue by the Native Authority, and nothing at all about the expenditure of such funds, chief Makongoro, as we shall see, were able to demand contributions, in cash and in kind, which enabled them to accumulate considerable personal fortunes. Such wealth was used for conspicuous consumption and to finance "development" projects which endeared them to colonial authorities.

Chief Makongoro as a beneficiary of Indirect Rule

Ikizu was a small chiefdom, about 300 square miles, located astride the main Musoma-Mwanza road some 35 miles south of Musoma, the district headquarters. Makongoro was appointed chief in February, 1926. He was the eldest son of Matutu Mwesa Gibwege, who was the tenth in the chronology of

---

167   Bretts, R.F. "Methods and Institutions of European Domination," revised by M. Asiwaju, *UNESCO General History of Africa*, vol. 7, *Africa Under Colonial Domination* edited by A. Adu Boahen: 316.

168   Pels, P. "The Pidginization of Luguru Politics: Administrative Ethnography and the Paradoxes of Indirect Rule," *American Ethnologist*, vol. 23, no. 4 (November, 1996): 742.

169   Liebnow, J. Gus, "Chieftainship and Local Government in Tanganyika," PhD dissertation, Northwestern University, 1955: 142.

170   See John Iliffe, "The Age of Improvement and Differentiation," in I.N. Kimambo and A.J. Temu (eds.) *A History of Tanzania* (Nairobi: East African Publishing House,1969): 137; Mamdani, *Citizen and Subject*, 138; Betts, "Methods and Institutions," 317.

171   Pels, "Pidginization of Luguru Politics," 750.

Ikizu rainmakers.[172] Before Makongoro's father died in 1926, he had wanted one Raphael Ngohira to succeed him as rainmaker. Physically, Ngohira was disfigured having suffered from small pox and was blind in one eye. According to Ikizu customs his disfigurement disqualified him from performing traditional rituals. Therefore he could neither be a rainmaker or chief.[173] Unable to have his first choice, Matutu is said to have chosen his grandson Webiro Kisone to succeed him as rainmaker and chief. On the death of his father Makongoro contested Webiro's right to succeed on the grounds that a grandson could not be chosen over a capable son.[174]

Born in 1894, Makongoro was 32 years old when he was appointed chief. Makongoro demonstrated his zeal to succeed by creating an administrative machine "of unusual strength, which enabled him to maintain absolute control over his chiefdom."[175] As we shall see, he did not only wield despotic powers, he changed important local customs which enhanced his authority and provided him with revenue for his personal use.

The Native Authority Ordinance (1926) did not give chiefs powers to tax and spend as they wished. The Native Authority treasury derived its finances mainly from rebates on the Hut and Poll taxes. The size of the rebates, which in many areas was limited to 20 percent, depended upon the number of taxpayers that a chief could claim. The rebate system stifled initiative on the part of many chiefs but especially those, like Chief Makongoro, who had "ambitious" projects that they needed to finance. In 1948, Ikizu had only 2,908 taxpayers.[176] However, these taxpayers owned considerable wealth in cattle. In 1925, they owned 15,668 cattle. In 1933, Ikizu taxpayers owned approximately 28,496 head of cattle. By 1950, the cattle population in Ikizu had risen to 38,486.[177] It was this wealth in cattle that Chief Makongoro ingeniously exploited.

Chief Makongoro realized that tax rebates were inadequate if he were to do what the colonial administration expected him to do in the name of "development" projects. He proceeded to change two Ikizu customs and these changes secured him two very important sources of revenue. In the mid-1930s a traditional custom called *marero* was altered at the instigation of Chief Makongoro albeit with the approval of the tribal elders.

> *Previously- whenever an adult male died, two heads of cattle were slaughtered by the heirs and the meat divided up amonst (sic) neighbours and relatives. Subsequently the custom was changed so that only one head was slaughtered and the second beast was handed over for use in furthering various public works. This meant in effect that an estate duty of one head of cattle was levied on the death of each adult male. The levy was often discharged by a cash payment of Shs. 100/- or Shs. 150/-[178]*

---

172   Tanzania National Archives (TNA), E.C. Baker, "Waikizu tribal history and legends," *Musoma District Book*, vol. 1, Sheet II.

173   Marwa, Sebastiani M. *Mashujaa wa Tanzania: Mtemi Makongoro wa Ikizu* (Peramiho: Benedictine Publications, 1988): 24.

174   Ibid. 29.

175   PRO, CO 622/1299, Chief Makongoro of Ikizu."

176   TNA, *Musoma District Book*, "East African Population Census," 30.

177   TNA, *Musoma District Book*, Annual cattle censuses for the years 1925, 1933 and 1950, 4.

178   Ibid. 4.

There is reason not to believe that many Ikizu elders supported Chief Makongoro's endeavor to change this customs. However, those who supported him probably did so for their own altruistic purposes.

The second custom that was changed at the instigation of Chief Makongoro involved the performance of what were known as *nyangi* ceremonies. *Nyangi* ceremonies were performed to mark important rites of passage. The most important *nyangi* ceremonies were those which marked male transition grades. The father or guardian of an adolescent transitioning into young adulthood had to supply beer and arrange to slaughter a beast or two. All elders would be invited to the feast. The black cow tail, *mkiraburu*, identified the newly initiated young adults.[179] Each carried the *mkiraburu* until they transitioned into the next grade.

The next grade was entered ten or so years after the first grade. An entrant had to prepare two feasts. One for the members of the grade whose rank he was leaving and one for those whose grade he was joining. The symbol for this grade of adulthood was a red cow tail called *siluli*. The highest grade would come ten or so years later. The symbol for the most senior grade, known as *Himaya*, was a white cow tail called *mkiru*. At the feast of investiture the holders of *siluli* and *mkiru* would be invited guests.[180] Within and between the three main grades existed minor ranks which one went through and each transition required a *nyangi* ceremony.

Prior to Makongoro's appointment as chief, all *nyangi* ceremonies were officiated and controlled by the elders who partook in the feasts prepared by entrants to new grades. After Makongoro became chief he assumed nominal control of all *nyangi* ceremonies and demanded payment from initiates into all minor and major *nyangi* ranks. Each entrant paid Chief Makongoro a goat for a minor rank and a cow for a major grade.[181] Honor and pride required that each Ikizu male go through one of the main three grades, namely the *mkiraburu*, *siluli* and *mkiru* grades. Any man who failed to do so could neither inherit property nor marry an Ikizu woman because no woman would accept him for a husband.[182] Therefore, Chief Makongoro was assured of payment for a *nyangi* ceremony at one time or other from all Ikizu men.

Furthermore, Chief Makongoro departmentalized the supervision of funerals and other rites of passage. Ceremonies dealing with circumcision belonged to the *Rusalange* department and those dealing with marriage belonged to the *Seega* department. The *Marero* department dealt with funeral matters and the *Himaya* department oversaw the transition into the topmost elder grade. Needless to say, the various departments facilitated the collection of "contributions" from bereaved families and the aspirants to the various minor and major *nyangi* grades.[183]

Chief Makongoro's success in manipulating and assuming control of all rites of passage may not have endeared him to the masses. However, as the local representative of the colonial state he probably believed there was nothing they could do. Moreover, as chief he was empowered to make bylaws, to adjudicate

---

179   TNA, *Musoma District Book*, vol. 1, Sheet 9, "Manners and Customs."

180   Ibid.

181   TNA, *Musoma District Book*, "Manners and Customs," Sheet 9.

182   Ibid.

183   Marwa, *Mashujaa wa Tanzania*, 52-53.

cases and to mobilize mass labor for public works. Subsequently, he did all these things independently of kin-based obligations and other traditional restraints.

The *marero* cattle that Chief Makongoro collected were used to feed people engaged in public works in the chiefdom. Communal labor was channeled into the building of dams, clearing of tsetse-infested bush, and the construction of roads. These projects served to raise Chief Makongoro far above other chiefs in official esteem. At the same time Chief Makongoro was coming under suspicion. As one official report noted, despite the efforts to improve the lot of his people, "no work was ever undertaken without the prospect of large scale financial profit to (Makongoro) himself."[184] Unbeknownst to his superiors was the actual extent of his wealth.

When Makongoro was appointed chief in 1926, he owned 250 head of cattle. By 1957 his head of cattle had increased to 2,500. As we have noted, there reason to believe most of the cattle were *marero* and *nyangi* related cattle. Besides wealth in cattle, Chief Makongoro owned three tractors, one Land Rover, and a trailer. One of the tractors, a diesel model, had cost Shs. 28,000.[185] Chief Makongoro owned a house in Musoma town which was valued at Shs. 95,000 and another in Ikizu was valued at Shs. 12,000.[186] Chief Makongoro could not have accumulated all this wealth from his salary of Shs. 585/- per month!

The salary paid to Chief Makongoro was supposedly intended to serve two purposes. The salary was intended to secure his allegiance to the colonial state at the same time as it was intended to compensate his loss of tribute from his people. As it turned out the salary was too meager to meet his financial needs and obligations. As we shall see, his needs and obligations called for and involved huge financial expenses.

To maintain his prestige and social standing Chief Makongoro engaged in what economists call "conspicuous consumption". Chief Makongoro allegedly had 80 wives and numberless children. He himself acknowledged to having 40 wives and 80 children.[187] Whether these figures are exact or not, to chiefs like Makongoro they show that polygamy as such and particularly its promise of a large progeny and a vast network of alliances were regarded as a criterion of prestige and public influence.[188]

Undoubtedly, Chief Makongoro's polygamous marriages and large progeny brought him prestige and public influence. However, that prestige came at a great cost to him. Besides paying bride wealth, he was expected to provide all his wives clothes and other necessities. His numerous children also needed to be clothed. The head teacher at Ikizu N.A. School estimated that half the annual intake of new pupils would consist of Makongoro's children.[189] A salary of Shs. 585/- per month could not even have sufficed to buy school uniforms for his children. Thus when district officials suggested that pressure should be brought to bear on parents in Ikizu to buy uniforms for their children, as was customary in all primary schools,

184   PRO, CO 822/1299, "Chief Makongoro", 5.
185   Ibid.
186   Ibid.
187   Ibid. 9.
188   Huber, H. *Marriage and the Family in rural Bukwaya, Tanzania* (Frisbourg: The University Press, 1973): 153.
189   PRO, CO 822/1299, "Chief Makongoro," 9.

Chief Makongoro was not supportive of this suggestion as it would have involved him personally in what he regarded as an unnecessary expense.[190]

As we have noted, since Chief Makongoro could not depend on his monthly salary to support his large family he had to find other means to augment it. Although the *marero* and *nyangi* contributions were the main source of Chief Makongoro's private "treasury", evidence suggests that the Chief's other sources included the imposition of arbitrary fines and contribution. In 1936, people in Ikizu were made to contribute through a mandatory collection Shs. 6,000/- to enable Chief Makongoro to buy a car. This collection had official approval, as did the collections for the war effort during World War II. Chief Makongoro undoubtedly knew that once official sanction had been granted, there would be no close supervision or accounting for what had been collected.[191] He therefore took liberty to demand contributions and to withhold funds as he pleased.

Chief Makongoro also engaged in trading which may have brought him substantial amounts of money. Among other things, he is said to have traded in cattle and his business contacts stretched as far as Kenya and Uganda. In 1929 he was reprimanded and ordered to pay the salaries of some headmen whom he had sent to Uganda to go look into his business affairs there that seemed to be going wrong.[192] However, after this reprimand Chief Makongoro seems to have gotten into the good books of successive District Officers.

Chief Makongoro's drive to build dams, roads, and other public works raised him above other chiefs in official esteem. A cursory examination of annual reports shows that Makongoro's personality impressed a number of District Commissioners over the years. In the annual report for 1939 he is referred to as "the hard driving Makongoro". The annual report for 1940 notes, "Makongoro deserves special mention for the driving power displayed". In the 1941 annual report it is noted that he is "especially to be congratulated upon his support for the War effort". In 1945 Chief Makongoro was awarded the King's Medal and was described as "a splendid Chief". In 1953 Chief Makongoro received the Coronation Medal and was praised as being the "outstanding personality" amongst the Musoma Chiefs.[193]

However, in 1958 official praise turned into official condemnation when the Chief Makongoro was accused of "illegal" hunting. This and other serious allegations caused the administration to consider deposing him. As we shall see, his untimely death "saved" him from being deported.

Chief Makongoro as a victim of Indirect Rule

The Native Authority Ordinance (1926) held chiefs accountable for their misconduct. If they were found culpable of criminal acts, they were subject to dismissal from office. They could be tried in a court of law like ordinary subjects. Thus, when Chief Makongoro was accused of illegal hunting he had to stand trial like any ordinary subject.

---

190   Ibid. 10.

191   TNA, *Musoma District Book*, vol. 1, "Irregularities by Chiefs," Sheet II.

192   Ibid.

193   PRO, CO 822/1299, "Chief Makongoro," 3.

It seems that Chief Makongoro's disregard for the Game Laws was not a secret in Ikizu and his "illegal" hunts were frequent. As it was noted at the time of his indictment:

Makongoro . . . went hunting very frequently indeed with his tractor and trailer and land rover. He drove his land rover and his son drove the tractor. He would kill as many as a dozen animals on each hunt and would off-load them at various huts on the return journey. There was a set tariff for the sale of these animals. His messengers would return to collect cash or seize a cow in payment on a subsequent day. The tariff charged was- Eland Shs. 120/-, Zebra Shs. 90/-, Wildebeest Shs. 80/-, Topi Shs. 50/-, Thompson's Gazelle Shs. 35/-.[194]

However, it is not surprising that the Game Department did not get earlier information on Makongoro's illegal activities because no game scout was stationed in the chiefdom.

The Game Department was also said to be very unpopular in Musoma District to the extent that people may deliberately have withheld information about hunting activities especially in the areas bordering the Serengeti Game Reserve. In any case, many people in Musoma district engaged in seasonal hunting activities which were condemned in various annual reports of the district's game department.

In the early 1930s the entire Musoma district was considered a Game Reserve and hunting was prohibited.[195] When the western boundary of the Serengeti Game Reserve was shifted towards Ikoma the eastern parts of Musoma district remained very close to the Serengeti. In fact, on many occasions European hunting parties entered the Serengeti Game Reserve from the Musoma side.[196] The Nata plains, where Chief Makongoro is said to have hunted "illegally", were only fourteen miles from Ikizu.

In August, 1957 Chief Makongoro was prosecuted on various counts for offenses against the Fauna Conservation Ordinance and the Penal Code. After long delays Chief Makongoro was finally found guilty by the Resident Magistrate, Musoma, in January, 1958, on the following counts:[197]

1st Count:- Hunting animals without a game license. Fine Shs. 2,000/- or 6 months in default.2nd Count:- Unlawful methods of hunting game. Fine Shs. 1,000/- or 3 months in default. 3rd Count:- Unlawful methods of hunting. Fine Shs. 1,000/- or 3 months in default. 4th Count:- Failing to record game animals killed on a license. Fine Shs. 200/- or 1 month in default. 5th Count:- Official corruption. 6 months' imprisonment. 6th Count:- Official corruption. 6 months' imprisonment. 7th Count:- Failing to surrender expired game license. Fine Sh. 1/- or distress in default.

Chief Makongoro pleaded guilty to the 1st, 4th and 7th counts, and the fines of which totaled Shs. 2,201/-. Chief Makongoro paid the fines.[198] He appealed against his conviction on those counts to which he had not pleaded guilty. In

---

194   PRO, CO 822/1299, "Chief Makongoro", 8.

195   TNA, *Musoma District Book*, vol. 1, "Natural History," Sheet I.

196   Ibid.

197   PRO, CO 822/1299, "Chief Makongoro", 1.

198   PRO, CO 822/1299, "Chief Makongoro," 2.

March the appeal was allowed by the Chief Justice and the convictions on 2nd, 3rd, 5th and 6th counts were quashed.[199]

Following the trial the Government commissioned an enquiry into the conduct of affairs in the Ikizu Chiefdom. The Governor appointed Mr. R. H. Gower, Senior District Officer, under sub-section 2 of Section 13 of the African Chiefs Ordinance, No 27 of 1953. Gower's enquiry revealed that "over many years Chief Makongoro's actions had been impelled almost exclusively by love of power and money".[200] The enquiry also revealed a grim picture of intimidation and extortion.

In all, Gower interviewed 129 witnesses, many of whom also submitted long written memoranda: "Some merely wished to record their desire to see their Chief return to rule in Ikizu. Others brought specific complaints of oppression suffered at the hands of the Chief, whilst others presented a more general picture of wide-scale oppression practiced in the Chiefdom during the 32 years of Chief Makongoro's rule".[201] Some specific complaints voiced by many witnesses deserve to be mentioned.

Many witnesses complained about the arbitrary fines imposed by Chief Makongoro. For instance, anyone who was late or missed turning up for communal work for a day or two had to pay a fine. These ranged from Shs. 50/- to Shs. 200/- and no official receipt was ever issued.[202] "Many witnesses complained that these communal works went on all the year round without allowing the people sufficient time for their own cultivation. Other witnesses mentioned having to work without pay in the Chief's own *shambas*".[203] According to Gower's enquiry, many witnesses cited examples of brutality suffered at the Chief's command. Although much of what many witnesses said may be held suspect, one case involved an actual victim whose testimony, Gower says, was corroborated by two other witnesses. Nyason Lugesha told Gower that in 1945 she had wanted to leave her husband. She was taken before the Chief who ordered her to be beaten. Three men who were later charged, convicted and imprisoned carried out the order. Nyason was seven months pregnant with twins and aborted that same day. She was operated on in Musoma and recovered.[204]

Chief Makongoro's order to have Nyason Lugesha beaten for wishing to leave her husband renders itself to many interpretations other than being a case of brutality. It is possible the Chief was making an example of Nyason for all those Ikizu "independent-thinking" women who were beginning to threaten to loosen the ties of matrimony. It is also possible that the Chief, as "customary" custodian of tradition, believed his order was to the effect of enforcing customary paternal control over marriage. The last interpretation is of particular significance. Traditionally, in Ikizu the jurisdiction over family disputes was a matter for clan members and elders. Under colonial rule this role was vested in Chief Makongoro and the native courts which supposedly used "customary law" to settle domestic disputes. However, as Mamdani has argued, "There was nothing customary about a (colonial) Native Authority whose rights extended to settling domestic disputes".[205]

Another curiosity is the decision to beat Nyason rather than sanction her behavior by other means. Moreover, in Ikizu divorce was acceptable. According

---

199   Ibid. 2.

200   PRO, CO 822/1299, "Chief Makongoro," 2.

201   Ibid. 2.

202   Ibid. 5.

203   Ibid. 6.

204   Ibid. 11.

205   Mamdani, *Citizen and Subject*, 48.

to H. C. Baxter, if a bride never went to her husband's village all the bride wealth and progeny thereof would be returned.[206] If the wife left her husband having borne him children the bride price and progeny was returned, but if the husband had performed the *Subo* ceremony bride wealth could not be returned.[207] In the case of Nyason, even if dowry was not returned, since she was already pregnant her husband would have had a legitimate claim to any child born.

Furthermore, the beating of Nyason was a manifestation of domestic violence[208] which, like legally sanctioned caning, was perpetrated in the name of "custom". Traditional gender-based oppression in Ikizu and other patriarchal societies emphasized the inferiority of women. Gender oppression, and the resultant violence against women, was part of a culture whose norms and values recognized a husband's prerogative to discipline his wife physically if he chose.[209] In the case of Nyason pre-colonial virtue was being maintained by a terrible punishment which was perpetrated in the name of "customary law". Moreover, Nyason's beating also suggests how in colonial Tanzania wife beating and child abuse were an integral part of the colonial social order! Juvenile criminals (less than fifteen years old) were legally sentenced to be caned. Between 1942 and 1956, 2,543 juvenile offenders were caned for various offenses against the law.[210] Wife beating and child abuse neither raised concern nor translated into statutory or institutional remedies.

There is no doubt Chief Makongoro carried high the banner of African tradition. Chief Makongoro was not just a "traditionalist" because of his polygamous marriages. According to Gower's enquiry, Chief Makongoro was opposed to Western influences that tended to undermine traditional authority and traditional values. Chief Makongoro was not in good terms with the Seventh Day Adventist Church (hereafter SDA) because he believed its adherents were opposed to the payment of *marero* and *nyangi* contributions. He therefore did what he could to frustrate Western missionaries in Ikizu chiefdom. In 1957 he refused to grant the SDA missionaries land to put in a borehole for their water supply. He also refused to consider the grant of a site for the Catholic Church in his area.[211]

Chief Makongoro was only interested in education as long as it did not involve the indoctrination of children with "new-fangled" ideas. In 1947 the Chief obtained official permission to start a fund with which to build "Bush" schools as an alternative to Mission schools. The fund, which was swelled by *marero* cattle, was used to build schools, pay teachers' salaries and procure school materials. A number of schools were opened but later some were closed and only three remained in operation in 1957, at *Sarawe*, *Salama* and *Hunyari*.[212] At the time the

---

206   TNA, *Musoma District Book*, vol.1, Baxter, H. C. "Waikizu Customs", Sheet I.

207   Ibid.

208   Domestic violence spans the range of violent encounters and includes physical assaults, sexual assaults, verbal assaults, intimidation, threats, extreme emotional or psychological neglect as well as death.

209   In Western cultures wife beating has been sanctioned by law at least since the days of the Roman Empire. The "rule of thumb" was an English common law which permitted a husband to beat his wife so long as the stick was not bigger than his thumb.

210   Figures are from respective annual reports of the Prisons Department.

211   PRO, CO 822/1299, "Chief Makongoro", 11.

212   Ibid. 9.

Government closed these three remaining schools in 1957, as they were still not registered, "Shs. 80,000/- were supposed to exist in the Fund, but only Shs. 5,000/- (had) been actually traced".[213]

Chief Makongoro is also credited with supporting *maendeleo ya wanawake* (women's progress) in his chiefdom. In 1957 his enthusiasm enabled the Social Development Department to set up Women's Clubs in Ikizu. However, the Chief was opposed to all efforts to break down the custom of female circumcision "on the grounds that this would destroy tribal custom".[214] Subsequently the Chief's enthusiasm for *maendeleo ya wanawake* cooled and Women's Clubs in Ikizu collapsed.

Despite some of the Chief's positive contributions, in his confidential report to the Governor, Mr. Gower portrayed Chief Makongoro in the most unfavorable terms:

> *After making allowances for the fact that some evidence was opinion and hearsay, and that some evidence was biased with ulterior motive, the general picture that is indelibly impressed on me as a result of my enquiry is that of a tyrannical Chief, who exercised complete control over his whole Chiefdom - his every action tainted with an overwhelming desire to line his own pocket. Makongoro struck me as a man who was ruthless, self centred and contemptuous of any views that ran contrary to his own.[215]*

Gower strongly recommended the deposition of Chief Makongoro "in the interest of good government".

Chief Makongoro deposed and exiled

After making due allowance for the exaggeration of witnesses at the inquiry, Governor Turnbull decided that sufficient evidence was forthcoming to justify the deposition of Chief Makongoro under Section 13(1) of the African Chiefs Ordinance (1953). The Order for Chief Makongoro's deposition was not, however, made at once. The explanation that the Governor gave the Secretary of State was that a number of legal and other difficulties had first to be resolved. The first difficulty that arose was the legal one of restricting Chief Makongoro's residence after he had been deposed. The Governor believed that Chief Makongoro's presence in or anywhere near the Musoma district would be a threat to law and order.[216]

At first, it appeared that if he were to be deposed it would necessary to prosecute him by the magisterial inquiry provided for under sections 15 - 20 of the African Chiefs Ordinance (1953). This would preclude him from entering certain chiefdoms in the territory. However, when this procedure was put into effect it was discovered that Chief Makongoro could only be kept out of certain chiefdoms but not out of townships, which did not fall within the jurisdiction of local chiefs.[217] There was nothing to stop Chief Makongoro from, say, settling down in Musoma town where he had a house.

---

213   Ibid. 10.

214   Ibid. 10.

215   Ibid. 14.

216   PRO, CO 822/1299, Saving Telegram to The Secretary of State for the Colonies, London, from the Governor, Dar-es-Salaam, dated 15 July, 1958.

217   Ibid.

It was then decided that the provisions of the Deportation Ordinance of 1921 (Cap. 38) must be used to deport Chief Makongoro, provided adequate evidence on oath could be produced to justify deportation. "At the beginning of July (1958)' wrote the Governor, `sworn evidence was received from Musoma, amply substantiating the allegation that Makongoro's presence would be a threat to law and order in Ikizu Chiefdom".[218] Twenty-two witnesses testified to the "oppression and terror that could again be expected in the area on his return".[219] During the inquiry Chief Makongoro was in Biharamulo, some two hundred miles west of Musoma, where he had been moved to "facilitate" a more conducive atmosphere for the Gower inquiry.

At the time that the Governor received sworn testimony from Musoma, he also received news that Chief Makongoro had been taken seriously ill of a heart complaint at Biharamulo. Thus although convinced that Chief Makongoro's deposition and deportation were both "most amply justified" the Governor was reluctant to take action against him "in view of the reported state of his health". However, another complication arose. This was the libel case against Mwalimu Julius Nyerere, the leader of TANU,[220] in which one of the libels alleged that the Musoma District Commissioner had "cooked up" a case against Chief Makongoro. Chief Makongoro was one of the witnesses for the Defense, and arrived in Dar es Salaam from Biharamulo on the afternoon of the 12th July and on that evening his illness was diagnosed as cirrhosis of the liver.

The case against Nyerere opened at 9 a.m. on 9 July 1958. The District Commissioner, Musoma, arrived in Dar es Salaam on the night of 8 July and "brought with him strong representations from the Provincial Commissioner, Lake Province, that Makongoro should be deposed forthwith":

His contention was that Makongoro might die at any time and, if he died before he had been deposed, it would thereafter be open to the Tanganyika African National Union to allege that Government had been unable to prove any matter of substance against him and had unjustifiably persecuted him to his death.[221]

On the strength of these representations the Governor made Orders on the 9th July deposing Makongoro as Chief under Section 13(1) of the African Chiefs Ordinance (1953) and deporting him to Tunduru[222] under Section 2 of the Deportation Ordinance (1921). The Orders were served on 14 July, 1958 while Chief Makongoro was admitted at the Sewa Haji hospital in Dar es Salaam.

Chief Makongoro died in Dar es Salaam on 25 September 1958. Mr. Nyerere himself made arrangements for the return of the ex-Chief's body to Ikizu where he was buried. "The funeral', wrote the Governor to the Secretary of State, `was turned into a considerable political occasion by the Musoma TANU branch".[223] TANU speakers and subsequent columns of *Mwafrika* `made something of a martyr of

218   Ibid.

219   Ibid.

220   TANU stands for Tanganyika African National Union, the nationalist party that led Tanzania to independence in 1961 under the leadership of Nyerere.

221   PRO, CO 822/1299, Governor's saving telegram, 15th July, 1958.

222   Tunduru is located in southern Tanzania and is approximately seven hundred miles from Musoma.

223   PRO, CO 822/1218, To Secretary of State from the Governor, saving telegram dated 15.11.58.

Makongoro.[224] One of the rumors circulating was that the Government had deposed Chief Makongoro because he opposed the introduction of District Councils.[225] The Government did nothing to dispel these rumors supposedly because:

> *First, it did not appear seemly to attack Makongoro either when he was dying or immediately after his death. Secondly, the allegations made about Government's motives did not attract a great deal of attention among the African public. Thirdly, those who paid the most attention to these allegations were the least likely to be affected by anything said in reply. Fourthly, a quasi-judicial enquiry is perhaps unsuitable for publication, since in its nature it makes allegations and averments which have not been tested in a court of law.[226]*

Furthermore, in the Governor's communication to the Secretary of State, it was emphasized that Chief Makongoro had not been deposed because he opposed the introduction of District Councils.[227] However, there is another possible reason why the government declined from responding to TANU's allegations. In adopting this approach the government observed one of the cardinal rules of effective propaganda, namely "avoid refuting the claims made by the opposition so that the original message is not spread further amongst those who may not have initially received it".[228]

Following the death of Chief Makongoro the Government had to deal with the issue of choosing his successor. The dispute that followed and how it was resolved marked a shift away from the arbitrary method of appointing colonial chiefs. On the day after the funeral a group of Makongoro supporters "elected" Hassani, a minor son of Chief Makongoro, to be his successor. Although the Governor had no doubt about the traditional methods used to "elect" Hassani, he questioned the lack of "concession whatever to the modern practice of adapting traditional methods to give the people a say in the choice of a Chief".[229] The Government proposed that "the new Chief be chosen in accordance with the popular will and without violating local custom".[230] Mr. Hans Cory, Government sociologist, and the District Commissioner were instructed to enquire into the most suitable way of selecting Makongoro's successor.

Chief Makongoro's successor was eventually chosen by a voting system, which was public and open to every Ikizu taxpayer. The voting system was founded on the use of the single transferable vote.[231] Out of 1,732 votes cast for 13 candidates on the first ballot Makongoro's son, Hassani, lay third in the voting with 377 votes.

---

224   Ibid.

225   Ibid.

226   PRO, CO 822/1218, Secretary of State for the Colonies, London, from the Governor, Dar es Salaam. Saving telegram dated 15.11.58.

227   PRO, CO 822/1299, The Governor, Dar-es-Salaam, to Secretary of State for the Colonies, telegram dated 30.10.58.

228   Rawnsley, Gary D. *Radio Diplomacy and Propaganda: The BBC and VOA in International Politics, 1956-64* (Macmillan Press Ltd., 1996): 22.

229   PRO, CO 822/1218, The Governor, Dar-es-Salaam, to Secretary of State for the Colonies, saving telegram dated 15.11.58.

230   PRO, CO 822/1218,The Governor, Dar-es-Salaam, to Secretary of State for the Colonies, telegram dated 15.11.58.

231   Ibid.

On the final ballot, Hassani and the rest having been eliminated, Matutu received 876 votes against 658 for his remaining rival and was duly declared chief.[232]

In a broader sense, Chief Makongoro's career is of interest in other ways. On the one hand, his career validates Mamdani's argument that "customary law consolidated the non-customary power of chiefs in the colonial administration".[233] Under indirect colonial rule the jurisdiction of Chief Makongoro included the arbitration of marital disputes which hitherto was the prerogative of one's kin and village elders. Under indirect rule Makongoro's power derived from his nominal control of previously autonomous social domains like the household, age sets, and initiation rites. However - and this is the crucial point - he did so without relying on the coercive force of the colonial state because there was no resistance against the changes he brought to bear on *marero* and *nyangi* customs.

On the other hand, the career of Chief Makongoro is a serious indictment of the policy of Indirect Rule as well as its affirmation. Chief Makongoro's career reveals one of the fundamental flaws of Indirect Rule. One colonial official remarked when Chief Makongoro was accused of "illegal" hunting: "It is a startling reflection on the present inability of many D. Cs. & D. Os. to get really "close to the ground". If one considers that all this happened within 30-35 miles of District Headquarters at Musoma where, I see, four Administrative Officers are stationed."[234]

Although the same official hastened to excuse the lack of supervision on "too much clerical work which ties personnel to their desks in the District headquarters", the fact remains that lack of supervision allowed chiefs like Makongoro too much latitude to do what they wished to do. It was also this lack of supervision, which indeed made Indirect Rule indirect, contrary to Mamdani's argument that it was a facade for direct rule.

The major obstacles to the close supervision of Native Authorities were the inadequacy of European administrative personnel and poor communications. "During the average interwar year', writes Heussler, 'there were some 150 to 170 administrative officers in the territory, including men on leave or otherwise unavailable for district postings."[235] Heussler concludes "No matter what they wanted to do on their own initiative or what headquarters instructed them to do, there were never enough men for the task."[236]

Personnel shortages forced District Officers to take chances that their chiefs would, as it were, do the right thing on their own! According to Heussler: "To some the position of a chief in his tribe was not a thing that Europeans need worry about as long as the man could be depended on not to cause trouble and to help with projects such as planting cotton . . ."[237] In some cases the gamble turned out fine, but in the case of Chief Makongoro the consequences were disastrous.

---

232   Ibid.

233   Mamdani, *Citizen and Subject*, 110.

234   PRO, CO 822/1218, The Governor, Dar-es-Salaam, to Secretary of State for the Colonies, telegram dated 15.11.58.

235   Heussler, R. *British Tanganyika: An Essay and Documents on District Administration* (Durham, North Carolina: Duke University Press, 1971: 23.

236   Ibid. 23.

237   Ibid. 19.

To know what was going on in their districts, District Officers had to go on tour. However, problems of communication and transportation limited the distances such tours could cover.[238] Remote parts were rarely, if at all, visited. Chiefs in remote areas easily escaped the scrutiny of District officials either by deliberately moving further from district headquarters[239] or by conveniently being absent when an Administrative Officer appeared.[240] The inability of many District Officers to get really "close to the ground" meant "nine-tenth of native life went on as always behind their backs and without reference to them".[241]

According to Arthur J. Wakefield, who worked for sixteen years in colonial Tanzania, the policy of Indirect Rule eventually became the main reason why the Colonial Service came to be regarded as "the political opponents of the people".[242] He further noted that:

> all "contact" of departments with the people is canalised through the one channel of District Commissioner-cum-Chief... The Service is not only foreign to the people, but its methods deprive it of developing real contacts; it has no roots in the lives of the people. Consequently individual officers rarely get inspiration from their service to the people.[243]

Thus while Indirect Rule provided an administrative structure of dealing with the mass of colonized people by less costly means, it turned out to be ineffective because it alienated the people from the administration and many European officials were frustrated by it and derived little satisfaction or happiness in their work.

In conclusion, it can be surmised that the policy of Indirect Rule in colonial Tanzania recognized the pre-colonial institution of chieftainship. However, the jurisdiction of chieftaincies was ill defined and many chiefs did not have independent sources of revenue other than the rebate from the taxes they collected for the colonial state. Chief Makongoro of Ikizu exploited the lack of close supervision to manipulate the customs and values of his people to secure their services and to create a resource base outside of official channels.

The British colonial endeavor in Tanzania was in part an exercise in institution building. The British policy of Indirect Rule sought to co-opt traditional rulers into the colonial bureaucracy with the objective of creating a colonial hegemony albeit "on a shoe-string" basis. The inability to provide close European supervision left many chiefs free to pursue their own agendas at the same time as they tried to do what the Government asked them to do. In so far as Imperial administrators were few in number and African chiefs were free to do as they wished, British control in Tanzania was more posture derived than absolute.

---

238   The suggestion by one Colonial Office bureaucrat that District Officers use helicopters (See CO 822/1299) Ordered on hypocrisy when all the time Governors were instructed to avoid heavy financial expenditures!

239   Graham, J. D. "Indirect Rule: the establishment of `chiefs' and `tribes' in Cameron's Tanganyika", Tanzania Notes and Records, no. 77 and 78 1976): 6.

240   Unfortunately a visiting car could be heard or spotted some distance before it arrived. This gave a chief the chance to hide if he wished.

241   Heussler, British Tanganyika, 16.

242   Wakefield, A.J. "Random Notes on the Colonial System", Mss. Afr s. 352, Rhodes House Library, Oxford, England. 2.

243   Ibid. 2.

5

The trial of Oldus Elishira (1955): Murder, Politics and Justice in Late Colonial Tanganyika

Introduction

Late in the afternoon on 23 February, 1955, a white settler named Harold M. Stuchbery was speared by a Maasai man named Oldus Elishira. The killing of 58-year-old Stuchbery caused fear among members of the white community at Ol-Molog in West Kilimanjaro. As we shall see, his death was neither thoroughly investigated nor was the case convincingly prosecuted. Efforts by his neighbor, Robin Johnson, to politicize the case did not attract much attention locally or abroad.[243] The murder itself raises a host of other questions regarding property rights, racism and prejudice, and the judicial process in late colonial Tanganyika.

This chapter examines the murder and the outcome of the trial to highlight the social, cultural, racial and political fault lines that would otherwise remain obscure to students of Tanzania history and jurisprudence. Details from the trial show that the court in colonial Tanganyika was more than a legal arena and the legal experts were more than "value-neutral" discoverers of the law. Of particular interest, although the court acquitted Oldus Elishira the Maasai community deemed it necessary to pay restitution to Stuchbery's widow.

---

243   *The Tanganyika Standard*, a daily newspaper, carried short columns about the case on 25 & 26 February; 2 March; 28 May; and 1 June, 1955.

At the micro level, the killing of Stuchbery was symptomatic of simmering hostilities between the European farmers at Ol-Molog and their pastoral Maasai neighbors. On the one hand, the settlers accused the Maasai of "trespassing" and exposing their beef and dairy cattle to bovine diseases. On the other hand, the Maasai were aggrieved because the settler farms obstructed the routes they used to the Tinga Tinga livestock market and in their seasonal migrations in search of pasture. At the macro level, the 1950s in colonial Tanganyika saw a rise in violent crimes against the person (such as assault and murder) and against property, such as burglary and larceny. Unable to receive police protection when they needed it, Europeans in Tanganyika resorted to vigilantism and guns sales rapidly increased.

The Ol-Molog Settler Community

In 1951, eight choice pieces of "virgin" land at Ol-Molog[244] were demarcated for settler farming out of land the government had alienated in 1947. There was intense competition to get these pieces. The "lucky" ones were the following: Piet Hugo, David read, Arthur Palfrey, Campbell Webb, Harold Stuchbery, George (aka Robin) Johnston, Sir Archibald McIndoe and Con Benson. Later, new arrivals included Brian Freyburg, Derek Bryceson, John Millard and Dr. Michael Wood. Some of these men were remarkable characters. Piet Hugo, a massive, strong and barrel-chested man, was an Afrikaner and a fighter pilot by training. Derek Bryceson, partially paralyzed in the legs from wounds sustained during the Second World War, was an ex-Royal Air Force pilot. In her memoir Erika Johnston describes him to have been stubborn as a mule.[245] Brian Freyburg was "an Englishman who looked like an athletic don". During the Second World War he was captured by the Italians, and "spent a lot of time escaping from Italian prisoner-of-war camps and being recaptured".[246] After the War he founded the African Flying Doctor Service and from 1958 to 1962 he was the president of the Tanganyika Capricorn Africa Society.

David Read was born and raised in Kenya and Tanganyika. His early childhood was not particularly comfortable. His mother and stepfather operated a store in Loliondo where they also tried their hand at farming. Twice his stepfather had to go try his luck panning for gold during the Lupa gold fever. On one of these trips he left the family with money enough only for flour and sugar which they survived on for eight months.[247] At the age of fourteen David could barely read or write.[248] However, according to Erika Johnston[249], David Read turned out to be "the real professional farmer in the area".

Con Benson was an eminent London merchant banker who purchased farm No. 8. But Mr. Benson seems to have been an "absentee landlord", who visited the farm annually. Doctor Michael Wood was a surgeon based in Kenya until 1957 when he and his wife, Susan Wood author of *A Fly in Amber*, moved to Ol-

244   Ol Molog is a Maasai name meaning "little pimples" which signifies the small hillocks that dot the landscape.

245   Johnston, Erika, *The Other Side of Kilimanjaro* (London: Johnson, 1971): 15.

246   Ibid. 15.

247   Read, David, *Barefoot over the Serengeti* (London: Cassell, 1979): 184.

248   Ibid. 184.

249   Johnston, *Kilimanjaro*. 14.

Molog. Robin Johnston was born in South Africa and grew up in England. He held an Honors Degree in anthropology and economics. He was also a trained pilot. Before he moved to Ol-Molog, he was in the Colonial Civil Service. His last appointment was as District Office at Kongwa during the infamous Groundnut Scheme. He resigned from the Colonial Service in 1951. At Ol-Molog, he initially co-owned his farm with Sir Archibald McIndoe, the renowned British plastic surgeon. It seems Sir Archibald only visited Ol-Molog for his annual vacation, when he would go hunting.[250] Johnston later bought out Sir Archibald's share of the farm which apparently soured their friendship.

Harold M. Stuchbery, the farmer killed by Oldus Elishira, was a retired veterinary doctor. He graduated with a DV Sc. from the University of Melbourne in Australia. After graduating he joined the Colonial Service. His last appointment was in Nyasaland (now Malawi). According to Erika Johnston, the opening up of Ol-Molog with this unusual assortment of men did not escape the attention of the English press, "who had some wild, uninformed theories about it".[251] How these men ended up at Ol-Molog is part of a broader history of European emigration to the colonies. An abbreviation of that history is necessary here.

Most accounts of British emigration start with the question of who migrated and who did not. To British aristocrats and the working class, the colonies offered little incentive for emigration. While to the aristocrat colonial life was too primitive, to the laborer there were few job opportunities since most of the menial jobs were performed by colonial natives.[252] Therefore the majority of European colonial societies were restricted in terms of class, probably most of them falling in the category of middle class. Certainly no two colonies were exactly alike, and colonial settler experiences evidently varied.[253]

When colonial rule was imposed in the 1890s, it was by force and conquest. The Germans, who first colonized Tanganyika, and later the British, assumed that their sovereignty extended to include claims over landed property. The Crown became the "owner" of all "waste and unclaimed" land, in many cases by concession or forfeiture. It was necessary that the ownership of these lands be primarily vested in the Crown so that their future disposal could be effectually controlled by the government.[254] It was this constitutional right that allowed colonial governments to sell or lease land to European settlers in Tanganyika. It was this constitutional right which also validated the settlers' claims to private landownership.

Permanent European settlement in Africa was largely a nineteenth and twentieth-century phenomenon. In colonial Tanganyika substantial immigration only occurred after World War Two. Many of the settlers, such as those at Ol-Molog, were either ex-servicemen or retired colonial civil servants. Between 1948 and 1958 the number of settlers doubled from 10,648 to 20,498, which called for an increase in the amount of land alienated for European settlement.[255] Despite

---

250   Ibid. 191.

251   Ibid. 17.

252   Christopher, A.J. *Colonial Africa* (London: Croom Helm; Totowa, NJ: Barnes & Noble Books, 1984): 122.

253   Ibid. 123.

254   Ng'ong'ola, Clement, "The state, settlers, and indigenes in the evolution of land law and policy in Malawi", *The International Journal of African Historical Studies*, 23, 2 (1990): 29.

255   Feierman, Steven, *Peasant Intellectuals: anthropology and history in Tanzania* (Madison: The University of Wisconsin Press, 1990): 164.

the safeguards provided in the Land Ordinance of 1923, and its subsequent amendments, land alienation for European settlement reduced the amount of land available for African use especially in particular localities of the Northern Province. This led to conflicts over land between settlers and Africans, the best known being the Meru land case.

According to Tidrick some Europeans were casting envious eyes on Maasai land as far back as the 1930s:

> *F. J. Anderson, a settler with a farm at Rasha Rasha, was the spokesman for those who felt that Masai District was wasted on the Masai. In a Legislative Council meeting in 1937 he accused the government of pampering the Masai... In 1942, after a long preamble once again accusing the government of "favoritism" toward the Masai, he asked in the Legislative Council if a thousand square miles of Masailand could be set aside for "settlement of fighting services personnel, when their job of destroying our foul enemies, who would make slaves of the Masai, is completed.*[256]

Anderson was reiterating what Lord Lugard had opined almost fifty years before. As far as Anderson was concerned, Maasai land use was not only wasteful but such wastefulness justified the alienation of their land for European use.

Anderson's request was initially refused on the grounds that the Maasai needed the land. Addressing the question in the Legislative Council, the Chief Secretary had this to say:

> *A large proportion of the [Maasailand] is unusable for other than pastoral purposes, owing to the unreliability of the rainfall, and for the same reason the bulk of the highlands included form an essential reserve of grazing for periods of drought... In Government's opinion the Masai make the fullest economic use of the land which their stage of development and tribal way of life permit and would not, in the conditions which prevail, be able permanently to maintain their present herds on an appreciably lesser area.*[257]

However by 1947 the Government had reversed its position and allowed the alienation of Maasai lands for European settlers. The Maasai were first evicted from the Sanya Corridor in 1947. In 1948 Ol-Molog, a dry season grazing area and ritual site of very great importance to the Kisongo Maasai was alienated to European wheat farmers.[258]

In the mind of the European settlers, finally the administrators had come to their senses and realized that they could not allow "these useless (Maasai) people to tie up thousands of acres of valuable agricultural land".[259] What the settlers did not realize was that the alienation of the supposedly high potential, relatively well watered areas occupied by the Maasai deprived them of an integral part of their grazing land. Thus the excision of Ol-Molog and other promising parts of

---

256   Tidrick, Kathryn, "Masai and their Masters: A Psychological Study of District Administration," *African Studies Review*, vol. 23, no. 1 (April, 1980): 24.

257   Quoted by Ndagala, Daniel K. *Territory, Pastoralists, and Livestock: Resource Control among the Kisongo Maasai* (Uppsala, 1992): 44.

258   Arhem, Kaj, *Masai and the State: The Impact of Rural Development Policies on a Pastoral People in Tanzania*, IWGIA Document (Copenhagen, 1985): 35.

259   Tidrick, "Masai and their Masters," 24.

Maasailand was liable to be resisted by the Maasai.

In the 1950s the Maasai like their Meru neighbors to the south were further deprived of land when the colonial government alienated more land to meet the increasing demands of immigrant white settlers. Both the Meru and the Maasai complained that the government had alienated their lands without consulting them.[260] A representative of the Meru Citizens Union twice took the case to the United Nations in 1951, but was unable to get the United Nations to force Great Britain to return the land to the Meru.[261] While the Meru were able to pursue legal action for their rights, the Maasai (who for some reason were unable to) may have chosen to take matters in their own hands, and knowingly or otherwise transgressed the settlers' private domain.

In the case of Ol-Molog the possibility of friction and trouble arising between the Maasai and the settlers was heightened by three factors: (a) the fact that the settler farms obstructed Maasai access to the Tinga Tinga livestock market, (b) the fact that Ol-Molog was a dry season grazing area and had places of great ritual value to the Maasai, and (c) the fact that the settlers were full of prejudice. The settlers' attempts to keep the Maasai off their private property clashed with the Maasai's need of an access route to the Tinga Tinga livestock market. It is partly because the Government realized the importance to the Maasai access route to the Tinga Tinga livestock market that it was prepared to construct a "fenced-in corridor" through Ol-Molog.

The alienation of Ol-Molog deprived the Maasai not only of dry season grazing land but also denied them access to ritual sites situated in this area. According to Ndagala, the restriction of movement was sometimes enforced with armed force: "On one occasion, the Arusha Company of the King's African Rifles (KAR) was employed to prevent Lolbene and Naberera Maasai returning from dry-season pastures in Sanya to their usual habitation."[262]

The Maasai not only abhorred these restrictions but they endeavored to contravene them. A vivid description of the impunity with which the Maasai disregarded these restrictions is given by Ndagala:

> They crossed the set boundaries into other Districts, broke into settler farms for water and grass, and voiced their grievances to the administrators at every available opportunity. It is also said that after the Maasai of West Kilimanjaro had learned that they were being restricted to given areas to protect settler cattle from disease, they designed revenge. They are said to have collected thousands of ticks from diseased stock, put them into small bags, and concealed them on settler land at night. Although the Maasai stock, said to be diseased had not come into contact with settler stock, the later soon contracted East Coast Fever from the "planted" ticks.[263]

This came to be known among settler circles as the "Masai- Chagga Conspiracy" because the settlers believed the Chagga had also participated.[264]

---

260   United Nations, Trusteeship Council, *Visiting Mission's Report, 1954*: 52-54.

261   Taylor, J. Clagett, *The Political Development of Tanganyika* (Stanford: Stanford University Press; London: Oxford University Press, 1963): 119.

262   Ndagala, *Territory, Pastoralists, and Livestock*, 43.

263   Ibid. 43.

264   Ibid. 43.

What further hindered "good neighborly" relations between the Maasai and European settlers was racial prejudice, especially on the part of some Government officials and individual settlers. In response to concerns about Maasai ritual sites at Ol-Molog and other areas in West Kilimanjaro, the District Officer of Moshi had this to say:

> . . . is it sound and right that [Maasai] should be given land... which can be put to greater economic use by Europeans, for no better reasons, than the preservation of barbaric customs; which should in my humble opinion be persistently steadily and gradually discouraged. . . No, for the sake of the Masai, peace and tranquility let us keep the Masai where they are. We cannot establish good grounds for resisting the alienation of these farms.[265]

This was characteristic of colonial disrespect for the customs and religious values of colonized peoples.

Consequently, in most cases Maasai intransigence was justified. A case in point was the Maasai need to have access to their ritual sites. One such ritual site was *Endoinyo loo'lmoruak* or Hill of the Elders where all *Olng'esher* ceremonies marking the transition from moran to elder for all Maasai are performed. The hill is located almost equidistant between Mount Kilimanjaro and Mount Meru. According to Ndagala this site is very important to the Maasai for two reasons: first, some Maasai believe the hill is a burial mound of the ancestor of all Maasai, and second, for purposes of the *Olng'esher* ceremonies, the site was chosen by Mbatiany, one of the most distinguished Maasai *olaiboni* or diviners.[266] However, the land on which this hill stands was alienated to a European settler as Farm No. 321.

Thus the Maasai with their cattle were in the habit of taking a short cut (usually at night) over these farms to get to the livestock market or on their seasonal migrations in search of pastures. Stuchbery and others believed that Maasai cattle exposed their farms to bovine disease. The farmers also accused the Maasai of stealing their cattle. Protests had been made to the Government, who were in the process of building a fenced-in corridor, through which the Maasai would be able to move their cattle. The fence was intended to prevent contact between livestock and the possibility of cattle theft.

On the afternoon of February 23, 1955, Stuchbery was told by his cattle herdsman that several "armed" Maasai were moving a small herd of cattle across the lower part of his property. Though he had had previous evidence of these movements by way of broken fences, spoor marks, etc., this was the first time that the Maasai and their cattle had actually been seen. Stuchbery snatched up his shotgun and, accompanied by the herdsman, drove down to waylay the Maasai.[267]

In due course, he confronted the Maasai and there was a scuffle. How and why Oldus Elishira stabbed Stuchbery with his spear is unclear. There are two conflicting accounts. According to Erika Johnston's memoir the sequence of events was as follows. When the Maasai saw Stuchbery's Land Rover approaching they bolted. Stuchbery sprang out and fired two shots into the air,[268] calling upon them

265   Ibid. 46.

266   Ndagala, *Territory, Pastoralists and Livestock*, 94.

267   Johnston, *Kilimanjaro*, 200, 209.

268   *The Tanganyika Standard*, February 25, 1955. 1.

to stop. The Maasai turned and waited for him to draw up to them. He told them that he was going to "disarm" them of their spears and take them to the police station.[269] He apparently told the Maasai that their cattle would be impounded until a case was taken against them.[270]

Stuchbery then proceeded to "disarm" the Maasai of their spears, *simis* and clubs.[271] He moved across to the first man and asked him for his spear. The man hesitated and then handed it over. The second man did the same and the spears were given to Stuchbery's herdsman to hold. Then Stuchbery drew up to Elishira and held out his hand for his spear. But instead of handing over his spear, Elishira grabbed Stuchbery's shotgun with one hand and with the other speared him through the chest.[272] As Stuchbery fell to the ground, the terrified herdsman fled. The postmortem showed Stuchbery had two stab wounds. It appears that Elishira stabbed him a second time as he lay on the ground. With Stuchbery dead or dying, his herdsman ran to report the incidence to Mrs. Stuchbery.

According to Elishira's defense lawyer, Dudley Thompson, Elishira[273] and his friends were just taking their cattle through what they believed was open land when Stuchbery confronted them and "arrogantly tried to chase away the Masai".[274] Whereas his friends ran off, Elishira just stood there. In Thompson's opinion, Elishira was not being obstinate, but rather was not used to being "shouted at in a strange language".[275]

When Stuchbery tugged at Elishira's spear, Elishira also tugged at Stuchbery's "stick". The tugging went on until Stuchbery's gun discharged. Supposedly the bullet grazed Elishira's arm. It was then that Elishira realized that Stuchbery intended to harm him and that is when he pulled his spear and stabbed him. Then Elishira wiped the spear off on the grass and went on with his cows.[276]

Immediately after Stuchbery's herdsman reported the killing to Mrs. Stuchbery, she alerted the police and a manhunt ensued. Supposedly the police thought the killer was a Maasai who was part of Mau Mau and it was announced that they were looking for a dangerous man.[277] As a result, the police rounded up dozens of Maasai for questioning and tortured some of them in the hope of getting a confession. Elishira was arrested two days after the killing of Stuchbery.[278] However, his arrest was not the result of the police manhunt. According to Thompson, when Elishira heard about the manhunt he went to the district commissioner's office at Sanya Juu and surrendered himself.[279] The district commissioner was none other than the brother of Peter Townsend who it was rumored Princess Margaret once wanted to marry.

---

269   Arrest by a private person without warrant was legal in colonial Tanzania.

270   Johnston, *Kilimanjaro*, 209.

271   *The Tanganyika Standard*, February 25, 1955. 1.

272   According to the court proceedings, reported in *The Tanganyika Standard* of May 28, 1955, Stuchbery tried to take the spear from Elishira.

273   In his memoir Thompson refers to Elishira as Oldtus bin Lisau.

274   Thompson, Dudley, *From Kingston to Kenya: the making of a Pan-Africanist Lawyer* (Dover, Massachusetts: The Majority Press, 1993): 123

275   Ibid. 123.

276   Ibid. 124.

277   Ibid. 124.

278   *The Tanganyika Standard*, February 26, 1955.

279   Thompson, *Kingston to Kenya*, 124.

It did not surprise Thompson that Elishira voluntarily gave himself up. According to Thompson, Elishira's behavior had something to do with a Maasai code of honor. Elishira supposedly surrendered himself because he was expected to own up to his misdeed. Furthermore, Thompson could not but admire what he calls a unique Maasai norm: "they will never tell a lie . . . They are very honest, regal people".[280] During the trial Thompson believed Elishira was going to tell the truth no matter what he told him to say.[281]

After his arrest and a preliminary investigation which took about three months Elishira was brought before the High Court at Moshi. Elishira was to be tried according to English law and, in any case, no lower court had jurisdiction to hear a murder case or the power to impose capital punishment. Be that as it may, the extension and application of English law in colonial Tanganyika was not without and qualifications.[282] When applied without limits or modifications, as it happened in Tanganyika, it was liable to lead to serious consequences. Of particular significance was the Penal Code's recognition and empowerment of "citizens" to make arrests. Stuchbery believed he was making such an arrest when he was killed by a man who obviously had no idea what a "citizen arrest" was and whether Stuchbery was justified to "arrest" him.

The trial of Elishira became a micro spectacle: a crowd of Maasai camped outside the courtroom and every day peered through its windows to see what was going on even though many possibly could not follow the proceedings. Inside the court a legal drama unfolded to determine whether a murder had been committed and whether or not Elishira was culpable. The trial was conducted by Justice J. S. Abernethy whose legal career was characteristic of most colonial judges in the sense that it started and ended in some colonial territory.

Judge Abernethy's career started with an appointment as legal adviser to the Borneo administration in 1936. In Borneo he also performed the duties of commissioner of lands, protector of labor and inspector of schools. While in Borneo, he also served as sessions' judge in 1946 and 1948. In 1949, he was promoted to the rank of resident magistrate and transferred to colonial Tanganyika. Two years later, at the age of 44 years, he was appointed judge of the High Court, a position he held from 1951 to 1958. Until 1957 judges of the superior courts in the colonies were appointed "at Her Majesty's pleasure", that is they could be removed without cause at any time.[283] After 1957 they could only be removed for good cause.

While many colonial judges were accused of "misdirecting the search for justice into arid channels of technicalities"[284], as well as rigidly applying English law without making an effort to understand the social conditions of the people to whom it applied, the way Justice Abernethy handled the Stuchbery murder case seems to exonerate him from such charges. He seems to have been exceptionally unconcerned with legal technicalities. More significantly, Judge Abernethy decided the case based on the mental state of the accused rather than on factual evidence

280   Ibid. 123.

281   Ibid. 123.

282   Allott, Anthony, *The Limits of Law* (London: Butterworths, 1980): 111.

283   Martin, Robert, *Personal Freedom and the Law in Tanzania: A Study of Socialist State Administration* (Nairobi: Oxford University Press, 1974): 6.

284   Ibid. 308.

from which intent to murder could be inferred. Furthermore, what makes Justice Abernethy's conduct unusual is that he acquitted an African accused of murdering a European! More will be said later about his attitude and judicial method.

When he was cross examined Elishira admitted that he speared and killed Stuchbery. Because of this admission, his defense attorney argued the case on extenuating circumstances, insisting that he could not be held responsible for his crime. Thompson argued that as a Maasai moran (warrior), Elishira could not have suffered the "indignity" of having his spear taken from him; that what Stuchbery did was "justifiable provocation" that caused Elishira to stab him.[285]

According to colonial Tanganyika's Penal Code, killing on provocation was defined as "the act which causes death in the heat of passion caused by sudden provocation. . . ."[286] The Penal Code also defined provocation as follows:

The term "provocation" means and includes, except as hereafter stated, any wrongful act or insult of such nature as to be likely, when done to an ordinary person, or in the presence of an ordinary person to another person who is under his immediate care, or to whom he stands in conjugal, parental, filial or fraternal relation, or in the relation of master or servant, to deprive him of the power of self-control and to induce him to commit an assault of the kind which the person charged committed upon the person by whom the act or insult is done or offered.

When such an act or insult is done or offered by one person to another, or in the presence of another to a person who is under the immediate care of that other, or to whom the latter stands in any such relation as aforesaid, the former is said to give the latter provocation for an assault.[287] The defense argued that Elishira was an "ordinary" and "proud" Maasai moran who in the presence of other Maasai men would not suffer the humiliation of being dispossessed of his spear.

In delivering his judgment Justice Abernethy said that although Elishira did not deny killing Stuchbery, he found Elishira's extra-judicial statement that he did so in self-defense to be convincing enough.[288] The judge also considered that although Elishira and his colleagues were trespassing, their trespassing was not criminal and Stuchbery had no right to take from them at gun point their spears, sticks and other weapons.[289] In the judge's opinion, Elishira was "certainly justified" in resisting Stuchbery's order that he surrender his spear.[290] In this regard, Justice Abernethy did not recognize Stuchbery's right to execute a "citizen's arrest" as sanctioned by the Criminal Procedure Code: Cap.20.[291]

There was an immediate outcry among the Ol-Molog settlers when Elishira was acquitted. Robin Johnston, Stuchbery's neighbor and an influential settler

285   Johnston, *The Other Side of Kilimanjaro*, 211.

286   Tanganyika, *The Laws of the Tanganyika Territory*. 175.

287   Ibid. 175.

288   *The Tanganyika Standard*, June 1, 1955. 1.

289   Ibid. 1.

290   Ibid. 1.

291   Tanganyika. *The Laws of Tanganyika Territory: in force on 1st January, 1947*. Rev. Edition, vol. 1 (Bradford and London: Watmoughs Ltd., 1948): 260.

in the area, did everything within his limited powers to protest against what he deemed a miscarriage of justice. According to Erika Johnston, although he sent a letter to the press they refused to publish it or to take up the settlers' cause.[292] We do not know why Mr. O.P. Blake, the editor of the only English daily the *Tanganyika Standard*, did not publish Johnston's letter(s). However, the *Tanganyika Standard* carried the news of the killing and reported about the trial and verdict. What is of significance is the way this was done. The breaking news headlines screamed, "EUROPEAN FARMER KILLED BY MASAI". Subsequent headlines read: "Masai moran detained", "Masai on trial for murder" and "MASAI NOT GUILTY OF MURDERING FARMER". Whether or not such headlines were intended to sensationalize racial relations or the "vulnerability" of settlers in colonial Tanganyika is a matter that requires a close scrutiny.

According to the Encyclopedia of American Journalism, sensationalism is described as "(1) detailed reporting of crime, sex, disaster, and monstrosity stories; and (2) use of emphasis, tone, and language to arouse interest in them".[293] It can be argued that based on this definition of "sensationalism" the headlines of all news related with the Stuchbery case intended to sensationalize the incident. Particularly relevant was the use of capitalized headlines. Newspapers ordinarily do not capitalize headlines unless something momentous happens.[294] The editor of the *Tanganyika Standard* may have considered the murder of a European by a "native" unusual and may have capitalized the headlines to stir up the emotions of the readers.

Furthermore, the capitalized headlines, "EUROPEAN FARMER KILLED BY MASAI" and "MASAI NOT GUILTY OF MURDERING FARMER" clearly evoked the editor's preconception of the defendant's guilt and could have inflamed passions for vengeance on the part of European settlers. To be sure, the news columns were suffused with biases because the editor, Mr. O.P. Blake, was reporting to a mainly European readership. Thus despite its subscription to a multi-racial society, the *Tanganyika Standard* could not quite refrain from using designations by tribe or by race. The fact that the *Tanganyika Standard* followed a moderately pro-European line of coverage of local and international news is not surprising.

The *Tanganyika Standard* and *Sunday News* were both owned by Consolidated Holdings which was based in Kenya. The first director of *Tanganyika Standard* was Captain C.B. Anderson, who was also the managing director of the *East African Standard* of Kenya. The first editor of *Tanganyika Standard* was J. Macnab. According to Hadji Konde he had a very patronizing attitude towards Africans.[295] The same could be said of O.P. Blake, the editor of the *Tanganyika Standard* throughout the 1950s.

The *Tanganyika Standard*'s racial undertones, especially in its news reports about the Stuchbery case, reflected the racial prejudices of its editor O.P. Blake. Whereas Stuchbery was mentioned by name, the accused was simply referred to as "Masai moran". Except once during the trial and when the verdict was reported

---

292   Johnston, *Kilimanjaro*, 211.

293   Paneth, Donald, "Sensationalism", *Encyclopedia of American Journalism*. New York: Facts on File, 1983: 451.

294   Lotz, Roy E. *Crime and the American Press* (Praeger, 1991): 106.

295   Konde, Hadji, *Press Freedom in Tanzania* (Arusha: Eastern Africa Publications Ltd., 1984): 16.

was Elishira referred to by his name. The newspaper reports also seem to have tried to sensationalize the killing to portray settler "vulnerability" in a hostile colonial environment. "Mr. H.M. Stuchbery', *Tanganyika Standard* reported, 'was attacked and killed by a Masai moran who speared him through the chest shortly after he challenged a group of tribesmen on his farm . . ."[296] Not only was the confrontation reportedly between "a European" and a group of "tribesmen" reminiscent of Tarzan stories, the way it was reported suggested an image of innocence and vulnerability on the part of the "European" and an image of "savagery" on the part of the "tribesmen." This in itself is not surprising because the most evocative norm among the settlers was the idea of being "civilized."[297]

Ol-Molog settlers like those elsewhere in the territory, believed they were law-abiding "citizens" who needed to do whatever it took to guard their private properties against trespassers. The fact that they themselves could be considered to be trespassers eluded them. Their imaged reality at Ol-Molog easily was fertilized with stereotypes of Maasai being "savages" who disrupted the endeavors of a pioneering community struggling quaintly in the "virgin" wilderness they had opened with their bare hands. On "their" hilly landscape of Ol-Molog the "civilized world" of the settlers met the "uncivilized world" of the Maasai. To the Maasai, however, settlers like Stuchbery were impudent trespassers.

Whereas Robin Johnson was personally not amused by the editor's refusal to publish his letter(s), other settlers at Ol-Molog were probably dismayed that the editor never ran an editorial about their security concerns or the killing of Stuchbery. Although the murder itself got front page coverage, in his editorial of 25 February, 1955, O.P. Blake found it necessary to editorialize about the lack of all-weather roads in the Southern Province! Likewise, the editorial of February 26 was about the importance of political stability in the territory. "Tanganyika', Blake wrote, `is today a land of economic promise, blessed with an able administration and with people of all races who place the interests of the country above all else. A political upheaval at this period in its history would be disastrous". Again, we do not know why Blake avoided comment about Stuchbery's killing in an editorial.

When the "not guilty verdict" was reported on 1 June, 1955, Blake made no comments in his editorial column about it. Instead he chose to discuss the threat of communism in colonial Tanzania; he warned that "the danger of Communist infiltration `through propaganda and the exploitation of grievances' [could] in no way be ruled out". In the same editorial of 1 June, he also emphasized the need for "orderly government", especially a government based on "partnership between the various [racial] communities". He concluded by warning against "Well-meaning but biased individuals who may endeavour to spread harmful propaganda" and "extremists" who were liable to bring disillusionment and economic suicide. Blake was indirectly trying to pre-empt any criticism of the verdict in the Stuchbery case; criticism which he believed could be detrimental to "orderly government".

Although Blake made no comments in his editorials about the verdict, *Tanganyika Standard* avidly reported Maasai reactions about it. *Tanganyika Standard* of 2 March, 1955 carried an interesting news report whose heading read, "Masai to open fund for dead man's family". According to the news article,

---

296   *The Tanganyika Standard*, February 25, 1955. 1.

297   Limerick, Patricia N. *The Legacy of Conquest: The Unbroken Past of the American West* (New York & London: W.W. Norton & Company, 1987): 36.

a baraza (council) of Maasai elders had met at Longido and had decided to open a cattle fund with which to pay restitution to the dependants of Stuchbery. Cattle contributed to the fund would either be sold and the proceeds handed over to the dependants, or the cattle would be given to the dependants to dispose of as they wished.[298] Why did the Maasai elders decide that payment of restitution was necessary? Was their decision to pay restitution an affirmation of Elishira's guilt? Why was the payment of restitution a communal responsibility?

Among the Maasai homicide is dealt with "according to the gravity of the matter, the degree of provocation caused and the element of chance or accident existing".[299] The Maasai also do distinguish between the murders of a Maasai by another (called l'oikop) from the murders of a non-Maasai, as well as between the murders of a relative, called en-gooki, and those of non-relatives.[300] The payment of restitution or enkurou is deemed necessary in all murder cases.

According to Maasai customs and tradition, when a person commits murder he or she is considered to be polluted.[301] The murderer must not only be cleansed but the cleansing must be accompanied with the payment of enkurou or "blood-cattle", which is made to the relatives of the deceased. This comes after the arbitration between the two families or clans by the elders has taken place. Normally arbitration would be initiated by the aggrieved family or clan. If immediate action is not taken by the relatives of the deceased, the relatives of the murderer can initiate arbitration for the customary payment of enkurou.[302]

Besides the need to cleanse the murderer, the payment of enkurou is intended to normalize relations between the families or clans. Before the cleansing and payment of enkurou no marriage between the clans of the deceased and the murderer can take place.[303] In some cases the relatives of the deceased will attempt to avenge their kinsman's death by killing the murderer.[304] Thus compensation is also intended to pre-empt any suspicions of deliberate ill will on the part of the murderer's family or clan as well as to pre-empt the possibility of revenge on the part of the family or clan of the murdered person.

How much enkurou is paid varies. According to Maguire, if the murdered person is a non-Maasai, but was known to and a friend of the murderer, twenty and nine cattle must be paid.[305] If the murdered is a Maasai, but no relative, compensation would either be twenty cattle and nine cattle, or forty cattle and nine cattle. According to Maguire, no penalty is laid down for murder of or assault on a stranger.[306] Maguire further explains the reiteration of the number nine in the enkurou prescribed as follows:

---

298   *The Tanganyika Standard*, March 2, 1955. According to the news report Mrs. Stuchbery, who was still living on the farm, was the deceased's second wife. A daughter by Stuchbery's first wife was then in her final year of study at St. Andrews University in Scotland.

299   Maguire, R.A. "The Masai Penal Code", *Journal of the Royal African Society* (October 1928): 12-18.

300   Ibid. 14.

301   One tradition has it that pollution occurs only if a man kills a woman. The man must undergo a ceremony of xpiation to be cleansed and purified to ward off any curse from the dead woman. Killing a woman is believed to bring not only bad luck such a man is socially disgraced.

302   Maguire, "Masai Penal Code", 13.

303   Ibid., 14.

304   Sankan, *Maasai*. 14.

305   Maguire, "Masai Penal Code", 15.

306   Ibid. 15.

A certain round number of cattle is settled upon as fine or compensation.
To this number (generally twenty or forty) must be added nine more for the
body of the murdered man, in order to wipe out the stain of blood which lies
between the rival parties. These nine cattle are accounted for according to the
orifices of the human body . . .[307]

The nine cattle which metaphorically "wipe out the stain of blood which lies between the rival parties" are in fact intended to pre-empt any retaliation and further spilling of blood.

The Maasai are not the only ones who compensate murder with "blood-money". According to Morris[308], among most of the pre-colonial East African societies when a homicide occurred, compensation was payable either by the killer or his kin, to the kin of the deceased. Among the Somali, a pastoral people like the Maasai, the payment of "blood-money" or *dia* is also a collective responsibility.[309] The objective of paying *dia* among the Somali is strikingly similar to the Maasai's *enkurou*. It is intended to compensate the loss of life and to forestall retaliatory action against the killer's clan.[310]

The collective payment of restitution for murder among the Maasai also has to do with their property rights. For the Maasai, cattle are the most valuable form of property. In the immediate family, livestock is inherited from father to son. However, as Arhem indicates, rights to livestock are at once individual and communal: "Clan mates and stock friends also have claims on the family herd. Control over livestock is stratified; it implies a set of vested interests involving individuals and groups outside and within the immediate family . . .[311] Therefore because of collective claims to the family herd, disposal of animals from it especially in regard to *enkurou* must be socially mediated. It is this social dimension of cattle that makes *enkurou* a collective rather than an individual's responsibility.

However by paying *enkurou* to the dependants of Stuchbery, the Maasai elders were not necessarily condemning Elishira. Rather they were acknowledging, as Maasai customary law required, the loss of life and the collective responsibility to pay the expected compensation for it. In their understanding, until *enkurou* was paid, the dispute between the families of the murderer and his victim would remain unsettled; in which case trouble was likely to occur. It is likely the Maasai elders feared possible reprisals either from the local settler community or from the government.

It is not clear whether twenty and nine cattle or forty and nine cattle were paid as compensation for Stuchbery's death. It is also not clear whether or not Mrs. Stuchbery accepted the Maasai's restitution for her deceased husband. What is interesting though is that the payment of "blood-money" raised a serious legal question for the colonial authorities. Since offences such as murder and manslaughter were within the exclusive jurisdiction of the "British courts", could a

---

307   Ibid. 15.

308   Morris, H.F. "The Award of Blood Money in East African Manslaughter Cases", *Journal of African Law*,
       vol. 18, no. 1 (Spring 1974): 104.

309   Contini, Paolo, "The Evolution of Blood-Money for Homicide in Somalia," *Journal of African Law*, vol.
       15, no. 1, (Spring 1971): 78.

310   Rigby, *Persistent Pastoralists* (London: Zed, 1985):155; Contini, "Blood-Money," 78.

311   Arhem, *Maasai and the State*, 10.

British court allow such compensation although under English law no such claim could be entertained? I am not aware how this problem was eventually resolved. However, in Somalia the colonial authorities there not only recognized payment of *dia*, but had it partially incorporated in the colonial administration of justice.[312]

Whether or not restitution in the Stuchbery murder case was accepted, it reflected the dualism of colonial Tanzania's legal structure. The payment of *enkurou* was an effort on the part of the Maasai elders to ensure justice was seen to be done according to their custom. In this sense, the murder set in motion two separate mechanisms of justice, each with its own rules. On the one hand, under Maasai customary law the homicide entitled Stuchbery's family to obtain blood-money from Elishira's clan as compensation for the loss sustained. On the other hand, Western criminal law required that Elishira be prosecuted and, if convicted, punished for having committed a criminal offence against society as a whole.

According to Erika Johnston the Maasai were more than "perplexed" about the "not guilty" verdict: ". . . the Maasai could not understand why their warrior had not been deservedly punished for his crime. Reliable rumour later had it that they had taken the law into their own hands and despatched the culprit themselves, shoving his body down an ant bear hole.[313] Erika Johnston was mistaken to think that Maasai ideas of guilt were in tandem with British law, in which case murderers are punished by a death sentence. On the contrary, according to Thompson the Maasai who attended the trial "had been sitting outside, staring in through the windows, not understanding anything that was going on -- simply wanting Oldtus returned to them alive."[314]

We have noted that after the verdict Maasai elders decided to pay *enkurou* as restitution for Stuchbery's death. As far as they were concerned, the payment of *enkurou* meant that justice was done. If Mrs. Stuchbery accepted the restitution, the Maasai would have regarded the matter settled without further punishment being necessary. Moreover, the idea of killing Elishira would be tantamount to the Maasai belief that to do so would have left two widows instead of one! Therefore it is inconceivable, according to Erika Johnston, that the Maasai "dispatched the culprit themselves."

Besides the legal ramifications of the Stuchbery murder case, the circumstances under which Dudley J. Thompson happened to be in Moshi and was asked to represent Elishira call for closer attention. Thompson, a Jamaican, was born in 1916 in Panama where his father was a school teacher. He was racially mixed, claiming African descent on his father's side and Jewish-Scottish descent on his mother's side. Although he was born in Panama he attended school in Jamaica. Having graduated from the Mico Teachers College, he was teaching when World War II began. At the beginning of the war he chose to enlist for the Royal Air Force. According to his memoir, reading *Mein Kampf* had made him dislike Hitler very much especially because of his denigrating remarks about Jews and `Negroes'.[315]

After the war he went back to Jamaica and resumed teaching. In 1947 he applied for and was awarded a Rhodes scholarship to study law Oxford University. While

---

312   Contini, "Blood-Money ", 80.

313   Johnston, *The Other Side of Kilimanjaro*. 211.

314   Thompson, *Kingston to Kenya*. 127.

315   Ibid. 22.

at Oxford he was involved in student politics and got elected president of the West Indian Students' Union. He recalls that the African students at Oxford criticized their West Indies colleagues for imitating the English and being brainwashed to believe that Africans were savages. Thompson admits that most West Indians mimicked the British and explains this to be the result of "the inferior status propaganda which had been sown in the West Indian educational system and which looked upon the African as a savage".[316]

While at Oxford Thompson became acquainted with George Padmore. Thompson acknowledges that nearly everything he knew about the Pan-African movement he learnt from Padmore.[317] He soon was caught up in the spirit of Pan-Africanism, especially its call for solidarity between Africans and people of African descent in the Diaspora.[318] After he graduated from Oxford he did a brief internship in the chambers of Sir Dingle Foot (a socialist) in London. Thereafter Thompson decided to go to East Africa. The decision, Thompson says, was a gut response to what he describes as a `call of the blood'.[319] In 1951, Thompson with his wife and two small children landed at Mombasa and set off for Moshi, "going on nothing but hope, faith and very little charity."[320]

Thompson first saw the Maasai when the family was on the road to Moshi. He writes: "There were the Masai with their long spears, resting on one leg, with the other lifted back, so they stood like flamingoes."[321] In Moshi, Thompson did occasionally see Maasai whose faces "had an extraordinarily peaceful expression." They also impressed him with their ability to "stride for miles with a graceful lope which combined a grace and dignity beautiful to behold".[322] His description and admiration for the Maasai was evidently at variance with those of European travelers and government officials. Thompson believed he could easily bond with the Maasai in ways that Europeans could not. In defending Elishira he saw an opportunity to practice law and to defend Maasai culture as he knew it.

As far as his African odyssey was concerned, Thompson did consider he was a "prodigal" son who had returned to the Motherland.[323] He says he knew his ancestors neither left Africa willingly nor did they take any worldly goods to squander on the way. However, Thompson did not call to question the evils of slavery any more than he exalted its positive side. Like Alexander Crummell,[324] Thompson believed slavery had contributed to the enlightenment of the slaves. According to Thompson, "We West Indians . . . who carried the blood of Africa in our veins, for our very survival had been forced to accept and adopt Western culture. This brought with it some advantages, and today we are in a position to contribute considerably to the progress of the Motherland."[325]

---

316   Ibid. 40.

317   Thompson, *Kingston to Kenya*, 45.

318   Ibid. 45.

319   Ibid. xi.

320   Ibid. 51.

321   Ibid. 52.

322   Ibid. 66.

323   Ibid. xii.

324   Crummell, Alexander, *Destiny and Race: selected writings, 1840-1898*, edited with an introduction by Wilson J. Moses (Amherst, NY: University of Massachusetts Press, 1992). See also Wilson Moses, *The Golden Age of Black Nationalism, 1850-1925* (New York: Oxford University Press, 1988, c1978).

325   Thompson, *Kingston to Kenya*, xii.

Needless to say, Thompson used his legal expertise effectively and specialized in defending mostly an African clientele in Moshi. At the time of the Stuchbery case the Maasai had already heard about and his affinity with Africans. It was Saturday and he was returning from a visit to an animal farm when he decided to stop by his office to get the mail. There he found a group of twenty Maasai seated on the wide pavement outside his office. Thompson says the group was under the guide and leadership of a French priest who acted as their interpreter.[326] They told him that they had walked over 100 miles to seek his representation as a lawyer. They told him they believed he could facilitate the immediate release of Elishira "so that they could take him home to face local trial, according to tribal rules".[327]

Thompson tried with difficulty to explain to the Maasai that the law had to take its course and that if Elishira was found guilty he could be hanged. According to Thompson, the Maasai did not understand that a guilty man could be hanged for murder as in their own words, "Who would then satisfy a second widow who would then go an empty bed".[328] In Thompson's opinion, this was the strongest argument he had ever heard against capital punishment.[329]

Thompson pledged to do what he could to get Elishira acquitted not just because he believed he was not guilty but because he believed the Maasai were victims of European injustices. One of these injustices was the alienation of Maasai land. Before the Stuchbery case Thompson used to conduct political seminars at his house in Moshi. He would start these seminars with the following invocation: "This is our land. It belonged to our ancestors. Anyone who tries to take it from us is evil and must be resisted".[330] It is for this reason that he downplayed the accusation of trespass in Elishira's trial.

According to Thompson, Elishira and his friends were grazing their cattle "following traditional paths from green to greener pastures as his forefathers had done for centuries. He had no knowledge of private holdings, titles or land boundaries; trespass to him was a concept unknown".[331] Besides, Thompson argued, Stuchbery was not only arrogant but fatally tactless in his attempt to drive the "intruders" off the land.[332] For Thompson such arrogance reflected nothing but racism on the part of Stuchbery.

The question of racism was close to Thompson's heart. His own family in Moshi was not spared of racial discrimination. Thompson's wife, Pearle, being part black and part white felt somewhat estranged from the European women. But what infuriated Thompson the most was what happened to his daughter Jo. Jo was of very fair complexion. When it was time for her to go to school Jo was admitted to the exclusively European school in town. A few days later, Thompson was informed that there had been a "mistake" and that Jo could not attend the European school. Knowing what the "mistake" was, Thompson wrote to the Governor. Although the Governor "sympathized", he could not do anything

---

326   Dudley Thompson to Lawrence Mbogoni, letter dated 8 September, 1995, in the author's possession.

327   Ibid.

328   Thompson, *Kingston to Kenya*, 125.

329   Ibid. 125.

330   Ibid. 72.

331   Thompson to Mbogoni, letter dated 8 Sept., 1995.

332   Ibid.

"since there were no plans to integrate the school in the near future" and therefore "admitting Jo would set a `dangerous' precedent".[333] After a year in Tanganyika Thompson's wife left with the children so that they could go to school in Jamaica.

Racism and prejudice were also behind the settlers' claims that Maasai cattle infected their cattle and that Maasai were stealing cattle from their farms. To begin with, the first claim appears to have been made out of ignorance of facts, namely that the Maasai endeavored to treat their cattle and although their herds were not grade cattle they were sturdy and disease resistant.[334] There is also reason to believe the settlers exaggerated the seriousness of diseased Maasai livestock because official reports throughout the 1950s did not indicate this to be of concern. For instance, not a single case of rinderpest was diagnosed in 1954 and 1955 in either local cattle or game in the Northern Province.[335] Instead, *Piroplasmosis* or red water was particularly troublesome amongst high grade and pure bred stock, and its source was not Maasai cattle which showed no symptoms of it.

Moreover, throughout the 1950s evidence suggests that the Maasai were amenable veterinary projects that the health of their herds. One British observer noted: "They are wealthy, and fully alive to the advantages to be derived from modern scientific improvements, are prepared to spend money on measures to improve and conserve their stock. In this respect they are somewhat in advance of other native tribes."[336] The fact that the Maasai were ready to take advantage of veterinary services to control cattle disease is evident in their demand for such services. In 1955, 153,197 calves in Maasailand were inoculated as part of the government policy of maintaining a high degree of herd immunity; the number was an increase of about 43,500 over the 1954 figures.[337] In 1956, 171,903 head of cattle were inoculated in Maasailand. About 8,500 vials of black-quarter vaccine were sold to the Maasai, as well as 1,100 vials of anthrax vaccine and over 5,000 vials of trypanocidal drugs.[338]

According to the 1959 Provincial Commissioner's report, ethedrin bromide was in great demand by Maasai cattle owners, who bought over 41,000 vials which cost 50 cents per vial. Thus in 1959 the Maasai spent over 20,500 pound sterling to buy ethedrin bromide. They also continued to seek the inoculating of their herds. To prevent the spread of rinderpest by buffalo and other game animals, about 107,120 Maasai cattle were inoculated in 1959.[339] In order to pay for these services the Maasai had to sell their cattle. In 1959 cattle sales by the Maasai reached a record figure of 32,369 head of cattle.[340] It was in this regard that Maasai considered any obstructions to the Tinga Tinga livestock unacceptable.

---

333   Thompson, *Kingston to Kenya*, 56.

334   Arhem, *The Maasai and the State*, 9.

335   Tanganyika. *Annual Report of the Provincial Commissioners, 1955* (Dar-es-Salaam: Government Printer, 1956): 88.

336   Quoted by Iliffe, John, *A Modern History of Tanganyika* (Cambridge: Cambridge University Press, 1979): 312.

337   Tanganyika. *Annual Reports of the Provincial Commissioners, 1955* (Dar-es-Salaam: Government Printer, 1956): 88.

338   Tanganyika. *Annual Report of the Provincial Commissioners, 1956* (Dar-es-Salaam: Government Printer, 1957): 105-106.

339   Tanganyika. *Annual Report of the Provincial Commissioners, 1959* (Dar-es-Salaam: Government Printer, 1960): 123.

340   Ibid. 123.

Despite Maasai readiness to spend money for veterinary services, these services Maasai were not adequately provided. According to Ehrlich, the colonial government in the postwar period spent more on roads than on agricultural and veterinary services, and extension services became increasingly difficult as independence approached.[341] According to Gulliver, the government spent very little money for veterinary services in Maasailand and gave very flimsy reasons for doing so:

> *The excuse for not providing such services was that the Maasai were too mobile, besides the shere (sic) difficulty of establishing such services in the wild extensiveness of Maasailand and the inevitable high costs of maintenance and low social and economic returns to the Government.*[342]

However, we have noted that the Maasai were not oblivious to the benefits of modern veterinary services, including the advantages of cattle dipping to fight disease.

Besides taking advantage of veterinary services to fight bovine diseases the Maasai, due to their long experience and keen observation of their natural environment, had developed what Kjekshus calls "an agro-horticultural prophylaxis" which for the longest had served them well.[343] For instance, tsetse infested areas were known to the Maasai and were avoided under normal circumstances. There is reason to suspect that settler concerns about "diseased" Maasai cattle were not only misguided but were perhaps raised for ulterior motives.

Traditional Maasai management of tick borne disease relied on an effective combination of transhumant movement, burning, and grazing sequences as well as hand grooming to remove ticks from individual animals.[344] Except for hand grooming, the other practices were seriously interrupted by land alienation and the fencing off of settler farms such as what happened at Ol-Molog. The settler-Maasai confrontation at Ol-Molog was a microcosm of this panacea for development.

While they focused their attention on the Maasai bogeyman the settlers were unaware of the danger that wildlife presented to livestock on their farms. Situated as Ol-Molog was between the Mt. Kilimanjaro, Amboseli and Loliondo game reserves, the areas settler farms were in very close proximity with game animals which could pass diseases to farm animals. The brown ear tick, *Rhipicephalus appendiculatus*, was known to carry parasitic protozoa of the genus *Theileria* both between cattle and from some wildlife, especially wild buffalo (*Syncerus caffer*), to cattle.[345] Besides *theileriosis*, many other diseases are transmitted between wildlife and domestic stock by tick vectors. Thus it was disingenuous on the part of the settlers to blame the Maasai for spreading cattle disease. Because they were so

341   Ehrlich, Cyril, "The Poor Country: the Tanganyika economy from 1945 to Independence", in D.A. Low and A. Smith (eds.), *History of East Africa*, vol. III (Oxford: Clarendon Press, 1976): 328.

342   Gulliver, *Tradition and Transition*, 239.

343   Kjekshus, Helge, *Ecology Control and Economic Development in East African History: The case of Tanganyika, 1850-1950* (London: Heinemann, 1977): 53.

344   Homewood, K.M. and W. A. Rodgers, *Maasailand Ecology* (Cambridge: Cambridge University Press, 1991): 184.

345   Giblin, James L. *The Politics of Environmental Control in Northeastern Tanzania, 1840-1940* (Philadelphia: University of Pennsylvania Press, 1992: 31.

obsessed with Maasai cattle contaminating their farms, they were at a loss to explain why their cattle got sick even when they had not come in contact with Maasai cattle. As a result the settlers resorted to Maasai conspiracy theories, including one that suggested that the Maasai deliberately planted ticks in settler farms.

As far as cattle thefts were concerned E. P. Wren, Acting Director of Public Relations, was concerned that these were on the rise in the Northern Province. In the period July 1, 1956 to June 30, 1957, about 1,476 head of stock was stolen. Of these, about 1,210 were recovered and the thefts resulted in the conviction of 50 persons.[346] By mid-1958, three-quarters of the Territory's strength of stock theft preventive officers were stationed in the Northern Province. Despite these efforts by the government stock thefts continued and resulted in the formation of several settler "vigilante committees". According to settler sentiments, the formation of these "vigilante committees" was their "vote of no confidence" in the government's ability to enforce law and order.

Meanwhile, the settlers were forced to concentrate their animals at night, behind fences of thorn, barbed wire, or cement. These nightly "confinements", unlike open paddocking, caused stock-owners to lose some 20% in milk and beef production.[347] To the settlers, cattle thefts were but one example among many flagrant breaches of law and order. In the words of the editor of *East Africa and Rhodesia*, they would not abandon their pursuit "unless they recognized the law to be a potent preventer and purposeful punisher of crime!"[348]

Regardless of settler sentiments and demands, the police force in late colonial Tanganyika was very understaffed and some policemen very incompetent to do much effective policing. In 1930, the police numbered 36 European gazette officers, 42 Europeans of other ranks, 67 Asians and 1,719 Africans. Accommodation and other facilities were wanting. Before World War II African police wore no shoes. It therefore amused Sir Charles Jeffries that the introduction of boots for all ranks in 1949 must have given "a tremendous fillip to recruitment and helped to attract an educated type of man."[349] Yet recruitment numbers remained low even after policemen were permitted to wear shoes. In 1954, the police force was 4,196 strong: 191 inspectors, 13 sergeant majors, 148 sergeants, 343 corporals and 2,753 constables.[350] Out of the 191 inspectors, 126 had work experience of less than five years; out of the 2,753 constables, 2,266 had work experience of less than five years.[351] By 1959, just two years before Independence, the numbers were only slightly higher than those for 1954. There were 263 police inspectors and 4,838 police of other ranks.[352] Of the 263 inspectors, 163 had work experience of less than ten years, and of the 4,838 rank and file 3,086 had work experience of less than five years.[353]

346   *East Africa and Rhodesia*, 12 June, 1958.

347   *East Africa and Rhodesia*, 17 July, 1958.

348   *East Africa and Rhodesia*, 8 May, 1958.

349   Jeffries, Sir Charles, *The Colonial Police* (London: Max Parrish, 1952): 115.

350   Tanganyika. *Annual Report of the Tanganyika Police, 1954* (Dar-es-Salaam: Government Printer, 1955): 4-5.

351   Ibid. 5.

352   Tanganyika. *Annual Report of the Tanganyika Police Force, 1959* (Dar-es-Salaam: Government Printer, 1960): 2.

353   Ibid. 4.

The weakness of the Police Department worried the new Governor, Sir Richard Turnbull, who was appointed in 1958. [354] He found out that the Department was not only numerically small for the size of the territory, but many of the policemen were young with little legal training and experience in Court.[355] Educational requirements for recruitment were exceptionally low. To join the Inspectorate the requirement was a Cambridge Overseas School Certificate or its equivalent plus a working knowledge of the Swahili language. For the rank and file, a recruit was required to have Standard IV education and a working knowledge of Swahili.[356]

The Governor was also alarmed by police inefficiency and lack of discipline. Many commissioned and non-commissioned police officers were routinely fired either for unsatisfactory conduct or inefficiency. In 1954 one police inspector was sacked for unsatisfactory conduct and four more were discharged "as unlikely to become efficient".[357] From the rank and file sixty were dismissed for misconduct, thirty were discharged for inefficiency, and one hundred and fifty-five were fined.[358] Drunkenness and sleeping on duty were said to be endemic.[359]

Likewise, the Criminal Investigation Department (hereafter CID) was grossly inefficient and understaffed. According to Sir Charles Jeffries, the CID detectives "resembled more the Bow Street Runners than the modern conception of a detective police officer".[360] The CID office in Dar-es-Salaam consisted of a very small staff which was only deployed for special cases throughout the Territory; there was also a photographic section and a fingerprint bureau. However, it was only in 1956 that a section dealing with "scenes of crime" was established. In 1955, because of shortage of CID staff at Headquarters assistance to District Police was given in only five cases.[361]

The Stuchbery case exposed the Police Department's Achilles' heel in a number of ways: the investigation and prosecution of the case was poorly done and medico-legal evidence was poorly collected and handled. In so far as the investigation went, there was no photographic evidence of the scene of crime. In terms of medico-legal evidence very little was collected and this little evidence was incompetently presented in court. According to Thompson, the police brought in two eminent doctors who, by showing how the victim's organs had been penetrated, were supposed to prove that Stuchbery was lying on the ground when he was speared. Their testimony was supposed to prove that Elishira did not kill him in self defense.[362] However, in their testimony each doctor reversed

---

354   Iliffe, *Modern History of Tanganyika*, 563.

355   Johnston, *Kilimanjaro*, 210.

356   Tanganyika. *Annual Report of the Tanganyika Police Force, 1959* (Dar-es-Salaam: Government Printer, 1960): 8.

357   Tanganyika. *Annual Report of the Tanganyika Police, 1954* (Dar-es-Salaam: Government Printer, 1955): 6.

358   Ibid. 6.

359   The 1954 police annual report noted that in many cases the men, owing to shortage of numbers, were called to do far too long hours and far too much night duty. Rest during the daytime for men on night duty presented a difficult problem. A man could hardly sleep in a small, hot, airless barrack room with his own or other people's children playing around.

360   Jeffries, *Colonial Police*, 116.

361   Tanganyika. *Annual Report of the Tanganyika Police Force, 1955*. (Dar-es-Salaam: Government Printer, 1956): 9.

362   Thompson, *Kingston to Kenya*, 126.

the sequence described by the other regarding how the organs were penetrated by the spear.

Furthermore, because the doctors ignored the possibility that Elishira may have acted in self defense, they did not examine his physical condition after he was arrested. Had they done so, Thompson argued in court, they would not have failed to notice the burn scar where the bullet had grazed Elishira's arm. In his cross-examination, Thompson suggests that the doctors' behavior was racially biased. When he asked one of the doctors to examine the scar, the doctor did and dismissively said "Obviously an old scar. . . . Probably got it climbing through barbed wire to steal cattle."[363] When Thompson suggested it was a burn scar the doctor scoffed, "No. . . Any fool can see that's not a burn." Thompson asked the doctor if Mr. Townsend who examined Elishira at the time of his arrest and believed it was a burn scar was a fool. The doctor did not answer.[364]

The prosecution was led by Crown Counsel John Ballard. Born in 1924, John Ballard attended Caterham School in Surrey, England. He did his undergraduate studies at Jesus College, Cambridge, where he graduated with a law degree. After his graduation and internship, he was called to the Bar at Middle Temple, London. In 1950 Ballard joined the colonial civil service and was posted to colonial Tanzania where he served as a cadet from 1950 to 1952. He was appointed Crown Counsel in 1953 at the age of 31. Thus when he prosecuted the Stuchbery murder case John Ballard had been crown counsel for only two years.

We do not know why Ballard joined the colonial civil service instead of pursuing a legal career in England. According to F.C. Gamble, a judge in colonial Uganda, the terms of service in the colonial legal service were not sufficiently attractive to a "rising young junior" to induce him to forsake a successful career at the Bar.[365] The wages were not sufficient to motivate one to excellence either. The starting salary was 630 sterling pounds sterling, with an increment limit set between 840 and 880 pounds sterling.[366]

As Crown Counsel, Ballard was expected to prove beyond a reasonable doubt that Elishira had maliciously intended to kill Stuchbery. The Penal Code defined "murder" as follows: "Any person who of malice aforethought causes the death of another person by an unlawful act or omission is guilty of murder".[367] We have noted that Elishira did not deny that he had speared Stuchbery. However, according to criminal procedure Judge Abernethy could not have automatically convicted him of murder. The judge was obligated to record the facts of the case as presented by the prosecution before he could determine whether the accused was indeed guilty.

From the beginning, Ballard was faced with several difficulties. These, as we have noted, included a shoddy investigation, contradictory testimony from the two doctors, lack of photographic evidence and lack of photographic evidence from the crime scene. While Thompson used positive stereotypes about Maasai

363   Ibid. 126.

364   Ibid. 127.

365   PRO, CO 822/71/5, F.C. Gamble, Judge, Kampala, "Conditions of Service: Magistrates and Crown Counsels in East Africa," memorandum dated 19 February, 1936.

366   Ibid.

367   Tanganyika. *The Laws of the Tanganyika Territory: in force on 1st January, 1947*, Rev. Edition, vol. 1 (London: Watmoughs Ltd., 1948): 174.

moran to argue that Elishira had acted in self defense when he stabbed Stuchbery, Ballard was apparently unable to come up with negative stereotypes to prove "malice aforethought" on the part of Elishira as defined by the Penal Code.[368] Yet "incriminating" stereotypes abounded. According to R. W. Hemsted, the Maasai lived "under conditions of indescribable filth in an atmosphere of moral, physical and mental degeneration".[369] Sir Charles Eliot, the Governor of Uganda, thought a Maasai resembled "the lion and the leopard, strong and beautiful beasts of prey that please the artistic sense, but are never of any use, *and often a very serious danger*"[370] (emphasis added).

Besides being "the terror" of their neighbors Maasai *moran*, unlike their elders, were alleged to be "instinctively" aggressive. According to one observer, to a Maasai fighting was an end in itself and the only occupation they considered worthwhile besides cattle-keeping.[371] The most chilling stereotype of Maasai as irrational barbarians and perpetrators of wanton destruction was that espoused by Reichard who says that for the Maasai *moran* "his only thought concerns killing and murder; he wants his weapon baptized in blood".[372] The question, however, is whether Ballard was aware of such negative stereotypes. If he was aware of them why did he not use them? We shall never know the answer to this question. What we can do is second guess him, which is next to impossible.

---

368   Ibid. 174.

369   Tidrick, "Masai and their Masters", 16.

370   Ibid. 28.

371   Cameron, *Equator Farm*, 125.

372   Quoted by Helge Kjekshus, *Ecology Control*, 11.

PART TWO

Film Production and Radio Broadcasting

6

Colonial Tanganyika on Film, 1935-1961

Introduction

The study of film as a medium of communication in colonial Tanganyika, like that of radio broadcasting, has attracted little research attention from students of Tanzania history.[273] By and large studies about cinema in Africa have devoted only a few pages to the film industry in colonial Tanganyika.[274] Yet colonial Tanganyika was the scene of several pioneering experiments in film production for African audiences in British Africa. Moreover, the literature on colonial film production in Africa deals overwhelmingly with the technical and policy matters and less with the propaganda value of the films themselves. [275] It was during World War II that the British government recognized that the film, like the radio, could effectively

---

273   Ssali, Mike H. "The Development and Role of an African Film Industry in East Africa with special reference to Tanzania, 1922-1984," PhD dissertation, University of California at Los Angeles, 1988; Rosaleen Smyth, "The Feature Film in Tanzania," *African Affairs*, vol. 88, no. 352 (July, 1989):

274   Ukadike, N. Frank, *Black African Cinema* (Berkeley: University of California Press, 1994): 33; Manthia Diawara, *African Cinema: Politics and culture* (Bloomington, IN: Indiana University Press, 1992): 1-3; Rosaleen Smyth, "The Development of British Colonial Film Policy, 1927-1939, with special reference to East and Central Africa," *Journal of African History*, vol. 20, no. 3 (1979): 437-450; Rosaleen Smyth, "Movies and Mandarins: The Official Film and British Colonial Africa," in *British Cinema History*, James Curran and Vincent Porter, eds., (Totowa, NJ: Barnes and Noble Books, n.d.); Rosaleen Smyth, "The Post-War Career of the Colonial Film Unit in Africa," *Historical Journal of Film, Radio and Television*, vol. 12, no. 2 (1992): 163-177.

275   PRO, CO 875/52/4, Norman Spurr, "Making Films for Africans," BBC broadcast, 5 February, 1950.

be used to deliver information and propaganda to illiterate African audiences. This chapter looks at film as a medium of communication in colonial Tanganyika with an emphasis on the development and use of "instructional" agricultural films for rural audiences from the late 1930s to the mid-1950s. The chapter also examines Hollywood's mania for safari-themed pictures and colonial Tanzania as the setting of MGM and Paramount Pictures films.

Colonial film productions in general were intended to act as a stimulant towards social and material progress. However, the choice of the themes and the content of colonial films tended to shift the blame for the shortcomings of colonial society from the State to the peasants.[276] Some of the films were based on reconstructed stories and real life experiences, but most were scripted fictional stories with "educational" messages in them. From the beginning, the preference was to produce and show "educational" rather than entertainment films. When William Sellers, a pioneer in the use of instructional films in Nigeria who became a key figure in the Colonial Film Unit (CFU), was asked why entertainment films made for Western audiences should not be shown to Africans, he had this to say: "There is overwhelming evidence that this would be a disastrous policy. Such films more often than not deliberately set out to falsify the facts of life, and would not only be misleading but even dangerous when shown to illiterate rural audiences in Africa."[277] What Sellers was really opposed against was the screening of entertainment films which portrayed whites in "undignified" roles, such as prostitutes, which could compromise the racial superiority of whites in the minds of Africans.

Since British imperialism rested on the myth of white racial superiority, it was imperative that colonial African audiences be shown film images that consolidated rather than undermined white racial superiority. This became the guiding principle for colonial film censorship. There were Europeans who believed that no African man should be allowed to see a picture of a white woman on the screen at all, irrespective of what she was doing. Even pictures of female film stars like Greta Garbo and Marlene Dietrich on display outside the cinema halls were deemed undesirable for Africans.[278]

For purposes of censorship colonial films were designated and labeled "instructional" or "non-instructional". Films that were labeled "instructional" included plays, light operas, travel pictures, etc., while reviews, musical comedies and other pictures of no educational value were categorized as "non-educational". To shield Africans from exposure to "undesirable" Western films colonial administrations used racial as well as social discrimination. Racial discrimination involved the licensing of films for exhibition to European and Asian audiences only.[279] Social discrimination included the use of legislation that fixed a minimum price of admission of one shilling and fifty cents plus an entertainment tax of one shilling per ticket for all films categorized as "non-educational".[280]

276   Hungwe, Kedmon, "Southern Rhodesian Propaganda and educational Films for Peasant Farmers, 1948-1955," *Historical Journal of Film, Radio and Television*, vol. 11, no. 3 (1991): 229.

277   Quoted by Malkmus, Lizbeth and Roy Armes, *Arab and African Film Making*, London: Zed Books Ltd., 1991): 19.

278   PRO, CO 323/1252/12, "Films Censorship: Institution of a Central Censorship in London."

279   The Governments of Kenya colonial Tanzania used both racial and social discrimination, whereas the Government of Uganda found racial discrimination to be undesirable.

280   PRO, CO 323/1252/4, "Film Censorship: Institution of a Central Censorship in London."

Ironically, while colonial film censorship attempted to "protect" Africans from the "corrupting" influences of Western films, European and North American audiences were shown films about Africa which distorted African reality especially by showing Africans "as creatures of odd appearance, quaint customs, insanitary habits and peculiar dances, in an aura of picturesque barbarism".[281] The misinformation caused by such distortions was the more worse considering that for the majority of the people in the west such films were the only source of information about Africa. Needless to say, this penchant for the exceptional and unusual is the colonial antecedent of modern day "parachute journalism" in which hordes of foreign journalists and camera crews have been attracted to trouble spots in Africa but the most they can provide are 30-second clips which trivialize events that are much more complex.[282]

Cinema as Propaganda

The purpose of colonial films was to transmit European-conceived ideas and values to the colonized African masses. It is in this sense that colonial films constituted a form of propaganda. The question however is why European film producers would want to transmit their ideas to Africans. The answer to this question is to be found in the nature of colonial rule which combined coercion and persuasion. Colonial films were essentially hegemonic because they were the embodiment of values and practices which served the interests of the colonial state.

From the viewpoint of the film producers the objective of "instructional" films was to educate the masses of illiterate Africans.[283] The assumption was that Africans had a highly developed sense of emulation which made film the ideal educational medium for them. However there is a difference between education and propaganda. According to Richard Taylor education teaches people how to think whereas propaganda teaches them what to think.[284] The assumption that Africans were good at emulation suggests that the films they saw were not supposed to teach them how to think but rather what to do. This chapter will analyze the themes and contents of chosen films to determine the kind of audiences they targeted and how the intended audiences reacted to these films.

Cinema, like literature, oral traditions and other aspects of culture, reflects a world view of things. In regard to the production and screening of "instructional" films in colonial Tanganyika, it is not only necessary to question the basic choices of subject matter but also the ideological assumptions behind those choices and their intended consequences. The answers to these questions, bearing as they do on film production and exhibition, will then be contextualized within the specificity of colonial relations to demonstrate the role of film in the intensification of commodity production.

The contextual dimension will reflect the power relationship between the colonizer and the colonized in which the differences (racial, cultural and economic) between the colonizer and colonized were seized upon and articulated

---

281   Smyth, "British Colonial Film Policy," 447.

282   McPhail, Thomas L. *Electronic Colonialism*, vol. 126 (Newbury Park, CA: Sage Publications, Inc., 1987).

283   PRO, CO 323/1252/30125, J. S. Huxley, "Report on the use of Films for Educational Purposes in East Africa."

284   Taylor, Richard, *Film Propaganda: Soviet Russia and Nazi Germany* (London: Croom Helm, 1979): 25.

in filmic language. The cinematic strategy used was the presentation of sequential images which emphasized the "primitive" in contrast with the "modern", the "uncivilized" in contrast with the "civilized". Such cinematic images also visually rationalized the objective of colonial rule: the European's objective was to uplift the African to an "acceptable" level of social, cultural and economic advancement.

The themes and contents of films reflected the numerous colonial policies through which the colonial administration sought to bring about change in people's attitudes and ways of doing things. Invariably the agent of change was a European, usually the district commissioner, who was portrayed pushing the frontiers of ignorance, disease and tyranny. Needless to say, the district commissioner was also the embodiment of European prejudices and cultural attitudes towards the subject people. In this sense, colonial films were racist in content and paternalistic in attitude.

However, the interests of the colonial filmmaker sometimes collided with those of his paymasters. While the CFU filmmakers were masters at putting ideas across their intended audiences, their intentions were not always in tandem with those of the colonial administration. From its inception the CFU, and later its units in the colonies, encountered resistance against the use of film as a medium for the betterment of the colonized. The nature of the conflict was succinctly explained in an address by C.Y. Carstairs given at the International Conference on "New Directions in Documentary Films" in Edinburgh in 1952. He said:

> [I]t is not much good showing the Nigerian film "Smallpox", and enthusing your audience about vaccination unless the Medical Department is at hand to vaccinate the new enthusiasts. An impulse not acted upon, or left in the air, is I think worse than none at all - it breeds frustration, and acts as a stopper against the next one.[285]

Coming from the Director of Information at the Colonial Office, the above statement reveals that colonial policy-makers were apprehensive that films could easily raise African expectations which colonial governments were not in a position to satisfy.

To be effective, Carstairs suggested, film use "must lead to useful action, and possible action". Thus, although he acknowledged that so far as subject-matter was concerned "there is no limit that need worry us", he was worried that film-makers could not just choose to make films about each and every subject. He emphasized that film production and usage be intimately integrated with the work and thinking of the colonial administration as a whole. For this reason, he argued, film production and distribution would have to be under the control of the local government.[286]

Some early contacts with the cinema

Ukadike strongly suggests that in West Africa the cinema was introduced by European missionaries.[287] Seeking to convert Africans, missionaries went to West Africa "armed not only with copies of the Holy Bible but also with film and slide projectors, which were used to facilitate the understanding of their evangelical

285   Carstairs, C. Y. "The Colonial Cinema," Corona, vol. 5, no. 2 (1953): 55.

286   Ibid. 54.

287   Ukadike, African Cinema, 30.

crusade".[288] It is not clear whether early missionaries to colonial Tanganyika used films and slides in their evangelical enterprise. However, J. Merle Davis, the originator of the earliest film experiment in colonial Tanganyika in the 1930s, realized the importance that the film as a supplementary visual aid could play in the missionary endeavor.[289] Davis also recognized the potential damage that films could do to Africans if allowed to carry bad influences from the "citadels of darkness" in the West.[290]

The Maryknoll Fathers, who arrived in Musoma on the eastern shore of Lake Victoria in 1946, also realized the potential of film in their evangelical work. In the early 1950s Maryknoll Father Albert J. Nevins was able to produce, with the help of Kenco Films, two films: Land of the Twelve Tribes and A Boy of the Bakuria.[291] Both films were in the English language and were obviously intended for western audiences. The narrative in Land of the Twelve Tribes, by Father Nevins, begins with a statement that Africans are "simple children of God". Then two white priests are shown visiting an old Luo chief. The party is entertained by tribal dancers, with painted faces, dressed in feather-plumed head gear and animal skins.[292] The close-up images of grass thatched huts portray very poor and squalid living conditions. Because the narrative does not explain the causes of these poor living conditions, the impression conveyed by the images is that Africans were to be pitied and needed to be "civilized." The missionaries were doing all they could to help.

A Boy of the Bakuria is about Kurya initiation rites. A boy's transition into adulthood required proof of courage and bravery which had to be demonstrated by success in hunting and stealing cattle. The initiate in the film first brings home an antelope that he has killed. There is a celebration dance with bedecked maidens and warriors dressed in leopard skins with feathered head gear blandishing spears. Then the boy must accomplish the second test of manhood, that of stealing cattle. He steals some cattle but is found and severely beaten and left for dead. Some strangers find him and take him to a missionary hospital. When he recovers a priest remonstrates with the boy, telling him it is not manhood to steal but that "it takes a man to serve God". The boy decides to become a Christian.

A Boy of the Bakuria was not intended to show African traditions in any positive light. The exception is the portrayal of the Kurya's sense of nature's balance. Before the boy hunter goes to the Serengeti plains to hunt, an old man tells him: "The great spirit of the sky gave the Kurya animals to hunt, but only for food. Kill only a small animal you can carry home. Do not be like the white man who kills all over the plain, just to kill." Evidently the Kurya did not consider hunting in the Serengeti to be illegal.

The Maryknoll Sisters in Musoma also had a film made about their activities there. The film, Bride of Africa, is about Obonyo, the daughter of Chief Hongo, who wants to become a nun. The film starts with a scene at the local church in the village of Kowak after a morning service. The narrator, the father of one of

288   Ibid. 30.

289   Davis, J. Merle, "The Cinema and Missions in Africa," International Review of Missions, vol. XXV, no. 99 (July, 1936): 379.

290   Ibid. 378.

291   Maryknoll Fathers and Brothers Archives, Maryknoll, New York.

292   In the film the Luo chief is wearing a suit with a colonial-style helmet which was popularly identified with European district commissioners.

the Sisters who was visiting from Wisconsin, observes: "I could see the innate simplicity and goodness of these dark skinned people. Their life is hard but they are cheerful". The comment may have been sincere but it betrays the subtle racism and stereotypic representation of Africans as "noble savages."

The narrative of *The Bride of Africa* extols the superiority of Western medicine over African witchcraft. Amago, Hongo's wife, is sick but the witchdoctor has failed to rid her of the devil inside. A messenger arrives to ask the Maryknoll Sisters for their help and they oblige. When the Sisters arrive in the village of Maguba they are met by Hongo who is characteristically dressed in animal skins. The Sisters' diagnosis of Amago's illness reveals that she is suffering from typhoid. Amago is given medication and recovers. The encounter with the Sisters leaves Obonyo very much impressed she wants to become a Sister too. She goes to school where she learns how to read and write; gets baptized and graduates at the ripe age of eighteen. By then a prospective husband, Wambura, has already paid 35 cows to Hongo as bride wealth. When Obonyo refuses to get married Wambura has her abducted. As Wambura and his friends celebrate, they get drunk and engage in a fight in which Wambura is pierced with a spear. His life is saved by the Maryknoll Sisters. As a result, Wambura renounces his claims on Obonyo and allows her to pursue her dream to become a nun. The contrast between "modernity" and "savagery" is obvious throughout the film, an evident carryover from earlier films about Africa.

Many of the American filmmakers who worked in Africa between the wars primarily regarded the continent like a zoo. Their favorite film locations were in East Africa and the Belgian Congo. Some of the filming expeditions had scientific credentials including those funded by the Smithsonian Institution and the American Museum of Natural History.[293] Notable among the earliest films produced in East Africa (colonial Tanganyika being one of the locations) were those filmed by Martin Johnson including *On the Borderland of Civilization* (1920), *Simba* (1924-1928), and *Congorilla* (1929-1932).[294] Johnson's films were, notably, explorer films and Africans contributed to their production by acting or inadvertently appearing before Johnson's camera. However, these films were primarily produced for commercial screening in Europe and North America. Intended for entertainment, Johnson's films divested, stripped, and deformed their African subjects to fit popular western images of Africans as "uncivilized". Africa was presented as "the land of odd animal species such as man-sized, scorpion-swallowing baboons that could lynch leopards".[295] African peoples were portrayed as "even odder and often more to be feared" than the inhabitants of the African jungle.[296] Johnson and other early filmmakers were quick to realize the commercial value of these fanciful and racist images. These early films set the tone and popularized the exotic imaging of Africa in western culture which has persisted to the present. The early Martin Johnson animal epics, such as *Congorilla*, find a parallel in some of Walt Disney's African productions, such as *The Lion King*.

---

293   McKinley, E. H. *The Lure of Africa* (Indianapolis: Indiana University Press, 1974).

294   Ukadike, *African Cinema*, 33.

295   Vaughan, J. Koyinde, "Africa and the Cinema," in Langston Hughes, ed., *An African Treasury* (New York: Crown Publishers, Inc., 1960): 85.

296   Ibid. 85.

However, it was between 1935 and 1937 that an attempt was made to produce films specifically intended for African audiences. The project, known as the Bantu Educational Kinema Experiment (BEKE), was sponsored by the International Missionary Council (IMC) based in Geneva. In 1932 the Department of Social and Industrial Research of the IMC sent a commission under J. Merle Davis to Northern Rhodesia and the Belgian Congo "to study the effect of the heavy industries of the Copper Belt upon native African life".[297] Among the findings of the commission were that (a) urbanization had undermined the social fabric of African life, and (b) there was a widening gap between "the outlooks and ways of life of the industrialized Native living in towns ... and those of his rural village".[298] Consequently, the IMC wanted to experiment the use of films towards arresting the moral corruption of the African by western industrial life.

While the BEKE's specific objective was to produce "instructional" films for the urbanized African, the IMC had a broader religious objective which included "the critical appraisal of all the forces - economic, social and political - which condition(ed) the life of the Christian community, and the utilization of these forces, where possible, as aids in the task of building the Kingdom of God on earth".[299] However, the problem was how to finance such a project because neither the IMC nor the Colonial Office was in a position to provide funding. The Carnegie Corporation of New York was subsequently convinced to provide funding for the experiment. Knowingly or unknowingly the IMC was blazing a new trail in the furtherance of European imperialism and the integration of Africans into the capitalist world economy. Film production was to become another instrument of globalization and the expansion of the frontiers of western consumerism.

Colonial Tanganyika was chosen to be the headquarters of the BEKE's experiment because the administration was willing to provide the required premises. The BEKE team arrived at the port of Tanga towards the end of June, 1935, and proceeded to its headquarters at Vugiri in the Usambara Mountains. While equipment was being installed at Vugiri, Latham visited Dar-es-Salaam, Tabora, Mwanza, Bukoba, Entebbe, Kampala and Nairobi. The object of this tour was to discuss the experiment with government officials and with leading missionaries; to make preliminary arrangements for a tour with the displaying unit at the end of the year, and to obtain ideas from officials of the various departments, missionaries, and other interested persons about subjects for filming and methods of treatment.[300]

Filming began at Vugiri on 26 July, 1935. Rain and cloudy weather, which continued late into August, interfered with photography. However, by working night and day seven films[301] were completed in less than six weeks after filming started. On 4 September, Latham and the displaying unit left Vugiri for a film-showing tour that would take them through central and southwestern Tanganyika to Northern Rhodesia and Nyasaland. On 27 November, the displaying unit

297   Notcutt, L. A. and G. C. Latham, *The African and the Cinema: An account of the work of the Bantu Educational Cinema Experiment during the period March 1935 to May 1937* (London: The Edinburgh House Press, 1937): 9.

298   Ibid. 9.

299   Ibid. 10.

300   Ibid. 121.

301   These were *Post Office Savings Bank, Tanga Travel, Tax, Hides, Tea, The Chief,* and *First Farce.*

returned to Vugiri after an absence of twelve weeks, having covered approximately 6,000 miles by road and given 46 displays to audiences estimated at a total of 36,500 Africans and Indians, and 670 Europeans.[302] On 14 December, the displaying unit started again, this time for a tour of the Lake Province, and went on through Uganda to Kenya. For this second tour, in addition to the first seven films, three new films, Soil Erosion, Co-operatives, and Gumu, were shown.

The BEKE was driven by an underlying sense of the power of film to shape ideas and attitudes. However, the stated and more specific objective was to use "the motion picture as an instrument of education and an aid for tribal society in the two-fold struggle it is making to preserve the old traditions and to adapt itself to the modern world".[303] This dichotomy between the modern and the traditional continued to be the underlying motif in subsequent films produced in colonial Tanganyika.

Between 1935 and 1937 the BEKE team in colonial Tanganyika produced approximately thirty-five short 16mm films with commentaries in English, Swahili, Sukuma, Kikuyu, Luo, Ganda, Nyanja, Bemba and Tumbuka.[304] These films were produced in two phases. In the first phase, from July 1935 to February 1936, thirteen films were made. Ten of these were shown in the first and second tours of East Africa in this period. The last three to be made were titled The Hare and the Leopard, a film based on parts taken from different African fables; Food and Health and More Milk, both of which were produced by Dr. C.R. Philip whose services came by courtesy of the Kenya Medical Department.[305] The following films were produced in the second phase: Healthy Babies, Progress, Soil Erosion at Machakos, Anaesthesia, Peasant Holdings, Preserving Eggs, Native Veterinary Assistants, Infant Malaria, Hookworm, Improved Agriculture, Coffee under Banana Shade, High Yields from Selected Plants, Coffee Marketing, Msukuma Farmer, Farm Implements, Labour Conditions at Geita Mine, Agricultural Education at Bukalasa, Uganda Boy Scouts, Milk from Native Cows, Cattle and Disease, Artificial Insemination of Cattle, and Marketing Export Native Maize.[306] Of the thirty-five films, nineteen were on agriculture and six on health.[307]

The predominance of agriculture-related films produced by the BEKE was not accidental. The explanation lies in the triple alliance between the BEKE on the one hand and the Colonial Office, the Carnegie Corporation and the governments of East Africa on the other. We have noted how from the beginning the IMC did not have the money to finance the BEKE. The money the BEKE got from the Carnegie Corporation only sufficed to carry the BEKE until July 1936. More money was needed for another year to complete the BEKE's program of films. It was therefore recommended that money should, if possible, be raised to carry on the experimental period until July 1937.

There followed a series of disappointments. Application to a large number of mining and industrial companies with interests in East Africa brought sympathy but no funding for the project. The Carnegie Corporation was also not immediately

---

302   Notcutt and Latham, The African and the Cinema, 122.

303   Malkmus and Armes, African and Arab Film Making, 19.

304   Diawara, African Cinema, 2.

305   Notcutt and Latham, The African and the Cinema, 48.

306   Ibid. 51-73.

307   Smyth, "Movies and Mandarins," 131.

able to make another contribution. It was then suggested that assistance be sought from the Colonial Development Committee (CDC). However, it was found that the CDC was precluded from making grants for purely educational purposes.[308] The BEKE therefore asked that application should be made to the CDC for a grant to the Governments of East Africa, "to enable them to obtain films intended to stimulate native production in the colonies, on the understanding that they should utilize the Bantu Educational Cinema Experiment for this purpose".[309] The CDC agreed to make a grant of 1,500 pounds if the East African governments would come up with 1,000 pounds sterling, which they did.

By the terms of the grant the BEKE was commissioned to supply 4,500 feet of films "specially designed to instruct the Natives of the areas concerned in agricultural methods, with a view to their making the best possible use of the resources at their disposal, and thereby increasing the quantity and quality of their output".[310] For colonial Tanganyika these terms were very opportune. Her economy during the interwar years was first characterized by stagnation soon after the war, followed by rapid growth in the late 1920s, collapse between 1929 and 1932, and a faltering recovery thereafter.[311] The time period 1935 to 1937, when the BEKE films were produced, was a period when Tanganyika's economy was struggling to recover. Thus the BEKE films were used to complement the administration's "plant more crops" campaign and other agricultural policies of the 1930s.

Furthermore, the significance of films like *Post Office Savings Bank* was not so much the emphasis on the stupidity of keeping one's money at home where it could easily be stolen, but the channeling of money into banks where it would be available for investment purposes. Iliffe notes that between 1938 and 1948 colonial Tanganyika's bank deposits rose from 1.8 million to 17.95 million pounds sterling, while bank lending increased only from 1.55 million to 1.8 million pounds.[312] The balance was, of course, deposited in London banks. Likewise, the film *Tax* which exhorted Africans to pay their taxes served a similar purpose. The Depression had brought hard times and shrinking labor and agricultural commodity markets. There was widespread tax defaulting. When World War II started many tax defaulters were systematically conscripted in lieu of their tax debts.

Moreover, films about health and related matters addressed problems that were at the heart of the imperial enterprise in colonial Tanganyika. Endemic diseases and poor sanitary conditions had to be combated because only a healthy population could engage in agricultural commodity production, wage employment and other activities that generated revenue for the government and provided Africans with the means to become "modern". The underlying theme was that of modernization. Visually and conceptually, the BEKE films counter-posed the idealized "modern" and prosperous versus the vilified "traditional" and primitive.

Ironically, the BEKE's untimely demise in 1937 was the result of lack of support by the Colonial Office and the East African governments. Evidently, following the Carnegie Corporation's reluctance to continue funding the experiment, the East African governments determined that by themselves they could not provide the

---

308   Notcutt and Latham, *The African and the Cinema*, 127.

309   Ibid. 128.

310   Ibid. 128.

311   Iliffe, John, *A Modern History of Tanganyika* (Cambridge: Cambridge University Press, 1979): 301.

312   Ibid. 302.

BEKE with adequate support.[313] However, rather than admit that the problem was inability to finance the BEKE, the excuses given by the East African governments included the alleged poor quality of the films and the undetermined value of films as a means of educating adult Africans.[314]

As the BEKE folded its operations, private film companies such as the British Fine Arts Pictures offered to step in and commercially produce films in Africa specifically for African audiences. Their overtures were unsuccessful in part because the Colonial Office was not ready to subsidize them.[315] There was also some official reluctance and suspicion about the commercialization of filming in Africa akin to suspicion about commercial radio broadcasting. A potentially large and important cinema trade in Africa could not be entrusted into the hands of fledgling commercial companies.[316]

Audience response to the BEKE films

The BEKE films were shown in rural as well as urban audiences. Thus audience reactions to the films varied from place to place. However, their effectiveness remains unclear. Five examples will suffice. The film *Hides*, an instructional film made at Korogwe with the help of the Veterinary Officer there, demonstrated the approved method of cleaning hides and drying them on frames in the shade in contrast to the popular method of pegging and drying in the sun. Although this film was appreciated among cattle-owning peoples there is no evidence that the "modern" method was widely adopted. Elsewhere the film aroused very little interest.[317] The film *Soil Erosion*, shot with the help of the Agricultural and Forest Officers at Moshi, was intended to demonstrate the causes of soil erosion and the methods of combating it. The BEKE noted that although many people in colonial Tanganyika followed the film's narrative, they were not familiar with the subject. For this and other reasons the film was omitted from the schedule of several shows in Tanganyika.

The film *Peasant Holdings* was about an experiment that was undertaken at Kingolwira, near Morogoro, that involved the reclamation of tsetse-infested land. A large area of land was cleared and African smallholders were offered fourteen-acre plots therein together with free building materials (sisal poles) and some assistance in the way of free food until the first crops were ready.[318] The smallholders had to plant crops recommended by the Agricultural Officer and adopt approved methods, including crop rotation. By the end of the BEKE's tenure it was concluded that the film had not been shown a sufficient number of times to judge of its merits.

Another film titled *Improved Agriculture* endeavored to portray the basic principles of improved agriculture, i.e. seed selection, crop rotation and the use of manure. The film simulates a situation where land becomes scarce and farmers are forced to cultivate the same piece of land over and over. The film shows

---

313   PRO, CO 323/1535/1413, Minute by Bowyer, 5 August, 1938.

314   PRO, CO 323/1535/1413, Freeman to Flood, 24 August, 1937.

315   PRO, CO 859/6/1406/23, Minute by G. Clauson, 17 July, 1939.

316   Ibid.

317   Notcutt and Latham, *The African and the Cinema*, 36.

318   Ibid. 55.

four peasants tilling their respective plots for five years; three have diminishing returns on their plots and one whose harvests increase instead of declining. The latter uses manure to replenish the soil. One farmer asks what one can do when animal manure is not available. The Agricultural Officer then shows them how compost can be prepared. According to the BEKE, audience reaction to the film was indeterminate.

However, the intended benefits in both *Peasant Holdings* and *Improved Agriculture* were to a great extent unrealistic. The results of the demonstrated farming methods portrayed in the films were only possible under very ideal conditions. Peasants must have realized the discrepancy between the ideal and the real conditions they worked in. Indeed applying manure and fertilizer could increase land productivity. Yet regardless of how fertile the land is, a good harvest will still depend on adequate and well distributed rainfall. Peasants were also probably not very convinced with the lazy farmer stereotype as an explanation for harvesting poor crops. In most rural areas peasants contended with vermin and pestilence that decimated a considerable amount of their harvests. The problem was exacerbated by the lack of game rangers and other services which the colonial government was not able to provide.

Another popular colonial stereotype was the notion of African farming as inherently backward. *Improved Agriculture* was both an indictment of African farming methods and an attempt to shift the blame for colonial agrarian conditions from the administration to the peasants. Shifting cultivation was condemned as wasteful because it destroyed the nitrogen in the top soil, and was said to be grossly inefficient because of shallow tillage which exacerbated loss of moisture through evaporation.[319] The later problem was identified with the crude farm implements that most peasants used. It was in this regard that the BEKE produced a film about the production of modern and more efficient farm implements.

The film *Farm Implements* was the only production that dealt with the use of modern farm implements. It shows the construction, adjustment and use of a plough, a ridger, a cultivator and a large harrow. The film is divided into these four sections, and in each section the implement is first shown working, then the construction details, and lastly a more elaborate section on its working.[320] The production of *Farm Implements* was ironic because in the early days of colonial rule in Tanganyika government officials discouraged African artisans from engaging in iron-smelting, forging and the production of iron implements. Import European manufactured hoes and machetes subsequently stifled and killed the local iron-working industry. Where artisanal activities had complemented agricultural production and the local ironsmiths produced farm implements as demanded, under colonial rule this internal interdependence was destroyed. The dependence on imported farm implements created during the colonial period has persisted to this day. It is not clear how African rural audiences reacted to the film *Farm Implements* knowing, as they did, that government was hostile to ironworking activities.

Despite the use of visual aids, including films and demonstrations, colonial efforts to introduce technological innovations met with minimal success. In some areas soil conditions were not conducive for plowing. A plowing demonstration

---

319   Mbogoni, Lawrence E. Y. "Ecological Crises and Food Production in Dodoma District, 1920-1960," MA Thesis, University of Dar-es-Salaam, 1981: 116-120.

320   Notcutt and Latham, *The African and the Cinema*, 68.

at Dodoma in 1925 proved futile because the soil was so hard the plough could not get in.[321] Local knowledge was not taken into account by the planners of the infamous Groundnut Scheme at Kongwa near Dodoma. The scheme failed and had to be abandoned in part because modern technology proved no match to Kongwa's soil conditions.

In 1937 the BEKE wound up the business of producing films in colonial Tanganyika. Although Latham had recommended to the Colonial Office that the BEKE continue the local production of films for Africans on a permanent basis, the suggestion met with some resistance. The administration supported the idea but the Colonial Office and the Kenya government opposed it. Lacking the financial wherewithal the administration could not pursue the venture alone. It would not be until after World War II that another attempt was made to produce films locally and the British Colonial Film Unit was specifically created for this purpose.

The British Colonial Film Unit

The Second World War, Smyth points out, gave considerable impetus to film-making because "the British Government looked upon films not only as an excellent means of entertaining soldiers but as an ideal vehicle for propaganda, particularly for illiterate audiences".[322] Therefore, in 1939 the British Colonial Film Unit (hereafter CFU) was established as part of the newly created Ministry of Information. The CFU was run by William Sellers and veteran silent-film director George Pearson. Sellers and Pearson subsequently came up with a remarkable theory of film-making for African audiences:

> Their basic assumption was that perception of moving images on film is something learned rather than inherent. The Unit's films were required to be simple in content, slow in tempo and have considerable pictorial continuity. It was recommended that film techniques should not go beyond the viewer's experience and that the use of montage, flashbacks and magnification be avoided.[323]

Needless to say, their theory reflected the pervasive European paternalistic attitude towards Africans. However, as Diawara suggests, there was more to it than mere paternalism: "They wanted to turn back film history and develop a different type of cinema for Africans because they considered the African mind too primitive to follow the sophisticated narrative techniques of mainstream cinema".[324]

Unlike the BEKE, which used 16mm films, the CFU shot its films in 35mm.[325] The Colonial Office requested the CFU to produce only instructional films. Colonial Office policy regarding the use of instructional films was first articulated in 1944 by the Advisory Committee on Education in the Colonies. In its report titled *Mass Education in African Society* the Advisory Committee not only recognized the film as an effective visual aid but encouraged its use, especially for adult mass education. The CFU received funding from the Colonial Development and Welfare fund beginning in 1947.

---

321   Mbogoni, "Ecological Crises," 127.

322   Smyth, "The Feature Film," 389.

323   Smyth, "The British Colonial Film Unit and Sub-Saharan Africa," *Historical Journal of Film, Radio and Television*,vol. 8 (1988): 3.

324   Diawara, *African Cinema*, 4.

325   Ibid. 3.

The CFU production team in colonial Tanganyika was under the direction of Rollo Gamble. By 1950 the team had produced a number of films including *Cattle Thieves* (1950), *Childbirth Today* (1949), *Marangu*, and *Water for Tomorrow* (1951). *Cattle Thieves* dealt with the problem of livestock theft which had worsened after World War II. The problem was especially serious in the Northern Province which is the setting of the film. The film shows some Maasai cattle rustlers being tracked by Anatoli, an inspector of the colonial police force. The culprits are apprehended when they attempt to sell the stolen cattle at a public cattle auction.

Childbirth Today is about the provision and use of prenatal services. The film encouraged expectant mothers to attend clinics for prenatal screening, childbirth and aftercare services. The setting of the film is on the coast which was one of the areas with high infant mortality. But the lessons of the film would have applied in many other places in colonial Tanganyika. The film also encouraged African girls to consider a career in nursing; the film shows a chief congratulating a local girl who has just completed her nursing training. The provision of prenatal and antenatal services was an alternative to the traditional methods offered by the *wakunga* (traditional midwives).

Marangu derives its name from a place in Kilimanjaro, one of the areas where coffee was grown and a prosperous and enterprising cooperative society, the Kilimanjaro Native Cooperative Union, was in full bloom. The film espouses the benefits of cash crop production. The film shows the people of Marangu "happy and prosperous" as a result of growing coffee for export. Involvement in cash crop production, the film suggests, avails one with an income with which one can spend on consumer goods thereby improving one's standard of living.

African responses to CFU films, 1944 to 1950

The main purpose of colonial films, regardless of whether these were "instructional" or for entertainment, was to justify European colonial rule. In 1943, colonial Tanganyika was chosen as the setting for the production of a full-length feature film titled *Men of Two Worlds*. The director was Thorold Dickinson, who described the film as "an intimate dramatic study of two races working side by side".[326] The film is about an educated African who returns to his village from abroad to teach. While teaching in his village, an outbreak of sleeping sickness occurs. The district administration orders the villagers to move to a new site, a decision supported by the African teacher. However, the local witch-doctor is against the decision and leads a local resistance which eventually becomes a battle of wills between those who support the teacher and those that support the witch-doctor.

According to Smyth, the West African Students Union (WASU) in Britain took exception to the filming and screening of *Men of Two Worlds* because they found the story-line and the characterization of the witch-doctor to be "harmful" and "unrealistic".[327] WASU's secretary-general, L. Solanke even wrote to the Under Secretary of State for the Colonies to protest the screening of the film. There is reason to believe educated Africans in colonial Tanganyika were likewise not very much amused by this film. But why were educated Africans offended by this film? Smyth notes that it is because it caricatured African tradition and suggested

---

326   Quoted by Smyth, "Movies and Mandarins," 135.

327   Ibid. 136.

that educated Africans were themselves traditionalists.[328] However, this may be a misconstrued interpretation of their reaction and loyalties.

To most educated Africans, in London as well as in Tanganyika and other colonies, *Men of Two Worlds* was "offensive" and "unrealistic" for entirely different reasons. On the one hand, the film was telling these educated Africans about a world they had either not seen or experienced, or preferred not to be reminded about. On the other hand, in their eyes the film's characterization of the witch-doctor was not only dehumanizing but created an image of a backward and terrifying Africa. The film, which stereotyped Africans as uncivilized and superstitious, probably made many educated Africans ashamed of their race and African heritage. Ironically, Europeans in colonial Tanganyika, as late as the 1950s, viewed educated Africans with contempt. Smyth is probably right that such films actually contributed to the anti-imperial mood among educated African audiences.[329]

However, if educated Africans were offended by the negative images of *Men of Two Worlds* and considered it racist, that suggests they would have been happier with more positive images. This raises the question about what would have constituted a "positive image". Most likely many educated Africans would have liked to see films in which Africans were portrayed as civilized. But civilized by whose standard? African condemnation of *Men of Two Worlds* was misplaced because its producers did not intend it to portray Africans positively. To portray them positively would have undermined the European "civilizing mission" in Africa.

Although we do not have evidence about how non-educated Africans received *Men of Two Worlds*, two hypothetical scenarios are most appealing. One is that tradition-bound audiences, especially in rural areas, would have sympathized with the witch-doctor's resistance to relocate the village because to do so meant leaving the graves of one's ancestors unattended.

In 1952 an audience survey of African reactions to CFU instructional films was conducted in rural Nigeria.[330] The principal finding was that people easily related to films with a familiar background: "But neither understanding nor familiarity was sufficient to get them to alter their behaviour".[331] Although no similar survey was done in colonial Tanganyika, the Nigerian findings may equally have applied to audiences there.

In Tanganyika, the film *Cattle Thieves* (1950) most likely amused audiences rather than teaching them any valuable lessons. To such audiences, the diligent Inspector Anatoli would have been praised; the colonial police force was despised due in part to the behavior of policemen. Be that as it may, *Cattle Thieves* helped to highlight a growing problem. Cattle thefts were very much in the news during the 1950s. The Northern Province was especially affected. Between 1954 and 1957 some 10,192 head of high grade cattle were stolen from settler farms in that province. The thefts were blamed on the Maasai. The severity of cattle thefts threatened the profitability of European dairy farming. In due course, the problem was brought to the attention of the House of Commons in London.

---

328   Ibid. 136.

329   Ibid. note 30: 346.

330   Smyth, Rosaleen, "The Post-War Career of the Colonial Film Unit in Africa: 1946-1955," *Historical Journal of Film, Radio and Television*, vol. 12, no. 2 (1992): 175.

331   Ibid. 175.

The police force in the Northern Province, limited by personnel and resources, was unable to stop the Maasai and others from engaging in cattle rustling.[332] In fact, due to the very small size of the Tanganyika police force, urban areas were given priority over rural areas because they were easier to patrol. Rural dwellers were left to fend for themselves. Consequently, cattle owners, both Africans and Europeans, resorted to vigilantism. Firearm sales and gun licenses rapidly increased. In 1957 a total of 24,605 gun licenses were issued.

Meanwhile, *Cattle Thieves* may inadvertently have glamorized the Maasai "warrior" tradition. It certainly did little to dispel the popular myth among the Maasai that all cattle in the world belong to them. The Maasai who saw the film may have laughed their heads off at the film's story line, especially the ease by which the culprits are caught. In the film, the culprits are caught when they try to sell the branded cattle at a public auction. The Maasai did not steal cattle in order to sell; they stole to replenish their herds or to slaughter the beasts for a feast.

According to Smyth, *Childbirth Today* proved popular with rural women.[333] It must have because it addressed a serious problem. It is not that rural expectant mothers needed to be persuaded to attend clinics; the problem was the shortage or absence of health services in many rural areas. In rural colonial Tanzania the provision of health services was the responsibility of the Native Authorities (NAs) which were introduced in 1926. However, due to lack of funds most NAs were unable to build dispensaries and maternity clinics. By 1950, the African population (estimated to be slightly over seven million) was served by only 61 Government hospitals and 428 dispensaries. The total number of hospital beds was 3,378 or one bed for every two thousand people.

Government-sponsored propaganda films, 1953-1955

In 1951, the administration started an interesting experiment which involved the production of entertainment films with story lines in Swahili.[334] The Governor, Sir Edward Twining, invited the African Film Production Company of Johannesburg to undertake the experiment. However, because the experiment turned out to be an expensive affair, and the administration was unable to get more money from the CD & W fund, the little that could be afforded was invested in the production of only a handful of films by 1953. The most popular of these were *Chalo Amerudi* (The Return of Chalo), *Dawa ya Mapenzi* (The Love Portion) and *Muhogo Mchungu* (Bitter Harvest).

The ideas for the script of *Chalo Amerudi* and the other films were supposedly elicited from African office and welfare workers.[335] In *Chalo Amerudi* we are presented with the dichotomy between urban and rural lifestyles in colonial Tanganyika. Chalo, the main character, is a civil servant in a government department. He is shown leading a profligate life in town; which is a typical colonial stereotype and something that the administration viewed negatively and

---

332   In 1954, the ratio of police to civilian population was 1:1,796; the ratio of police by territorial size was 1:81 square miles.

333   Smyth, "Career of the Colonial Film Unit in Africa," 171.

334   Smyth, Movies and Mandarins," 139.

335   Smyth, "Feature Film in Tanzania," 391.

sought to discourage. It was one of the evils of associated with urban life where one was out of the reach of traditional authority.

Chalo receives news that his father has died and decides to go to his village for the funeral. When he arrives he discovers that his wife has been having an affair with another man. Not only does Chalo beat up his wife's lover but he decides to stay in the village. This plot begs a number of questions: why did Chalo go to town without his wife? Why did his wife cheat on him? Why did the cuckolded Chalo quit his job and stay in the village? Evidently, the producers did not ask these questions. However, we know that colonial wage employment in Tanganyika was uncertain, which explains why someone looking for a job would not have taken their family to town with them. The wife would either follow later after the man was settled or in most cases would just stay in the village. Such family separations were common and caused infidelity by both husbands and wives.

The theme of rural versus urban life was repeated in *Muhogo Mchungu*. Juma, the main character, is a peasant whose main dream is one day to live in town. When he finally goes to town he gets in trouble right away. Dropped in the middle of town he has no clue about how he can safely cross the street amid such traffic. His other experiences include losing all his money to a trickster in a game of cards; a thief snatches his bag which he recovers with the help of a policeman; and finally, when Juma tries to seduce a woman he meets in the street he is severely beaten by the husband and is left unconscious in the street. A truck almost runs over him but stops just in time. The truck driver recognizes Juma and takes him back to the village. Back in the village Juma swears never to go to town again.

Muhogo Mchungu accurately dramatizes the hazards of town life for those unaccustomed to it. However, the message that town life can be nasty did not deter people from venturing to urban centers. For most primary school leavers the pull of urban life was the opportunity to get a job. High expectations and rural unemployment were the most important causes of rural-urban migration in colonial Tanzania. Regardless of the vagaries of town life as portrayed in *Muhogo Mchungu*, many people believed that town life was easier than rural life. Given the opportunity, those who could go to town never gave much thought about what dangers awaited them there. By the 1950s the problem of rural-urban migration was so serious that the government decided to take legal measures.[336]

The documentary films of Bernard W. Kunicki

Bernard W. Kunicki was a freelance photographer who first visited colonial Tanganyika in 1950. He had been hired by the British Airways Corporation to make promotional films for the airline. Kunicki was so impressed by the beauty of Tanganyika's natural environment he wondered why not much filming had been done to promote Tanganyika abroad. Tanganyika's natural beauty not only converted Kunicki into an ardent fan but he made it his life ambition to portray the positive side of African life. In 1952 Kunicki made the first colored film for the East African Tourist Travel Association.[337] The same year he produced *Kinship of the Creature*, a nature film. *Kinship of the Creature* shows wild animals "as they

---

336   The Townships (Removal of Undesirable Persons) Act was amended in February 1958 to facilitate the repatriation of large numbers of "undesirables" living in various towns.

337   Bernard W. Kunicki was interviewed by the author in London on July, 7, 1998.

are" rather than as things with quaint habits; not as dangers faced by some intrepid cameraman, or as targets for a hunter's gun. According to Kunicki, the purpose of filming *Kinship of the Creature* was to mobilize support for the conservation of wildlife in colonial Tanganyika.

After 1952, Kunicki made several short films among which were *Cotton of Tanganyika* and *Coffees of Tanganyika*. He contributed the material he had gathered for these films to the Colonial Raw Stock. Kunicki told the author that he preferred to make several short films instead of one epic: "To my mind it is more important to keep East Africa in the public eye through a continual series of short, interesting films, than to make an epic - which is seen once and then forgotten. If these short films can reach a wider world audience so much the better."[338] It is not clear whether or not Kunicki's films attracted worldwide attention. The point, however, is that he was an individual who took it upon himself to promote Tanganyika abroad more than the Public Relations Department ever did.

In 1960 Kunicki started filming *Tanganyika National Parks*, which came out in 1961. As the name suggests, it was a film about the splendor and pageant of wildlife in colonial Tanganyika's national parks. The film opens with shots of kopjes in the Serengeti Game Reserve. There follows several scenic shots of vegetation characterizing the seasonal changes in the Serengeti which are the cause of the seasonal migration of the Serengeti's multitude of wildlife.

Kunicki's endeavors to film in colonial Tanganyika were not without obstacles. One of these obstacles was bureaucratic red tape. Kunicki was subjected to the same restrictions which commercial filmmakers with more resources faced such as getting a license and having one's scripts checked by government before filming was permitted.[339] Kunicki also complained that the Block brothers, owners of the Norfolk Hotel in Nairobi, interfered with his filming career. He did not say what they actually did.

MGM and Paramount Pictures: the making of *Mogambo*

Most of Hollywood's feature films during the earlier part of the twentieth century were produced in studios and sets located in the United States of America. For instance, Tarzan films were all filmed in the United States even though they depict "jungle life" in Africa. One of the very few exceptions was when in 1952 John Ford took his creativity and imagination to the Kagera River where he filmed part of the feature film titled *Mogambo*. Besides the Kagera River location, *Mogambo* was also filmed on location in Okalataka (French Congo), Isiola (Uganda) and in Kenya (with backdrops of Mt. Kenya, Mt. Longonot and Lake Naivasha).

John Ford is said to have disliked shooting a film in a studio if he could get it into a natural setting; he preferred natural settings to studios because he liked fresh air, the wide spaces, the mountains and the desert. His choice to shoot *Mogambo* in equatorial Africa was mitigated in part by personal circumstances. During the summer of 1952, Ford was in the midst of a financial battle with Herb Yates who he suspected was pocketing money from his last film *The Quiet Man* when MGM approached him about making *Mogambo*, a remake of an earlier

---

338   Kunicki Personal Archives, letter from B. Kunicki to D.O. Mathews dated 11 September, 1952.

339   Kunicki Personal Archives, letter from D.O. Mathews to Bernard Kunicki dated 3 December, 1951.

movie titled *Red Dust*.[340] Sam Zimbalist at MGM wanted the remake to feature Ava Gardner, Grace Kelly, and, again, Clark Gable. However, Zimbalist wanted a change of location from French Indo-China to East Africa. In July 1952, Ford accepted MGM's offer.[341]

In August 1952, Zimbalist sent Jim Havens to survey locations in East Africa. Havens spent six weeks driving all over East Africa in a Land Rover: "Everywhere he went he made careful notes on roads, the quality of the water, the cooperativeness of the local officials, the proximity of medical facilities, and the location of the nearest landing strips. Havens chose two principal locations: the Serengeti Plain of Tanganyika, where the grazing animals numbered in the millions, and the Kagera River of Uganda, which had spectacular rapids and waterfalls."[342] *Mogambo* was the biggest picture ever shot in Africa; the schedule called for sixty-seven days on location, the logistics involved were mind-boggling,[343] and the personalities were so varied and volatile.

Mogambo was to be an MGM-British production in the sense that with the exception of Ford, Wingate Smith, cinematographer Robert Surtees, and the three American stars, the entire company was to be English. In September 1952, Ford and the other Americans left for London, where they spent three weeks preparing the picture and casting the lesser roles. On October 16, Ford, Surtees and Smith left London for Nairobi, Kenya, where they were met the next day by Havens and Norman Reid, their safari guide. The cast began arriving in Nairobi in the first week of November. The arrival of Ava Gardner and Frank Sinatra, her husband at the time, was greeted with a lot of fanfare.

Ava Gardner felt a special attachment to *Mogambo* not only because she would be co-starring with Clark Gable but because the film location was in Africa "amid authentic scenes of unrivaled savagery and awe-inspiring splendor."[344] In preparation Ava had to submit to "a hellacious series of shots for smallpox, yellow fever, cholera, typhus, typhoid, and God knows what else."[345]

Mogambo's crew arrived in Nairobi at the beginning of the Mau Mau crisis. Due to concerns for their safety MGM had sent its own thirty-man police force.[346] While in Nairobi they were also under the protection of both the Lancashire Fusiliers and the Queen's African Rifles. For added security everyone was in the cast was issued a weapon. Clark Gable, an experienced hunter, got a high-powered hunting rifle, while Ava was given "a presumably more ladylike .38 police special revolver."[347] Moreover, to secure immunity from Mau Mau attacks MGM reportedly made a secret payment of fifty thousand dollars to Jomo Kenyatta.[348]

---

340   This was a classic safari film that MGM had made in 1936 with Mary Astor, Jean Harlow, and Clark Gable. *Red Dust* was filmed in French Indo-China.

341   Ford, Dan, *Pappy: The Life of John Ford* (Englewood Cliffs, NJ: Prentice-Hall, Inc., 1979): 252.

342   Ibid. 252. Reference to the Kagera River being in Uganda is only partly true. Much of the river is actually in Tanzania (what was then Tanganyika).

343   MGM had organized the largest safari ever put together and had rented every safari vehicle in East Africa.

344   Gardner, Ava, *Ava: My Story* (New York/Toronto/London/Sydney/Auckland: Bantam Books, 1990): 178.

345   Ibid. 178.

346   Ibid. 179.

347   Gardner, *Ava: My Story*, 179.

348   Harris, Warren G. *Clark Gable: A Biography* (New York: Harmony Books, 2002): 329.

Ayman Scott notes that "*Mogambo* did exactly what it was supposed to – make money, and quite a bit of it."[349] *Mogambo*'s worldwide gross earning was $8.2 million.[350] What Scott does not say is what the film did to promote tourism in East Africa in general and in Tanganyika in particular. On the one hand, the portrayal of Gable as a catcher of wild animals for zoos encouraged professional collectors to comb East Africa for live species as well as trophies. On the other hand, the film's romantic scenes portrayed East Africa as a place where Europeans could come and shed all their inhibitions. As Scott notes, the randiness of the original *Red Dust* (filmed in the confined quarters of a Malayan rubber plantation) was replaced by "a comparatively demure attitude toward infidelity in the far courtlier remake."[351] Mrs. Nordley (Grace Kelly), a dutiful wife, is lured into adultery by the primitive sensuality of Africa.[352]

The logistics of Making Mogambo

The budget for *Mogambo* was $3.1 million dollars. This amount covered expenditures that included payments for African labor for menial tasks like clearing land and film "extras". In his memoir Tim Harris, who was in the early 1950s the district commissioner of Bukoba, gives an interesting account about the logistics of clearing land for a landing strip requested by MGM. Clearing the selected place required the leveling of a number of large ant-hills as well as bush and trees. Since Bukoba did not have heavy earth-moving equipment MGM hired the needed equipment from a multinational company which was at the time engaged in road construction in neighboring Uganda.[353] The landing strip, according to Ava Gardner, was an eighteen-hundred-yard runway that was built in a whirlwind five days: "Every day, supplies and mail were flown in from Nairobi on sturdy old DC3s, and exposed film stock, carefully packed in dry ice, would be flown out."[354]

Harris was also intrigued by a rather unusual request, namely the need to protect some animals that MGM had flown in from Nairobi for the film (a baby elephant and baby rhino, a leopard and, later, a rather out of place black panther). Apparently, the safety of the animals was part of MGM's insurance policy. MGM also requested permission to employ local inhabitants as casual labor and extras. However, local officials as well as MGM were concerned that wages paid to Africans should not "disrupt" the local economy.[355]

According to Harris, the "MGM encampment was a real oasis in the middle of the African bush, with a restaurant tent in the care of that renowned cateress and expert in coping with African conditions, Mrs. (Ma) Stafford, one-time manager of the Southern Highlands Club, and later of the Dodoma Hotel." Ava

---

349   Scott, Ayman, *Print the Legend" The Life and Times of John Ford* (New York: Simon & Schuster, 1999): 424.

350   Ibid. 424.

351   Ibid. 424.

352   Ibid. 419.

353   The hiring of the equipment from the multinational company was facilitated by the Governor of Uganda, Sir Andrew Cohen.

354   Gardner, *Ava: My Story*, 179.

355   Harris, Tim OBE, *Donkey's Gratitude: twenty-years in the growth of a new African nation – Tanzania* (Edinburgh/Cambridge/Durham: The Pentland Press Ltd., 1992): 243.

Gardner recalls that the encampment was three hundred tents strong: "And if you think those were just for sleeping, think again. My God, we had tents for every little thing you could think of: dining tents, wardrobe tents with electric irons, a recreation room tent with darts for the Brits and table tennis for the Yanks, even a hospital tent complete with X-ray machine and a jail tent in case anybody got a tiny bit too rowdy."[356]

The encampment was the venue of numerous sundowners, including one which was attended by the Governor of Uganda, Sir Andrew Cohen. As Harris notes:

> "His visit provided an interesting insight into the protocol of the film-making world. At the sundowner party that night it was the Director, John Ford, and the stars who were the focal point in whose honour the party was being given, not the Queen's Representative. I had already, of course, noticed the comparable class distinction and social segregation in the dining-room, where it was my good fortune to be allocated to the same table as that remarkable and delightful and most talented raconteur as well as actor, Donald Sinden."[357]

In this MGM "oasis" in the middle of nowhere there was a clash of personalities. According to Dan Ford, his grandfather did not get along very well with Clark Gable: "The two men had many things in common – including a fondness for periodic bouts with the bottle – but as professionals their styles were very different. Gable was careful, methodical, and a notoriously slow study who didn't like spontaneity and change. If he was interrupted in the middle of a scene, he'd have to go back and start at the beginning."[358] However, Ford and Gable's bouts with the bottle were regular rather than periodic episodes as Dan Ford suggests. According to Warren G. Harris, Gable's biographer, Gable's "shakes" began causing problems, as John Ford, a heavy drinker himself, would not permit many retakes due to Gable's condition.[359]

The biggest logistical nightmare was probably the sheer enormity of the picture and the sixty-seven-day shooting schedule; it apparently put enormous pressure on its director, John Ford. Dan Ford notes that by the time his grandfather arrived in Tanganyika, "he was bone-weary and fed-up: tired of being hot by day and cold by night, of being wet, filthy, and bug-bitten. The African sun was wilting him like a batch of fresh-cut flowers, souring him like a pitcher of flesh milk. He yearned for the comforts of civilization, for the luxury of a hot bath, air conditioning, and the room service of a really good hotel."[360]

In Tanganyika, John Ford was afflicted with amoebic dysentery and stomach cramps which, according to Dan Ford, "took a heavy psychological toll before they were arrested. Every day his mood grew blacker, and every minor failure became a calamity. Instead of approaching the last scenes of the picture with enthusiasm,

---

356   Gardner, *Ava: My Story*, 179.

357   Harris, *Donkey's Gratitude*, 244-5. Scott Ayman gives a different version of this event. The governor
       invited the actors and Ford to spend a weekend at the Governor's House. Gardner, Sinatra, Kelly,
       Sinden, and Gable boarded the unit airplane to Entebbe, Uganda. Ford followed later. See, Scott, *Print
       the Legend*, 421.

358   Ford, *Pappy*, 254.

359   Harris, *Clark Gable*, 331.

360   Ibid. 255.

John began looking for ways to cut the location work short. He rewrote several long dialogue scenes so that they took place inside of tents and rescheduled them for London."[361] In late January 1953 the company left Tanganyika and went back to London. However, Jim Havens stayed in Tanganyika with a second unit to shoot the animal scenes.[362] The filming location in Kagera reverted to bush after the film unit left.

The last Hollywood film to be shot in Tanganyika was *Hatari* (shot in 1961 and released in 1962) starring John Wayne. Because the film was about animal catching for zoos it was shot on location in Arusha. Kenneth M. Coleman describes it thus: "*Hatari* was a John Wayne film with a solitary female (Elsa Martinelli) who jumps into Wayne's bed, apparently to counter any tendency to see homoeroticism in the otherwise exclusively male cast. . . . The movie is about male bonding, with Africa as the mere setting and animal catching from trucks as the requisite dangerous activity."[363] After the filming was done the trucks were donated to the Tanganyika Game Department.

---

361   Ibid. 255.

362   Ibid. 255.

363   Cameron, Kenneth M. *Africa on Film: Beyond Black and White* (New York: Continuum, 1994): 134.

7

Radio Broadcasting in Colonial Tanganyika, ca. 1951-1961

> Communication between peoples widely separated in space and thought
> is undoubtedly the greatest weapon against the evils of misunderstanding
> and jealousy, and if my fundamental invention goes some way towards
> averting the evils of war, I shall not feel that I have lived in vain.
>
> Guglielmo Marconi[364]

Introduction

Guglielmo Marconi's successful production of the first transatlantic wireless signal on December 12, 1901, would change both the nature of international diplomacy and the legitimating of political authority within individual states.[365] It should be noted, however, that Marconi's achievement did not go beyond the transmission of the usual signals in codes. The honor of the first transmission of the human voice over the radio waves belongs to an American, R.A. Fessenden

---

364   Quoted in Rawnsley, Gary D. *Radio Diplomacy and Propaganda: The BBC And VOA in International Politics, 1956-64* (Macmillan Press Ltd, 1996): 1.

365   Washburn, Philo C. *Broadcasting Propaganda: International Radio Broadcasting and the Construction of Political Reality* (Praeger: Westport, Connecticut, London, 1992): xvii.

of the University of Pittsburg, who did it in 1902.[366] Fessenden is also credited with making the first broadcast in history. On 24 December 1906, he succeeded in transmitting both speech and music from his experimental station which later was registered as KDKA, Pittsburg.

Radio broadcasting began in Britain in 1922. However, in the case of colonial Tanganyika half a century would pass before radio broadcasting was introduced and used as an instrument of political power.[367] According to J. Grenfell Williams, former Head of Colonial Service at the British Broadcasting Corporation (hereafter the BBC), practical difficulties with transmission, and the fact that early radios were made to run on mains electricity, prevented the introduction of broadcasting in many parts of tropical Africa before World War II.[368] Before World War II very few households in East Africa had mains electricity and those that did virtually none were occupied by Africans.[369]

Moreover, the need to introduce broadcasting in the colonies before World War II may have been pre-empted by the introduction of the BBC's Empire Service in 1932. On December 19, 1932, the BBC Empire Service started regular broadcasts to the far-flung parts of the British Empire. The intended purpose of these broadcasts was to offer Britons living overseas "some share of the amenities of the home country and of metropolitan interests and culture".[370] Eventually the Empire Service was relayed by the local radio services in many colonies such as India, Singapore, Kenya, Gold Coast, Nigeria and various West Indian islands. The Gold Coast and Nigeria had a wired system of loud speakers in people's houses around Accra and Lagos.

Furthermore, while Marconi saw his invention as an unprecedented contribution towards easing the problem of communication, many colonial proconsuls at first did not necessarily desire an effective means of mass communication such as the radio promised to be.[371] According to Graham Mytton, officials in colonial Tanganyika and elsewhere had good reasons to be suspicious of the power of radio. Although they could control radio broadcasting as an institution, they suspected that they could not control what people would actually listen to on their radio sets.[372] It is therefore not surprising that many colonial officials were initially either ambivalent or downright hostile to the

---

366   Ladele, Olu, V.O. Adefela and O. Lasekan *History of the Nigerian Broadcasting Corporation* (Ibadan University Press, 1979): 2.

367   However, in neighboring Kenya local radio transmission was introduced in 1928 with the colonial settler community as the main beneficiary.

368   Williams, J. Grenfell "Broadcasting in the African Colonies", *BBC Quarterly*, 6, 4 (Winter 1951-52): 217.

369   Radios that could run on batteries were expensive and/or cumbersome. It was the invention of the transistor in 1948 and the production of cheap transistor radios from 1948 onwards which transformed the situation. Transistor radios did not require mains electricity but could be run on small, cheap flashlight (torch) batteries.

370   British Broadcasting Corporation (hereafter BBC), *Empire Broadcasting* (London, 1936): 2.

371   Governor Edward Twining of Tanganyika (1949-1958) believed the cinema was "probably the most powerful agency for propaganda and instruction". See PRO, CO 875/67/6, Twining to Blackburne, dispatch dated 20 April, 1950.

372   Graham Mytton, British Broadcasting Corporation (BBC), Director of World Service, interviewed 14January, 1998, London.

introduction of radio broadcasting in the colonies.[373]

By the mid-1930s, there was increased fear in top government circles in Britain that the Empire was being threatened by German and Italian propaganda broadcasts especially prepared for overseas listeners. It was in this context that the then Secretary of State for the Colonies, J. H. Thomas, appointed a committee chaired by the Earl of Plymouth to consider and recommend ways by which broadcasting services could be introduced in the colonies. Thus from the British Government's vantage point, broadcasting in the colonies was, from the outset, to be an instrument of the state, a means of advancing government objectives.[374]

After broadcasting was introduced in Tanganyika in 1951 the radio became one of three basic means of mass communication. The other two were the press and the cinema. All three, in varying degrees, were employed to communicate information about Government activities and policies. Of the three media the most effective was the spoken word coming over the radio, especially where the speaker was known to his audience either personally or by reputation. The "magic" of hearing a voice coming from far away Dar es Salaam not only popularized radio listening but contributed to the growth of radio ownership in colonial Tanganyika. It is therefore surprising that students of Tanzanian history have ignored this fundamental aspect of mass communication. This chapter is intended to fill this lacuna.

British colonial administration in Tanzania relied on both coercion and consent. The police, courts and prisons were the coercive institutions of the colonial state. The mobilization of consent was the prerogative of the Public Relations Department (hereafter PRD) and the mass media including the Tanganyika Broadcasting Corporation (hereafter the TBC). Although the administration financed the establishment of vernacular newspapers, it felt that due to mass illiteracy the radio was the most effective transmitter of information; more so than newspapers. At independence in 1961 not more than ten per cent of the country's African population could read and write.[375]

Insofar as the objective of radio broadcasting in colonial Tanganyika was to inform, we must consider broadcasting as a communications activity with a beginning and an end. In this regard Harold Lasswell's model will be applied to analyze the utility of radio broadcasting in Tanganyika.[376] According to Lasswell, a convenient way to describe a communications act is to answer the following questions:[377] Who says what, in which channel, to whom and with what effect? On the basis of these hypothetical questions Lasswell proceeded to show how each

---

373   Randal Sadleir, interviewed January 20, 1998, London. According to Randal Sadleir, who worked as District Commissioner and later as Public Relations Officer in Tanganyika from 1948 to 1959, many colonial officials believed money intended for broadcasting could better be invested towards improving social services in the districts where many lived without electricity, indoor plumbing or telephone communications.

374   Heath, Carla W. "Broadcasting in Kenya: policy and politics, 1928-1984", PhD dissertation, University of Illinois at Urbana-Champaign, 1986: 87.

375   Mytton, Graham *Mass Communication in Africa* (Edward Arnold, 1983). No official figures or estimates are available for the year 1961.

376   Harold D. Lasswell, "The Structure and Function of Communication in Society" in *The Communication of Ideas: a series of addresses*, edited by Lyman Bryson (New York, 1948). For a critique of Lasswell's model see Mytton, *Communication in Africa*, 5.

377   Lasswell, "Communication in Society", 37.

of these questions produces a different area of media research namely (a) media analysis, (b) control analysis, (c) content analysis, (d) audience analysis, and (e) effect analysis. The objective of this study is to look at all the above five aspects in relation to radio broadcasting in colonial Tanganyika. But first, some background about colonial public relations in colonial Tanganyika.

The Public Relations Department

Although an information officer was first appointed in 1939, the administration did not create a Public Relations Department until in 1949. Eight years later Governor Sir Edward F. Twining remained unsatisfied with the work of the PRD and especially in regard to their inability to publicize Tanganyika abroad. He was very much concerned about "the difficulty of educating that part of the public in England, America and elsewhere who take interest in African affairs". In a letter to S.H. Evans, dated 14 February, 1957, the Governor specifically blamed the PRD for Tanganyika's lack of publicity overseas.[378] The Governor seriously entertained the idea of employing a professional to do the job. However, his efforts to get one were not successful.

Twining's concern with publicity was the greater because the territory was a United Nations Mandate and there were periodic visits by UN missions. Therefore the international image of the administration mattered very much to Twining and the British Government. Governor Twining's concerns about Tanganyika's lack of publicity overseas eventually led him to accept the commissioning of a book on Tanganyika which he expected would give the administration the kind of publicity he wanted. The book project was the brainchild of the Corona Club of the Colonial Office which agreed to pay the author half the cost.[379] The author was one Mrs. Helen Stahl. However, when Governor Twining received the typescript of the book in January, 1958, he was not happy with it. In a letter to Gorell-Barnes, he wrote: "To say that I am disappointed would be a masterly understatement. The book does not produce the kind of publicity we want, nor would it reach the audience that we had intended it for. We were hoping for an easily readable informative volume which would appeal to the average reader and tell him something about Tanganyika".[380]

Governor Twining was so convinced the book would do colonial Tanganyika little good and could cause his administration a great deal of harm. He was therefore prepared to do two things:

> *We can pay Mrs. Stahl and not publish. We in Tanganyika are perfectly prepared to pay our share of buying her out, and to face with equanimity the tittle-tattle that may spread itself around Chelsea and Bloomsbury about our stuffed-shirtedness, our myopia and our nestling in cocoons of righteous self-esteem. . .*

> *Alternatively, we can pay Mrs. Stahl her fee and have the book re-written by someone like Dobson or J.C. Clarke (both of whom are on leave pending*

---

378   PRO, CO 1027/134, E. Twining to S.H. Evans, dated 14 February, 1957.

379   The Corona Club was established in 1900 by the then Secretary of State for the Colonies. I am not clear what its original objectives were but later the Club was preoccupied with a book project on the History of the Colonial Services. By 1962 it had 2,754 members of which 1,203 were still serving overseas.

380   PRO, CO 1027/296, E. Twining to W.L. Gorell Barnes, dated 20 January, 1958.

retirement and are still closely in touch with real events and situations in Tanganyika).[381]

For publicity's sake Governor Twining was prepared to do anything. It is also interesting to note that the British and American audiences the Governor wanted to be informed about Tanganyika were indeed very ignorant about colonial affairs.

The ignorance of the average person in Britain about Empire matters was revealed by a survey that was conducted for the *Daily Graphic* by Mass Observation in 1948.[382] The survey was conducted because of the great Empire issues then pending, and was primarily aimed, through a series of questions, at discovering two main facts: what people knew about the Empire and what their feelings were about its future. A cross-section of the public was taken and a national sample of 2,078 persons was interviewed. The findings were startling: Seventeen per cent could name no part of the British Empire; more than half (56 per cent.) could name no event that had taken place in the Empire recently; and only one in three could define the difference between a Dominion and a Colony.[383]

The most knowledgeable occupational group was that which comprised professional, managerial, and higher clerical workers. Housewives, unskilled operatives, and people over the age of sixty, were the least well-informed sections of the population.[384] It is noteworthy that even the best-educated occupational group, and those people who had travelled widely overseas,[385] were far from being fully informed about Colonial matters. The survey served a useful purpose because it brought to the attention of those responsible for framing a Colonial information policy the true state, not so much of public knowledge, as of public ignorance of colonial affairs.

The British public's ignorance about colonial affairs was also symptomatic of an imperial information order which emphasized the flow of news and information from London to the colonies and not the other way around. This state of affairs had been the cause of concern at the conference of Information Officers held in Nairobi in September, 1943. At that conference a Captain Tyfield noted that the BBC from time to time received from the Army in Kenya recorded material intended for broadcasting. He lamented the fact that "no reports had yet been received as to the reception these programs had met with in England".[386] After the war, the BBC occasionally aired a program "East Africa Calling" on its General Overseas Service. However, the BBC Home Service hardly any news about East Africa.

The war-time neglect of colonial news both in the BBC Home Service and the BBC World News continued after the war. By the late 1950s, Kenya officials were still complaining about the BBC's limited reportage of Kenyan affairs as well as

---

381 Ibid.

382 PRO, CO 875/72/2, "Government Information Allied Service: Social Survey."

383 Ibid.

384 Ibid.

385 Precisely three-quarters of all those who had been abroad were men, and the great majority (83 per cent.) were recruited on account of war or peace-time service with the Forces and Merchant Navy. When, however, those persons who had only been abroad on account of their service with the Forces are removed, it appears that nearly one-fifth more women than men had actually travelled.

386 The BBC, Written Archives Centre (hereafter WAC), Caversham, File E 1/21 "East African Broadcasting, 1943-1947".

about factual errors when anything was actually reported.[387] The BBC explained that the reason why not much about East Africa was featured in the BBC's world news was because it was difficult to compress the world news into nine and a half minutes.[388] However, another reason could have been the lack of professional journalists. During this period East Africa was covered by Reuters and the nearest regular BBC correspondent was stationed in South Africa.[389] It was not until late in 1959 that Douglas Willis was appointed BBC News Correspondent and was based in Nairobi, Kenya.

While British people were not regularly treated to news and events about East Africa, they were fed stereotypical images about Africans through the BBC's "The Kentucky Minstrels".[390] This radio series, which ran from 1933 until 1950, was the most popular blackface production in United Kingdom radio history. Blackface minstrelsy in the UK, like that in the USA, caricatured blacks drew upon racist white conceptions about Africans and African-Americans. Blackface minstrelsy endeavored to confirm the racial inferiority of people of African descent.[391]

Meanwhile, in colonial Tanzania itself the PRD tried, despite the limitation of resources and personnel, to publicize Government policies. As African demands for self-government intensified, and Radio Cairo intensified its anti-British broadcasts, the PRD was called upon to conceive a "counter-propaganda drive". In September 1958 Randall Sadleir, Senior Public Relations Officer, who until then was working in the Northern Province, was transferred to Dar-es-Salaam for this purpose. According to the Chief Secretary, Arthur Gratten-Bellew, Sadleir was soon able to achieve "some success with his somewhat unconventional approach to the problems presented by the increased political tempo".[392]

According to Sadleir, although he was not trained in public relations his experience as District Officer Cadet and District Commissioner in Tanganyika from 1948 to 1957, and his Irish sense of humor, enabled him to do his job quite well. He held an unusual understanding of the African intelligentsia and colonial politics. Soon after his posting to Dar es Salaam he wrote:

> The African intelligentsia in Dar es Salaam and elsewhere with whom I have mainly to deal with are at the moment suffering from an almost pathological attack of nationalism: their fear, suspicion and ignorance is almost beyond belief. To the difficulties of inheriting the potted skills and cultures of a thousand years in the hot-house atmosphere of the last fifty, are added their exposure to the unprecedented propaganda blasts of the present age. Great patience is required at times to listen to their distorted nonsense, but it becomes easier to bear when one realises that from all quarters of the globe they are regaled with accounts of racial oppression in South Africa, integration at the point of

387   PRO, CO 1027/330, "Criticism of the BBC in East Africa, 1957-1959."

388   Ibid.

389   Ibid.

390   Pickering, Michael "The BBC's Kentucky Minstrels, 1933-1950: blackface entertainment on British Radio", Historical Journal of Film, Radio and Television, v. 16, n. 2 (June 1996): 161-196.

391   Blackface minstrelsy originated in the United States of America. Created by white Americans, antebellum minstrelsy relied on blackface and caricatures of African-Americans to amuse audiences that were predominantly white. Blackface minstrelsy simply portrayed Black people as creatures of ridicule.

392   PRO, CO 1027/134, Chief Secretary, Tanganyika to W.A.C. Mathieson, Colonial Office, secret telegram dated 9 September, 1958.

the gun in the United States, "imperialism" in North Africa and the Middle East, and now (the last straw) race riots in the United Kingdom...

The more the Africans learn the more conscious do they become of their present great inferiority to the rest of the world, and in my opinion it is only human that they consciously or sub-consciously must place the blame for this state of affairs on the "imperialist" invader. Like France, which could forgive England everything except being liberated by her, so need we expect no gratitude for our African achievements, and the slightest trace of arrogance, patronage or condescension ... leaves a bitter wound on their hypersensitive emotions.[393]

For Sadleir, extraordinary public relations methods were needed to meet an extraordinary situation. He endeavored to replace the age-old "chats around the camp fire" with informal contacts in bars, football grounds and homes.[394]

Despite his sensitivity to African emotions and his sympathetic understanding of African aspirations, Sadleir proved very adept at pulling the wool over the eyes of Tanganyika nationalists.[395] To this end Sadleir employed three main strategies:

(a) "Taking the lid off", i.e. encouraging the people to express their opinions freely and fearlessly rather than keeping them bottled up in the back streets. (b) Identification - doing one's best to identify oneself with the people's aims and aspirations, listening to their more outrageous comments with a grave sense of humour, and winning their confidence by practical help where possible, and trying in general to give a sense of proportion to their nationalistic urge. (c) "Taking the wind out of their sails", i.e. pointing out that there (was) little real difference in aim between, say, a TANU election manifesto and the policy of Her Majesty's Government with regard to Tanganyika's future.[396]

Besides inviting trade union officials, newspaper editors, college students and the like to his weekly radio talk program, Sadleir endeavored to wine and dine any African he considered worthy of the effort. Once every two weeks Sadleir invited a dozen or so Africans, including politicians and journalists, for an informal tour to places of interest in Dar es Salaam. After the tour he entertained them to beer at the Breweries followed by lunch at the COZY CAFE "where informal discussion (took) place in a convivial atmosphere".[397]

According to Sadleir, the objective of his informal tours was "to try and show selected leaders drawn from all walks of life how the country 'ticks over' so that they will realize that self-government is not just a matter of raising a flag with an elephant on it over Government House!"[398] The value of the tours was enhanced by the inclusion of newspaper reporters, photographers and broadcasting recording personnel, "who thus ensured that the whole country got a vicarious profit from

393   PRO, CO 1027/134, Sadleir's note attached to secret telegram from Chief Secretary, Tanganyika to W.A.C. Mathieson, Colonial Office, dated 9 September, 1958.,

394   Ibid.

395   In an interview with the author, Sadleir noted that the only exception was Julius Nyerere whom he failed to tice to any bar for an informal chat or to his popular radio program "Majadiliano". When I asked him why he was unable to get Nyerere to participate in his radio program Sadleir suggested that Nyerere thought the program was below his status.

396   PRO, CO 1027/134, Sadleir's note dated 9 September, 1958.

397   PRO, CO 1027/134, Sadleir's note dated 9 September, 1958

398   Ibid.

the tours".[399] However, in Sadleir's opinion most important work of all was the day to day informal contacts with African leaders in Dar es Salaam.[400] He spent most of his time in Livingstone Street "where little offices of newly formed trade unions spring up like mushrooms overnight".[401] Eventually Sadleir opened an office in Livingstone Street right "next to a charcoal burners shop".[402]

Sadleir also made special efforts to court the editors of *Mwafrika*, the mouthpiece of the nationalist party the Tanganyika African National Union (TANU), "in order to make it slightly less irresponsible".[403] He occasionally invited the editors to his house for a meal or a drink. Although he did not delude himself into believing that his efforts could do anything to make what he called "the lunatic fringe nationalists" less implacable in their hatred of British rule, he hoped that his efforts would help "to keep them above ground than below it". In my interview with him Sadleir emphasized that he tried to do anything he could to pre-empt the possibility of a crisis in colonial Tanganyika similar to Kenya's Mau Mau crisis. But what Sadleir feared was already happening in many places upcountry. In 1958 numerous incidents and confrontations involving the police and the public occurred in Mtwara, Sumbawanga, Geita and Mwanza which the Government immediately blamed on "irresponsible and ignorant hooligans" within TANU[404]

The Tanganyika Broadcasting Corporation

In colonial Tanganyika, like elsewhere in British Africa, radio broadcasting was used as a propaganda instrument by the colonial administration. This was neither inadvertent nor accidental. As Mytton has convincingly argued, it is not possible to think of politics, colonial or otherwise, in isolation from communication.[405] In Tanganyika the exercise of colonial power involved various forms of communication which included the popular *baraza* and "fire-side" chats.[406] However, unlike the popular *baraza* (public meeting) and local newspapers, the radio proved to be the most effective in overcoming the barriers of distance and illiteracy. Hitherto the administration had no easy means of contact with the masses because of Tanganyika's geographical conditions and the underdevelopment of its transportation system. District Officers spent considerable time travelling on foot to inspect their domains and meet with their subjects. But travelling on foot one could cover very limited space and meet with only a limited number of people. Consequently, prior to the advent of radio broadcasting the Government and other agencies were able to communicate effectively with only a small proportion of Tanganyika's population.[407]

---

399   Ibid.

400   Ibid.

401   Ibid.

402   Sadleir's letter to the author dated 14 February, 1998.

403   PRO, CO 1027/134, Sadleir's note dated 9 September, 1958.

404   *The Tanganyika Standard*, April 16, 1958.

405   Mytton, *Mass Communication*, 6.

406   Communication being defined as an interpersonal relationship, either direct or indirect, involving the transfer of information in the form of explicit statements of fact to messages whose objective is to influence an audience's view of the world.

407   Mytton, *Mass Communication*, 5.

Echoing in tone the media policies of other British territories after World War II, the administration in colonial Tanganyika specifically intended to make radio broadcasting a tool for managing the "political awakening" of the African and to counter "misinformation" from so-called agitators, both from within and from without. From the perspective of the Colonial Office the "twin births", to borrow Zaffiro's term,[408] which necessitated the urgency of managing the African political awakening were the increasing tempo of African nationalism and the spread of communism.[409] More specifically, radio broadcasting in the colonies was to be used "to combat the growth of Communist influence, not only by direct counter propaganda but also - and perhaps chiefly - by the positive projection both of the accurate appreciation of the democratic point of view and the principles upon which (Western) civilization is based".[410]

In colonial Tanganyika, the events of World War II and the need to provide news and propaganda led to the introduction of what may actually have been the prototype of broadcasting in the colony. In 1940, the Public Works Department presented to the Government a van fitted with a microphone and loud speaker. The van was dubbed the "Mobile Unit for Broadcasting".[411] The van was used to give daily news bulletins in Swahili at all important centers in Dar es Salaam. Further broadcasts were given at the Police Barracks twice a week, and a weekly bulletin was read to Indians in Gujerati and Hindustani every Sunday evening.[412] The Liwali (headman) of Dar es Salaam supplied local news of interest which was incorporated in the bulletins. The Swahili broadcasts were very much appreciated and attracted big crowds especially in the New Market and Ilala areas.[413] A year later a similar broadcasting van was constructed by the Divisional Engineer of the Posts and Telegraphs Department for use in the upcountry town of Tabora.

In the meantime, wireless reception sets with loud speaker equipment for broadcasting news from radio station 7LO Nairobi were becoming popular. It is estimated that in 1940 between thirty and forty such sets were in operation throughout Tanganyika.[414] Thus interest in listening to the radio or the news already existed when the administration of colonial Tanganyika decided to build a local radio broadcasting station in 1951. The following description and analysis of the history of broadcasting and listening to the radio in Tanganyika from 1951 to 1961 is based on Lasswell's model as described in the introduction.

---

408   Zaffiro, J. "Twin Births: African Nationalism and Government Information Management in The Bechuanaland Protectorate, 1957-1966", *The International Journal of African Historical Studies*, vol. 22, no. 1 (1989): 51-77.

409   Charles Armour, "The BBC and the Development of Broadcasting in British Colonial Africa 1946-1956", *African Affairs*, vol. 83, no. 332 (1984): 362; See also: PRO, CO 537/6585, "Memorandum on the Development of Broadcasting in the Colonies."

410   PRO, CO 537/6585, Secretary of State for the Colonies, Circular dispatch dated 29 March, 1949, "Broadcasting in the Colonies." See also, Armour, "Development of Broadcasting", 362.

411   PRO, CO 875/8/5, "PROPAGANDA: Tanganyika progress reports."

412   Ibid.

413   According to the "PROPAGANDA; Tanganyika progress report" for 1941 as many as 1,000 Africans sometimes assembled at these centers to hear the news.

414   PRO, CO 875/8/5, "Tanganyika progress report for 1940."

(a) Medium analysis

Radio broadcasting in colonial Tanganyika was established in 1951, with a grant from the Colonial Development and Welfare Fund (hereafter CD & W).[415] In a sense, Tanganyika benefited from an upsurge of interest in wireless broadcasting in the Colonial Office,[416] which made possible the provision of monies for the purchase of transmission equipment and receivers.[417] Initially, only a small transmitter was installed at a cost of less than 10,000 pounds sterling. Because its transmission range was a short distance of 40 kilometers or 24 miles it only covered Dar es Salaam and its suburbs. Indeed, the radio was then known as *Sauti ya Dar es Salaam* (The Voice of Dar es Salaam).

The studio of *Sauti ya Dar es Salaam* was a blanket-lined attic in a building on Kichwele (now Uhuru) Street. The aerial, a dipole, was hung between a palm tree and a casuarina tree! It was connected to a Hallicrafter BC610 transmitter, which was fed from a Tannoy PA amplifier, with inputs from a Decca record player and single 4021A microphone.[418] Three one-hour broadcasts a week were started in July 1951, with Thomas Marealle (later to become paramount chief of the Chagga) as announcer and program producer. In 1955 a bigger 20 kW Marconi transmitter was installed at the new studios under construction along Pugu Road. In May, 1956, Governor Twining opened the new studios and a single program with territory-wide short and medium wave coverage began.[419] The total cost for the new studios, transmitter and 50 receivers for African community listening came to 80,000 pounds sterling, of which 55,000 pounds came from the CD & W fund.[420]

From 1951 to mid-1956 the broadcasting agency was known as the Tanganyika Broadcasting Service (hereafter TBS). The control of broadcasting was vested in C.A.L. Richards, the Commissioner for Local Development who, in turn, was responsible to B. Leechman, the Member for Social Services. Initially the language policy of TBS was to use Swahili and later replace it with English.[421] A former school headmaster, Mr. C. Ryan, was seconded to TBS specifically for the purpose of developing English as the medium of broadcasting.

On July 1, 1956, a statutory public Corporation created by Ordinance took over the operation and control of broadcasting from the Government's Department of Social Development. The new Corporation was named the Tanganyika Broadcasting Corporation (hereafter TBC) and had a Board consisting of eight unofficial and two official members, one of the official members being the Director of Public Relations.[422] The membership of the Director of PRD on the TBC Board

---

415   Konde, Hadji S, *Press Freedom in Tanzania* (Arusha: East African Publications Ltd., 1984): 44.

416   Armour, "Development of Broadcasting", 362.

417   Without this grant broadcasting probably would have come to much later to colonial Tanzania. The administration was simply not ready then to use its meager resources to introduce radio broadcasting.

418   *Ariel*, 9 September, 1981.

419   According to the PRD the new transmitter ensured comfortable listening throughout the territory under normal conditions. However, according to many informants in some upcountry areas occasionally the radio would just go off.

420   PRO, CO 875/67/7, "Broadcasting. Tanganyika",

421   However, officially no broadcasting to Europeans was contemplated.

422   While the interests of the Director of Public Relations were to promote a positive image of the colonial administration, it is not clear what the interests of the other Board members were and whether or not they were at variance with those of the Director of Public Relations.

suggests how from its inception TBC worked closely in tandem with the PRD. It was the PRD which provided TBC with a daily world and local news service in Swahili, a weekly news digest and a monthly review.[423]

The TBC Ordinance, No. 4 of 1956, stipulated the duty of the Corporation and general powers in relation thereto as follows:

> It shall be the duty of the Corporation to operate and maintain a broadcasting service as a means of information, education and entertainment for the public of the Territory and to develop the service to the best advantage and interests of the Territory.[424]

However Sec. 16 of the Ordinance empowered the Government to prohibit the broadcasting of any matter or matter of any class or character which might be contrary to the public interest.

The first Director-General of TBC, Thomas Wightman Chalmers, came to colonial Tanganyika on secondment from the BBC. Chalmers was a man of great experience. At the BBC he was Controller of the *Light Programme* from 1948 to1950. He was the Director of the Nigerian Broadcasting Corporation from 1951to 1956, and Controller, BBC Northern Region, 1956-1958. Colonial Tanganyika was fortunate to secure his services. However, those services did not come cheaply. He was hired under very favorable terms of service: a salary of 3,000 pounds sterling per annum, a 20% gratuity, free housing, transport and travelling expenses, free medical care plus a fully paid leave in England after every 30 months of his 5-year contract.[425]

Chalmers was expected to work closely with the TBC Board of Governors. However, the TBC Ordinance did not specify the Board's duties and functions. What the Ordinance specified was that "the manager of the broadcasting service (i.e. Director-General) shall be responsible for the control and day to day management of the broadcasting service".[426] The undefined relationship between the Board and the Director-General did not pose any problems in part because of the European predominance in its membership. Later, as we will see, when in 1961 the Board became predominantly African, fears of political influence necessitated a clear definition of that relationship. In any case, as Director-General, Chalmers was fully in control of the day-to-day running of TBC and used his authority to shape TBC as he wished.

Chalmers consciously endeavored to Africanize TBC as soon as was practical to do so. Chalmers maintained a very informal relationship with the top echelon of the BBC and exploited these contacts to send Africans to the BBC for training. Thus in 1959 he was able to send David Wakati to the BBC on secondment for two years, which was rather unusual. The same year two of the Swahili program staff, Athumani Magoma and Ellie Mbotto, went on a BBC training course in London. At the same time Chalmers recruited Paul Sozigwa, who had graduated

---

423   Tanganyika. Public Relations Department. *Annual Report, 1956* (Dar-es-Salaam: Government Printer, 1957): 9.

424   BBC, WAC, File E 1/1 510/1, *Tanganyika Broadcasting Corporation Ordinance, 1956* (Sec. 13) (hereafter TBC Ordinance).

425   Chalmers Personal Collection, *Tanganyika file*, Grattan-Bellew to Tom Chalmers, letter dated 24th October, 1957.

426   BBC, WAC, File E1/1 510/1, "TBC Ordinance, Sec. 8 (3)".

with a BA from Makerere, as Assistant Swahili Program Organizer. To enable the planned expansion of programs, five program assistants and ten technical assistants were recruited in December 1959; all of whom had sat for their O Level School Certificate.[427]

At the beginning of 1961 a new Board was appointed by the Governor under its first African Chairman, John Keto, who was at that time on the teaching staff of St. Andrew's College, Minaki. For the first time also the Board had a majority of African members namely, Dina Sawe, Sheikh Juma Mwindadi, C. Mwinchande and Sebastian Chale. At this time Chalmers and the Board turned their attention towards preparing TBC "materially, physically and psychologically" for Independence Day (December 9, 1961) and after.

However, the transition to Independence was not an easy one. During the February session of the House of Assembly, formerly the Legislative Council, some of the African members severely criticized the TBC. What prompted this criticism was a request by the TBC for an additional 12,000 pounds to run the English program. One member, Lawi Nangwanda Sijaona, objected to the use of English (and Gujerati) in broadcasting and thought the English program was unnecessary.[428] He also criticized TBC for not providing up to date news:

> I tune to the TBC at 8 o'clock for news. The news is very scanty. You sometimes have events taking place in Tanganyika and a better report of them is given in neighbouring territories, such as Kenya, and there you will hear of events taking place on the same day in Tanganyika being broadcast to people over the KBS.[429]

Sijaona reiterated the importance of radio broadcasting and how those who were responsible for it could use it for sabotage. He called for the Government to take over TBC and run it as a department of the Government.[430]

However, Chalmers worked hard behind the scene to pre-empt, if not to postpone, not only Government takeover of broadcasting but interference with the day to day running of the TBC Chalmers believed this could be done by convincing the TBC Board, which was now predominantly African, to accept the idea that the integrity of TBC depended on its independent status. In this regard he sought the advice of Hugh Carleton Greene who was at the time Director-General of the BBC. Greene referred Chalmers to the Whitley Document in the BBC Beveridge Report of 1931.[431] Greene alerted Chalmers to specific ideas in the Whitley Document which he believed would be useful. One such idea was that the responsibilities of the TBC Board members ought to be "general and not particular" and that he could ensure that board members would work with the Director-General and decide upon major matters of policy and finance, but that they leave the execution of that policy and the general administration of the Service in all its branches to the Director-General and his competent officers.[432] Greene also advised Chalmers to pay close attention to the suggestions or complaints of the Board members.

---

427   TBC, *Annual Report, 1959* (Government Printer, Dar es Salaam, 1960): 2.

428   Tanganyika. *Legislative Council Debates*, 15 February, 1961, 116.

429   Ibid., p. 117.

430   Ibid., p. 117.

431   BBC WAC, File E 40/202/2, H. Carleton Greene to T.W. Chalmers, letter dated 10 January, 1961.

432   Ibid.

Chalmers, it seems, was able to convince John Keto, the African Chairman of the Board, to accept Greene's suggestions especially regarding the relationship between the Board and the Director-General. In a memorandum to Board members dated December 23, 1961, Keto reiterated, almost verbatim, Greene's suggestions to Chalmers about what the functions of the TBC Board ought to be.[433] Thus, Keto wrote, the "Board cannot run or even supervise the day-to-day business of the Corporation, which is of great technical and administrative complexity. Broadcasting is a professional business, and must be left to professionals".[434] Keto further noted, "Our main concern should be in matters of broad policy both in the programme and financial fields, not in matters of detail, which should be for our officers to consider. As a Board, we should take joint decisions; our interest should be general and not particular".[435] Keto also called upon members of the Board to "take the opportunity afforded by the item `Board Points' in the Agenda, to raise any particular issue of less than major character".[436]

(b) Control analysis

Our control analysis must start with an overview of broadcasting policies. Besides the intentions of using radio for propaganda, colonial broadcasting policies were also informed by the recommendations of the Plymouth Committee which in 1936 "envisaged colonial broadcasting as not only for entertainment, but rather for enlightenment and education".[437] For that purpose, the Plymouth Committee "strongly recommended that wherever possible broadcasting activities should be developed in the colonial territories as a public service by the governments concerned".[438] Thus as early as 1956 the PRD was proposing that a broadcasting unit should be set up within the department "whose job would be to explain government's policies and actions to the people, to act as a channel for all government publicity, and to negotiate with the Corporation (the TBC) for such time on the air as was necessary to carry out these purposes".[439]

In November 1956, the first step was taken; with the help of the Schools Broadcasting organization, "news commentaries were initiated to follow the news daily or several times a week."[440] According to the PRD: "The value of these was proved during the Middle East crisis when a series of nine commentaries explained the reasons for the British and French action and by presenting a

---

433   Indeed, reading the memorandum one gets a feeling that the author of the memorandum could as well have been Chalmers himself.

434   BBC WAC, File E 40/202/2, The Chairman to Board Members, "The Board and the TBC," memo dated 23 December, 1961.

435   Ibid.

436   Ibid.

437   Wilkinson, "BBC and Africa", 177.

438   PRO, CO 537/6585, "Broadcasting in the Colonies – Policy." The main argument against commercial broadcasting in principle was that its main motive would be to make a profit. Therefore, it was believed, commercial broadcasting would cater primarily for its sponsors, and would offer more entertainment programs and venture into less popular, educational programs only as window-dressing to impress critics.

439   Tanganyika. Public Relations Department, *Annual Report, 1956*, 9.

440   Ibid., 9.

balanced picture did much to reassure the people".[441] However, Britain's failure to force Gamal Abdel Nasser to hand back the Suez canal demonstrated Britain's waning power not only in the Middle East but soon also in Africa.[442]

In addition to material supplied to TBC by the PRD Press Section, officers of the PRD took part in a number of broadcasts including those covering the meetings of the Legislative Council.[443] One of these officers was none other than Mr. T. R. Sadleir. Sadleir organized and moderated an unrehearsed weekly discussion program in Swahili called *Majadiliano* (Discussion). His discussants were members of the public and the discussions covered a number of controversial subjects including racial discrimination in public toilets.[444] *Majadiliano* took place from 8:30 to 9:00 on Thursday evenings and was repeated on Sunday evening every week.[445] Sadleir considered his program an antidote to the anti-British broadcasts by Radio Cairo.[446] The program wound up in May, 1959 after Sadleir was transferred to the Co operative Society. Its replacement known as *Je hii ni Busara?* (Is this Wisdom?) was not very popular.

Furthermore, the PRD co-operated with TBC in recording programs from the Provinces and in establishing and encouraging listener groups in various parts of the territory. The opening during 1958 of the United Kingdom Information Office (hereafter UKIO) in Dar es Salaam was a timely reinforcement in the sphere of information dissemination, both in English and the vernacular. Co-operation between the PRD, TBC and the UKIO was close both in the preparation and in the distribution of news. Particularly valuable to the colonial mass media was the timely reception by the UKIO of communiqués from the Central Office of Information in London everyday at 7 pm local time.[447]

(c) Content analysis

To appreciate what people listened to on their radios in the 1950s and how programming evolved up to 1961, our attention must first focus on how broadcast schedules were structured, that is, when the programs were aired. From the very beginning TBS and its successor, TBC, operated on set schedules so that listeners knew when and where on the dial they might find a program. However, from 1951 to 1956 the TBS station came on the air for very short periods each day. When it commenced broadcasting in 1951, TBS was on the air only one and a half hours each day. Subsequently more time and programs were added. By January 1957, TBC was on the air for six hours daily with Swahili programs taking sixty-three per cent of air time.[448]

---

441 Ibid., 9.

442 Shaw, Tony, *Eden, Suez and the mass media: propaganda and persuasion during the Suez crisis.*

443 Tanganyika. Public Relations Department. *Annual Report, 1958* (Dar-es-Salaam: Government Printer: 1959): 2.

444 Ibid., p. 2.

445 Sadleir's note in PRO, CO 1027/134, dated 9 September 1958.

446 Randal Sadleir, interview, 20 January, 1998. In my interview with Sadleir he also mentioned that the Portuguese authorities in Mozambique periodically jammed his program but he did not say why.

447 PRO, CO 1027/522, "U.K. Information Office – Tanganyika."

448 The remaining time was taken by English broadcasts. Attempts to introduce broadcasting in Gujerati failed.

Between 1958 and 1961 broadcasting hours were doubled to twelve hours. The following are programs for 1 December, 1958:[449]

Morning

6:15 a.m. Jambo	7:39 a.m. Editorials (BBC)
6:45 a.m. Habari za Jana	7:45 a.m. Local News (English)
7:00 a.m. Morning music	8:00 a.m. Close
7:30 a.m. BBC News	

Afternoon

12:15 p.m. BBC News	2:00 p.m. BBC News
12:30 p.m. General Overseas Service (BBC)	2:15 p.m. Close

Evening

5:30 p.m. Maombi ya Wanawake	7:30 p.m. Aina ya Twiga
6:00 p.m. BBC Kutoka London	7:45 p.m. Wajibu wa Raia
6:15 p.m. Tommy Steel	8:00 p.m. Habari za Leo
6:30 p.m. Kuran Tukufu	8:15 p.m. Michezo (Sports)
6:45 p.m. Habari za Ulimwengu	8:30 p.m. KAR (King's African Rifles) Hewani
7:00 p.m. Jimbo Lenu	

English programs

9:00 p.m. BBC World News/Home News from Britain
9:14 p.m. Local News, Weather Report, Commercials
9:25 p.m. Week-End Sports
9:30 p.m. "Journey into Space"
10:00 p.m. "Melody aqnd Song," The Melachrino Orchestra/Voices of Walter Schumann
10:30 p.m. Close

---

449   BBC WAC, File E 1/1/510/1, "Tanganyika Broadcasting Corporation."

Prime time was obviously in the morning and in the evening.[450] As can be discerned from the programs above, the TBC tried to cater to a wide range of interests.

However, a major component of TBC programming in the late 1950s was entertainment. First, broadcasting music programs was inexpensive. All that was needed was a gramophone and a stack of records. In those days copyright restrictions were not seriously enforced.[451] Second, music was one of the traditional popular-entertainment forms. The music aired was familiar and uplifting. The most popular genre was African "jazz" music performed by Swahili and Congolese artistes. This so-called "jazz" music was actually dance music that was heavily influenced by Caribbean rhythms.

Another component of programming in the 1950s was the broadcasting of sporting events; especially popular were the live broadcasts of Sunlight and Gossage soccer tournaments.[452] The live broadcasts of Sunlight and Gossage soccer tournaments enabled TBC to create a territorial radio-listening audience. Although the announcers of soccer matches were all men, other programs had female announcers. The most popular female broadcasters were Deborah Chihota, Khadija Saidi and Violet Maro.[453]

A closer look at the sample of daily programs above shows an interesting mix of music and informational programs. Thus in the morning the news was placed between two *Jambo* programs, and BBC News followed immediately after *Morning music*. In the evening *Wajibu wa Raia* (Civic Duty) and the news came before a sports program. The TBC strategy was to use entertainment as bait; a captive audience stayed tuned for other non-entertainment programs.

Moreover, when listeners lost interest in a program they had the freedom to tune in to other stations such as the Kenya Broadcasting Corporation (KBS), the Uganda Broadcasting Corporation (UBC) and many others.[454] Surfing the airwaves was a freedom unique to radio broadcasting. Whereas newspapers could be censored or their distribution carefully controlled, the African listener was free to tune to a station of his liking, including those of neighboring countries and as far away as Cairo, Bonn and Washington, D.C. This freedom gave listeners access to other news and views which they could compare with those aired by TBC. This freedom, of course, undermined the Government's efforts to prevent foreign propaganda from being heard.

---

450   Radio signals are transmitted by "ground" and "sky" waves; "sky" waves reflect off the ionosphere only after sunset and cover greater distance than "ground" waves.

451   BBC WAC, Tom Chalmers to Miss Chandler, letter dated 11 August, 1958. In this letter Chalmers explains how difficult it was for him to explain to his staff the intricacies of copyright.

452   The Sunlight Cup competition was an annual event in which each Province sent a team to Dar es Salaam. The Gossage Cup was also annual but it involved the national teams of Kenya, Tanzania and Uganda; the venue rotated between the three capitals, Dar-es-Salaam, Kampala and Nairobi.

453   Women also played a big part in operating technical equipment in the TBC studios. One of these operators was Agnes Kufa.

454   TBC, *Audience Survey Report 1960*, 7.

(d) Audience analysis:[455]

In colonial Tanganyika, as in other colonies, broadcasting involved a triple relationship between the manufacturers of equipment, broadcasters, and audiences. In the beginning this tripartite relationship was riddled with many difficulties. Since broadcasting in Africa was not initiated by manufacturers for the purpose of selling transmission equipment and receiving sets, public policy makers in the colonies and in Britain had a hard time convincing British manufacturers to make radios that Africans could afford to buy and maintain.

Harry Franklin, the pioneer of radio broadcasting in Northern Rhodesia (present day Zambia), eventually was able to convince the Ever Ready Battery Co. in London of the potential market for receivers in Northern Rhodesia, Southern Rhodesia and Nyasaland. Ever Ready then designed and manufactured the "saucepan radio".[456] The "saucepan" set, which was mass-produced and easy-to-maintain, came to be known as the poor man's radio.[457] By 1949 several British manufacturers were producing receivers at a whole sale price of three or four pounds sterling.[458] The "saucepan" set offered "a really world-wide market for British industry".[459] However, because the receiver and the battery, which was about 8 inches by 3 inches by 5 1/2 inches, each weighed just over seven pounds, the "saucepan" set was not portable. It was a disadvantage that led to its replacement by the portable "transistor" radio (invented in the United States of America in 1948) which was equally cheap. Adding to the disadvantage of the "saucepan" was its prohibitively expensive battery which cost 1 pound sterling.

While radio broadcasting was a new medium, its development was very much shaped by colonial Tanganyika's social, political and cultural realities which in turn were re-shaped by radio broadcasting. Following the decision to set up a broadcasting service the Government had to contend with two major problems: how to apply the known techniques of broadcasting to a new audience entirely unfamiliar with them and how to bring broadcasting to many people as possible. The first was a technical problem which pertained to transmission and reception, while the second was an administrative problem that had to do with listening facilities for those who could not afford radios.

Due to problems with electrical storm interference, long-wave transmission was never considered as an alternative to short-wave or medium-wave transmission. Rather it was decided that it would be cheaper to use the short-wave transmitter on the high-frequency band. But the size of the country (750 miles by 600 miles) and its population being denser along its edges, coupled with

---

455   The only audience survey in this period was conducted for the TBC by the Market Research Company of East Africa in 1960. The sample involved 1,733,067 rural households and 78,800 urban households. The survey sample included 31,195 rural households and 7,449 urban households with radio sets.

456   PRO, CO 537/6585, "Broadcasting in the Colonies, Policy." The set was designed for short-wave reception and was housed in a substantial metal cabinet with provision for the back to be sealed and so prevent interference with the adjustments.

457   Wilkinson, J.F. "The BBC and Africa", *African Affairs*, vol. 71, no. 283 (April 1972): 179.

458   PRO, CO 537/6585, Secretary of State for the Colonies, circular dispatch dated 29 March, 1949.

459   PRO, CO 537/6585 "Broadcasting in the Colonies." In the first six months of production, these receivers were not only selling in Northern and Southern Rhodesia and Nyasaland, for which countries they were specifically produced, but also in Singapore and Malaya and in various countries in Africa - the Belgian Congo, Basutoland, Bechuanaland, West Africa and Kenya.

the necessity of locating the transmitter at Dar-es-Salaam, presented difficulties even for shortwave coverage. A type of aerial used effectively in those days for "local" broadcasting on shortwave (as opposed to international broadcasting on shortwave) was one which fired the transmitter energy directly upwards in a relatively narrow solid beam. That solid beam of energy was then reflected from the ionosphere at a mean height of some 250 miles so that a considerable area around the transmitting station was illuminated more or less evenly by the reflected beam.[460] However, the maximum range at which such a transmission could be used with advantage was limited to some 400 to 500 miles from the transmitting station. The distance from Dar-es-Salaam to the shores of Lake Victoria, with the highest population density, is greater than this range.

The problem of how best to bring broadcasting to as many people as possible was identified by Mr. W. E. C. Varley in a 1946 survey.[461] For a population the majority of whom scratched a poor living from the land or poorly paid urban jobs, the affordability of radio sets required either some form of subsidy for the supply of sets or a very considerable reduction in the price.[462] There was also the problem of lack of electricity in the rural areas which required that the radios that Africans used had to be battery-operated.[463]

Varley also suggested that community listening was probably the best way to bring radio broadcasting to as many people as possible. The Government accepted the idea and procured 30 receivers for distribution to community listening posts all over the territory. In major towns community listening posts were strategically placed close to the African residential quarter. In addition, several departments were encouraged to set up community listening facilities, as were native authorities, estates and other large employers of labor.[464] Most likely the administration envisioned the power of radio broadcasting in the administrative changes that could take place within hours of a radio announcement. For the first time the Government could speak directly to the people without having to compete with other voices.[465]

Besides the community listening posts, listening to the radio soon became a family pastime as more and more people bought their own radios. There is no exact way of knowing how many people listened to the radio. If we assume that for every receiver there were about 6 to 10 listeners,[466] the numbers of listeners would have been considerable based on available receivers. Based on estimates of about 1,400

---

460   Roberts, W.A. "The Technical Development of Broadcasting in Colonial Territories: Tanganyika," dated June, 1953, in Chalmers Personal Archives.

461   BBC WAC, File E1/21, Varley, W.E.C. *Broadcasting Survey of the British East African Territories*, dated April 1948.

462   Williams, "Broadcasting to the Colonies", 218.

463   These needed periodic recharging. Eventually listeners developed ingenuous ways to recharge radio batteries one of which was to put them on top of house roofs during the day.

464   PRO, CO 875/67/7, "Broadcasting – Tanganyika."

465   An important aspect of colonial communication was the position and role of District Commissioners who, by virtue of their positions acted as intermediaries between the Central administration and the masses. They could and did choose what information they wanted to pass on either way. Sometimes orders were either not communicated or information that was intended for colonial subjects was often too long delayed.

466   Wilkinson, J.F. "The BBC and Africa", *African Affairs*, vol. 71, no. 283 (April 1972):176.

receivers in use in 1951,[467] there would have been approximately 14,000 listeners when broadcasting started in 1951. In 1956, *Baragumu*, a Government Swahili daily newspaper, estimated that there were approximately a quarter million TBC listeners in Tanganyika. *Baragumu* also estimated that TBC received 200 requests per week to hear a favorite record played.[468] The popularity of listening to the radio was also reflected by the number of new receivers imported per year as well as the number of radio licenses sold per year. Table I shows figures of transmitters, receivers and licenses for the years 1951-1961.

Table I: The growth of radio and its audience, 1951-1961.

Year	Number of Transmitter	Number of Imported Receivers	Licenses sold	Estimates of actual numb er of sets in use
1951	1 SW	N/A	-	1,400
1952	1SW 1MW	N/A	-	-
1954	1SW 1MW	19,045	-	-
1955	1SW 1MW	21,225	-	-
1956	2SW 1MW	11,418	-	60,000
1957	2SW 1MW	14,685	-	-
1958	2SW 2MW	10,721	20,480	-
1959	3SW 2MW	12,486	18,176	-
1960	3SW 2MW	12,479	18,000	72,232
1961	3SW 2MW	14,488	34,404	-

Source: Mytton, Graham, Mass Communication in Africa (London: Edward Arnold, 1983): 110.

As can be seen, the number of imported receivers peaked in 1955 and thereafter averaged about 12,000. The demand for radios was phenomenal given the fact that in 1946 Varley had observed the virtual absence of radio sets among Africans. It can also be seen from Table I that the number of licenses sold was significant although the figures do not tally with the estimated number of actual sets in use. For a variety of reasons such as lack of accessibility, forgetfulness, not to mention deliberate evasion, many people who owned a radio did not comply with the regulation that each year they must purchase a license for it.[469] The loss

467 Mytton, *Mass Communication*, 110.

468 *Baragumu*, May 10, 1956.

469 BBC WAC File E 1/1 510/1, Tom Chalmers to Sir Beresford Clark, letter dated May 2, 1959. A licence fee of Shs. 10/- per set was introduced in January, 1957. Licenses were issued by the Posts and Telecommunications Administration, which retained 15 per cent. of the fee. Due to inefficiency and the fact that Post Offices in Tanganyika were not to be found in many parts of the Territory, the Posts and Telecommunication administration was logistically incapable of enforcing the collection of radio fees.

of revenue to the TBC from non-payment of radio fees amounted to thousands of pounds sterling. It is possible that fewer than half the total number of set owners paid. Based on the total number of sets imported between 1954 and 1958 which was 77.094 sets, payment of fees in 1958 should have brought in Shs. 770,940/- in revenue. But in that year the TBC realized only Shs. 204,800/- from radio fees! Evaders were encouraged by lack of prosecution. The prosecution of offenders was made virtually impossible because "the Ordinance (was) so worded that proof (had) to be adduced that a defendant was actually using a set without a license", something that was very difficult to prove.[470]

In May 1960, an audience survey was conducted for TBC by the Market Research Company of East Africa based in Nairobi, Kenya. Although Chalmers was unhappy with its "slightly dubious statistics", for a first attempt in an uncharted field it was not too bad.[471] According to the survey by 1960 listening to the radio had become a regular habit for all races in Tanganyika. Table II shows responses, by race, to the question: "If without a radio, would you miss it?"

Table II: If Without A Radio, Would You Miss It?

Race	No opinion	Very much	Quite a bit	Not much	Not at all
	%	%	%	%	%
Europeans	2.8	45.9	30.3	13.8	7.2
Asians	3.1	57.4	21.1	11.7	6.7
Arabs	2.3	56.8	19.9	13.4	7.6
Africans	2.0	53.1	22.5	18.4	4.0

Source: TBC, Audience Survey, 1960, 11.

The 1960 audience survey also determined that income was a significant factor in radio ownership, especially among Africans. The survey showed that 73% of the Africans who owned a radio earned between Shs. 101/- to Shs. 500/- per month.[472] The majority of African radio owners were people with a regular income. Dr. Peter Kitundu told the author that people in Iramba District who could afford to buy radios during the 1950s were mostly traders, teachers and medical assistants.[473] Professor Lloyd Binagi from Tarime, North Mara District, voiced a similar opinion. Prof. Binagi told the author that his father, a headman and a court assessor, was one of the first people in his village to buy a radio.[474]

In colonial Tanganyika radio owners conveyed news heard over the radio to their neighbors. This "relay function"[475] can be determined by analyzing what

---

470   BBC WAC File E 1/1 510/1, Tom Chalmers to Sir Beresford Clark, letter dated 2 May, 1959.

471   Chalmers Personal Archives, T.W. Chalmers to R.S. Postgate, letter dated 14 February, 1961.

472   TBC, Audience Survey Report, May 1960, Prepared by The Market Research Company of East Africa, Nairobi, Kenya, 5.

473   Formerly a physician at Winona Hospital, Minnesota, interviewed 30 November, 1997.

474   Professor at the University of Wisconsin-Whitewater, interviewed 6 December, 1997.

475   Lasswell, "Communication in Society", p. 48.

they heard (or thought they heard) and how they passed this information to their neighbors. Evidence suggests that as relay agents African listeners represented the weakest link in radio broadcasting in Tanganyika. Several factors accounted for this weakness. Most of the factors were pre-dispositional and environmental. Most people listened to the radio while doing chores and other things as table III indicates. Consequently, listeners could and did distort what they heard over the radio.

Table III: What do you do when listening to the radio?

Race	Just listen	Sew or knit	Do house work	Read	Write	Do odd jobs	Do paid jobs
	%	%	%	%	%	%	%
European	75.2	2.8	2.8	13.8	-	0.9	1.8
Asians	79.3	3.5	1.6	7.8	1.2	2.7	2.3
Arabs	67.3	-	2.0	4.1	-	4.1	22.5
Africans	78.3	2.2	2.5	12.3	0.2	1.7	1.6

Source: TBC, Audience Survey, 1960, 15.

Furthermore, in remote districts poor reception and fading accounted for lack of clarity of what was being said which may have caused listeners to misunderstand what they heard. Such distorted news was then passed on to others. Besides problems with poor reception, some people deliberately exaggerated and distorted what they clearly heard or provided incomplete information by repeating what appealed to them the most.

Finally, education was an important factor in the relay of information by radio owners. According to the 1960 audience survey, 6% of the African respondents had no formal education; 16% had 1-4 years of education; 12.2% had 5-6 years of education; 17.5% had 7-9 years of education; and 39.0% had 10-12 years of education.[476] Thus 34.2% had no more than six years of education, a level of education that could not have equipped them with analytical abilities, say, to understand and explain world events.

(e) Effect analysis

There is no exact way of knowing the political influence of radio in colonial Tanganyika. Analyzing audience research data collected by TBC and reading letters written by listeners to TBC are two ways of determining the reaction of listeners to radio broadcasts. However, these methods are not without doubts, especially since many listeners may not have bothered to write or could not write because they were illiterate.

However, radio broadcasting most likely influenced the turnout and results of the 1958 and 1959 Legislative Council elections. In these elections Africans

476   TBC, Audience Survey Report 1960, 5.

for the first time went to the polls to choose who would represent them in the Legislative Council. Since these were the first ever elections in colonial Tanganyika, the electoral process had to be explained in order to be understood.[477] The amount of air-time that TBC allocated to the coverage of the elections and the issues that dominated the airwaves show how the Government tailored the information about the elections and how TBC was an important factor in mobilizing people to vote.

At 9:15 p.m. on August 20, 1958, Governor Richard Turnbull addressed the country by radio. In his speech he emphasized the significance of the elections in relation to the constitutional changes that could lead the country towards self-government. He urged listeners who were qualified and wished to vote to register as soon as possible.[478] In a single speech the Governor reached more people than the district and provincial officials had been able to do for months. By tying the issue of self-government to the impending elections set for September 1958, the Governor indirectly suggested that Africans would only have themselves to blame if self-government was delayed. It appears that his message was clearly understood. Before the speech only 7,000 people had registered to vote. However, thousands more registered after the speech as 60,000 turned out to vote in September.[479]

In 1959, TBC allocated more air time to programs laden with political content. The program "Today in LegCo" aired all the sessions of the Legislative Council in English and Swahili. Two major speeches by Governor Turnbull were relayed live from the opening sessions of the Legislative Council on 17 March and 15 December respectively. The speeches were translated into Swahili and Gujerati were respectively.[480]

Besides its political influence, broadcasting clearly influenced people's decisions to purchase items that were advertized over the radio. According to the 1960 audience survey, over the counter medications topped the list of items that respondents said they bought as a result of radio advertisements.[481] Batteries, cooking fat, toothpaste and margarine followed in that order. Thus radio advertisements were very instrumental in propagating mass consumerism in colonial Tanganyika.

The introduction of radio advertisements was a departure from a policy that discouraged the commercialization of broadcasting. When officials at the Colonial Office debated about colonial policy for broadcasting in the late 1940s there were two points of view. One view was that broadcasting should be a public service operation, largely funded by government subvention and supplemented by license revenue.[482] The second point of view favored commercial operations run by private companies granted a contract by government to establish broadcasting stations, accept advertizing revenue and provide government with air time when

---

477   In *The Tanganyika Standard* of October 26, 1957, Mr. G.W.Y. Hucks, the Supervisor of Elections, lamented the lack of African enthusiasm to register to vote and blamed it on ignorance and especially the fear that if one registered to vote and did not they would go to jail.

478   PRO, CO 822/1522, "Talk given on the TBC by His Excellency the Governor at 9:15 p.m. on 20 August, 1958."

479   PRO, CO 822/1456, "Supervision of Elections – Tanganyika."

480   TBC, *Annual Report, 1959* (Dar-es-Salaam: Government Printer, 1960): 4.

481   TBC, *Audience Survey Report 1960*, 52.

482   BBC WAC File C. 138, Armour, Charles, "From Saucepan Radio to Satellites: the Development of Broadcasting in Africa."

required.[483] The public service point of view prevailed.

Change of attitude at the Colonial Office toward commercial advertizing by radio and the fact that the TBC was unable to raise enough revenue from licenses were two factors that encouraged the TBC administration to venture into advertizing. Beginning on November, 1, 1956, TBC allowed "spot" advertizing for a limited period of approximately five minutes each evening following the BBC and Local News. TBC charged Shs. 20/- per night for 30 worded ads and 50 cents per extra word.[484] Initially only advertisements in English were accepted. Subsequently advertisements in Swahili also began to be aired and eventually came to surpass those in English.[485] Obviously the advertisers must have realized the opportunities that TBC afforded them to reach the African consumer via the Swahili programs.

Because of colonial Tanganyika's limited industrial development TBC's ads were mainly from commercial and industrial firms based in neighboring Kenya. It is not surprising therefore that in September 1959 TBC appointed Ian McCulloch as its Advertizing Representative in Nairobi, Kenya.[486] In order to maximize revenue from ads TBC increased the number of Swahili entertainment programs and cut down informational programming. In 1960 policy changes were made to provide more air time for advertisements. As Chalmers noted, "The conflict between God and Mammon is as real in radio broadcasting as in other spheres of activity".[487] Thus what the Colonial Office had initially feared about the commercialization of broadcasting came to pass.

However, the transition from informational to entertainment broadcasting also reflected customer preferences. Whatever the merits of TBC's output of talks and discussions in 1960, it was entertainment programs that made a mass appeal. By 1960 entertainment programs were still of a comparatively simple kind, and still relied on the use of gramophone records by popular African, European, Arab and Asian musicians. Judged by box-office standards TBC's request programs in 1960 must be reckoned a smash hit. The monthly total of post-cards rose from 2,700 in January to 9,600 in December.[488] The windfall in postage stamps alone must have brought a cheer to the Postmaster-General!

School broadcasting

School broadcasting in colonial Tanganyika was started in August 1955. Initially the broadcasts were for half an hour and the programs included world affairs and English.[489] At that time the Government provided 200 radios to African primary and middle schools regardless of whether or not they were run by the Government, Native Authorities, or the Missions. The radios enabled 17,000 pupils to listen to

---

483   Ibid.

484   BBC WAC File E 1/1 510/1. At the time Shs. 20/- was equivalent to one British pound.

485   T BC, *Annual Report, 1959*, 9. In December 1958 "spot" advertisements in Swahili and English totaled 71 and 63 respectively; in December 1959 there were 280 Swahili and only 72 English advertisements.

486   Ian McCulloch later resigned following his appointment as Public Relations Officer to the Government of Kenya. He was succeeded by Peter Colmore, a well known figure in the advertising and entertainment industry in colonial East Africa.

487   TBC, *Annual Report, 1960*, (Dar-es-Salaam: Government Printer, 1961): 4.

488   Ibid., 5.

489   *Mwangaza*, 9 May, 1956.

schools broadcasts that were eventually to become an established feature of the educational system in Tanganyika.[490] By 1960 there were about 360 schools on TBC's distribution list, i.e., they were registered for listening. From their inception school broadcasts formed an important part of TBC's output, and their extent and expertness placed them ahead of any other British African and Caribbean territory.[491] TBC was thus able to share its experience with other territories, whose representatives attended the Conference on Radio in Education held in London in July, 1959.

The Advisory Committee on Education in the Colonies pointed out in *Mass Education in African Society*, a 1944 policy paper, that growing political consciousness among the natives was a primary concern. The Committee emphasized that character training (i.e. the shaping of behavior such as obedience, submissiveness, passiveness, etc.) be a part of the colonial school curriculum. Subsequently the Department of Education in Tanganyika carefully oriented the content and teaching of history, current affairs and other subjects to this end.

In 1959, TBC started experimental broadcasts to secondary schools. Their immediate success encouraged TBC to plan for a regular series in 1960. Most of the material broadcast to secondary schools came from the accumulated stock of recordings of the BBC Colonial Schools Transcription Service (hereafter CSTS).[492] The CSTS was started in 1952 with the aim of encouraging broadcasting services in the colonies to build up their own school broadcasts. It was financed by a grant from the CD & W Fund. The grant was renewed in October 1955 on the explicit understanding, which was communicated to Colonial Governments in 1956, that CD & W assistance would not be continued after 1958. Funding was later extended until March, 1960.

According to Chalmers, the Director-General of TBC, the accumulated stock of recordings held by CSTS was not only essential in the running of the TBC's school programs, without them school broadcasts in Tanganyika would have been well-nigh impossible.[493] Colonial Tanganyika had no local expertise to sustain its school broadcasting service. TBC's schools broadcasting unit consisted of two people who between them had to organize nearly 200 hours of broadcasts to schools per year.[494] In anticipation of the ending of CSTS assistance the BBC had reissued on long-playing discs some of its best school programs. By 1960, CSTS had something like 600 programs recorded which would be available after CD & W funding ceased on March 31, 1960.

The problem according to Chalmers was that these recordings were only satisfactory for "static" subjects and not for science subjects. Therefore the discontinuation of CD & W funding for CSTS adversely affected TBC's school broadcasting. It is no secret that there was a serious shortage of teachers in colonial Tanganyika. Whilst school broadcasting could not replace face to face classroom instruction, it could provide an immense stimulus to students and the teachers as well.

---

490   Sturmer, Martin, "The Media History of Tanzania", PhD dissertation, Afro-Asiatisches Institute, Salzburg, Austria (1998): 80.

491   TBC, *Annual Report, 1959*, (Dar-es-Salaam: Government Printer, 1960): 7.

492   Ibid., 7.

493   *The Times*, 12 July, 1960, letter to the editor by Tom Chalmers.

494   Ibid.

In the meantime, TBC continued to strive to improve the reception of its school broadcasts. In 1959 considerable improvement in long-distance reception was improved by the use of an additional transmitter on the 31 meter band from 11:00 a.m. till noon. Indirect evidence of its effectiveness came in the increased correspondence from schools in the Western and Lake Provinces, where difficulties of reception had previously been encountered.[495] Furthermore, discussions were held between TBC and Messrs. Twentsche Overseas Trading Company Ltd. about the possibility of producing a transistor set for schools that would be pre-tuned only to TBC frequencies.[496] Whether such a set was produced and distributed is unknown by the author.

Moreover, while BBC remained the source of school material, news and editorial comment, it also provided training for TBC's African personnel. The very first trainees at BBC were Athumani Magoma and Ellie Mbotto. David Wakati from Zanzibar, who would later become Director-General of Radio Tanzania, was also trained at BBC and was one of the pioneers of the BBC Swahili Service together with Oscar Kambona, Nasor Malik, and Tryphon Wagi.

In conclusion, we can say that radio broadcasting revolutionized communications in colonial Tanganyika. Unlike the colonial press, TBC had monopoly of the air waves which, with the exception of external broadcasts by Radio Cairo, would not locally become a contested arena until the 1980s. Thus as a tool for managing information TBC was used by the colonial administration to effectively control the flow of news and other information to a predominantly African audience which bore the brunt of colonial rule.

The radio broadcasting colonial Tanganyika was also a significant contributor and influential in the globalization of consumerism. Commercial advertisements created new needs that were satisfied by commodities produced by local and foreign manufacturers. Bombarding listeners with commercials, TBC more than anything else succeeded in integrating Africans into the capitalist system. TBC radio programs also endeavored to inculcate the ideals that were central to the functioning of the colonial system such as civic duty and being a good farmer. Radio programs helped to inculcate in the emerging African middle-class the tastes and mannerisms of the European middle-classes.

Finally, while the majority of people in colonial Tanganyika lived under a suffocating blanket of poverty they could listen to TBC at a neighbor's house or those in town from a communal listening post. Otherwise, they could catch on what was going on from a radio owner when they met at the local beer club or from gossip. Thus, for those who could not read listening to the radio became a significant source of information. As the momentum towards independence increased people clamored more and more for news and information about what was going on in Dar-es-Salaam and elsewhere in the country. In 1960, a restaurant owner in Dar-es-Salaam unwisely refused to admit a crowd clamoring to hear the broadcast of a speech by Julius Nyerere. He sustained considerable damage to his furniture.[497]

---

495   TBC, *Annual Report, 1959*, 8.

496   Ibid., 8

497   Chalmers Personal Archives, "Broadcasting in East Africa", by Derrick Sington.

PART THREE

Affairs of the Heart in Colonial Zanzibar

8

Dr. Pitchford's love affair with Ms Gool Talati

Introduction

The British Empire provided many opportunities to doctors who were willing to emigrate to seek new careers in the service of British firms, white settler communities and colonial administrations. In Africa, doctors were far removed from the pressures and controls exerted by the General Medical Council of the United Kingdom. The conduct of those employed by colonial administrations came under the purview of the Colonial Office in London. Although colonial medical officers were subject to bureaucratic discipline, the Secretary of State for the Colonies had the discretion of referring to the GMC cases of serious professional misconduct for disciplinary action. Between November 23, 1858 and December 31, 1990 the GMC held public disciplinary proceedings involving 2,015 cases of individual practitioners: "Some 2,316 separate charges were dealt with, the difference between the number of practitioners and number of charges relating to the 301 cases where the same practitioner was involved in more than one subsequent charge."[498] Thirty of these cases were from Africa, excluding Egypt.

The number of cases referred to above is probably less a measure of medical sin than of cases the GMC could handle comfortably. According to Stacey, it was not the intent of the GMC to rack out and haul up all miscreants for disciplinary

---

498 Smith, Russell G. Medical Discipline: *The professional conduct jurisdiction of the General* Medical Council, *1858-1990 (Oxford: Clarendon Press, 1994): 97.*

action.[499] Moreover, as the case at hand will show, dictates of leniency and cronyism influenced individuals or bodies not to report all cases to the GMC. Among the number of cases cited above 346 involved improper sexual or emotional relationships with patients or their families, dealing in indecent materials, acts of criminal indecency, unnatural sexual offences, impropriety with patients, and seduction of patients.[500]

The Medical Act 1858 originally gave the General Council power only to direct the Registrar to erase the name of a practitioner from the Register by which decision the practitioner was barred from practicing medicine. However, by 1932 the Council's Standing Orders provided for the announcement of decisions by the Council President together with "such terms of reprimand admonishment or otherwise as the Council shall approve."[501] There were two cases of sexual misconduct reported and dealt with by the GMC from colonial Africa. One, in 1903, involved adultery with Mrs. T. that led to a divorce case in which the doctor was named.[502] The other, in 1944, involved adultery with a patient Mrs. B. and writing improper letters to her.[503] In the first case the doctor's name was erased from the Register for 114 months after which it was restored. In the second case the doctor's name was erased from the Register for 24 months after which it was restored.

Ethical prohibitions and the severity of censure then and now for improper sexual and emotional relationships with patients presume that such relationships have deleterious consequences for patients. According to Franz Moggi, Jeannette Brodbeck and Hans-Peter Hirsbrunner, data available to date shows that physical contact such as kissing, fondling genital parts, and sexual intercourse has negative consequences on the patient, ranging from the impaired ability to benefit from treatment to deterioration in psychosocial functioning.[504]

Dr. Pitchford's infatuation with Miss Gool Talati

In 1934, the Acting British Resident in Zanzibar informed the Colonial Office in London regarding ethical misconduct by Dr. Henry Otley Watkins-Pitchford, Medical Officer, which had necessitated disciplinary action under Colonial Regulations.[505] It had been discovered that Dr. Pitchford (married with 3 children) was romantically attracted to Miss Gool Talati, a fourteen year-old Parsee school girl, who had previously received professional treatment from him. The relationship involved the exchange of love letters and a one- time clandestine rendezvous in the garage of a friend where hugging and kissing took place.

Upon discovery of the relationship by the school authorities the Acting Resident, out of respect for the family's feelings as well as to avoid a public scandal affecting the good name alike of the Government service, the European community, and

---

499   *Quoted by Smith*, Medical Discipline, 99.

500   Ibid. 103.

501   Ibid. 124.

502   Ibid. *Appendix, 250.*

503   Ibid. *Appendix, 283.*

504   Moggi, Franz, Jeannette Brodbeck and Hans-Peter Hirsbrunner, "Therapist-Patient Sexual Involvement: RiskFactors and Consequences," *Clinical Psychology and Psychotherapy, 7 (2000): 54-60: 55.*

505   Public Record Office (PRO), CO 850/42/2 Acting British Resident, Zanzibar, to Secretary of State for the Colonies, Confidential dispatch dated 12th April, 1934.

the medical profession, suggested to Dr. Pitchford the alternative of resignation and early departure from Zanzibar or of availing himself to an enquiry by the Executive Council under Colonial Regulations. Dr. Pitchford elected to submit to an enquiry.

A committee of the Executive Council was appointed and constituted of A. N. Doorly, the Attorney-General, Wm. Hendry, the Director of Education, and B. Spearman, the Acting Director of Medical and Sanitary Services. Dr. Pitchford was assisted by J. P. Jones, Provincial Commissioner. Proceedings began on the 31st of March, 1934. The Attorney-General, who chaired the committee, called upon Shavakshaw H. Talati through whose complaint this matter had come to the notice of Government to testify. Talati identified himself as Gool's uncle and noted that she was 14 years old; she was born August 1919 in Bombay. He stated that he was first informed by Sister M. Adalinde, principal of St. Joseph's Convent School, that she suspected Dr. Pitchford was carrying on a romantic correspondence with his niece through another student called Eva Deacon. Sister Adalinde also told him that because of her suspicions she appointed someone to watch Gool and this person saw Gool going to and returning from Dr. Freeth's garage. It was at this meeting that Gool and Dr. Pitchford embraced and kissed.

Talati further noted that the family invited Sister Adalinde to the Talati residence to assist them in getting a confession from Gool. On the promise she would not be punished by her parents Gool confessed: "She said that Dr. Watkins-Pitchford sent communications through Eva Deacon, that at first she refused to accept them but Eva Deacon induced her to read them and that Eva Deacon herself wrote the replies." Talati also explained how his niece happened to become Dr. Pitchford's patient and how their relationship developed thereafter. Gool's father had taken her and her sister to see Dr. Pitchford to have their eyes examined:

"After having made his acquaintance as a result of the treatment taken, Dr. Watkins-Pitchford once invited all the (Talati) children to a tea-party at his house saying he was very fond of children. We noticed that he used to meet our children on the main road and used to talk to them. One day he advised my brother that his eldest daughter had very weak eyes and that she should be stopped studying at the (Convent) school. My brother accepted his advice, but we now suspect that Dr. Watkins-Pitchford may have done this in order to remove her from his way in getting into touch with her younger sister, who always hitherto accompanied her to school."[506]

When asked why he was the one who made the complaint, Talati said that his brother Pirojshaw (Gool's father) was so shocked that he was unable to do so himself. Talati also said he was the one who was first informed of the matter and Pirojshaw asked him to deal with it. Talati complained directly to the Chief Secretary, not through the Director of Medical and Sanitary Services, because he was in the Secretariat himself as Chief Clerk. He said that when he made the complaint he did not wish the matter divulged to anybody other than the Chief Secretary and the Resident: "I desired to keep the matter as secret as possible. I only asked for protection for the girl and that such action should be taken as to stop Dr. Pitchford's course of conduct."[507]

---

506   PRO CO 850/42/2 Enclosure 2 in the Acting British Resident's confidential dispatch of 12th April, 1934.

507   Ibid.

Jones called only one witness for the defendant, one William R. D. Crarey, Acting District Engineer in the Public Works Department. Crarey testified that he had been friends with Dr. Pitchford for some 7 years and was his confidant to a certain extent.[508] He stated that Dr. Pitchford had spoken to him some fifteen months earlier about Gool although he did not know the girl's name then.

> *"I knew who he was talking about as he pointed her out to me. I think he said he would get to know her. I think she was then dressed in the 'sari'. (Parsee women's dress, not worn by young children). At that time I thought she was about 18 to 20 years old. I formed this idea from her height and dress. Since I returned from leave in September 1933 Dr. Pitchford has made further references to the girl. He said she looked extraordinarily nice and was a perfect girl. He appeared to be enamoured of her. I did not consider the affair serious at all at the time. Later he told me that he was sending notes to this girl. I was perturbed at this and pointed out the danger of sending notes. He replied 'there is nothing serious in it' and that he contemplated no immoral purpose, but that it was merely a flirtation."[509]*

Crarey went on to testify that during the last six months he had noticed some change in Dr. Pitchford. He seemed to be abnormal about this girl. The sight of her seemed to have a very disturbing influence on him. According to Crarey, Dr. Pitchford was an ordinary sort of man who "was very susceptible to the charms of women."

In his exculpating statement Dr. Pitchford said he was acquainted with Gool long before she became his patient. Whenever they met they would nod to each other and say "Good afternoon" or "Good evening." According to Dr. Pitchford, she always responded and was very cheery and affable:

> *"I, being normally somewhat unduly susceptible, became increasingly anxious to cultivate the friendship of a girl who was acknowledged even by members of her own sex to be very pretty and freely bestowed smiles whever (sic) we saw each other. It is not usual for Parsee ladies to bestow smiles upon Europeans, and so I imagined I was very much favoured and, to some small extent, was foolishly proud of that fact."[510]*

Furthermore, Dr. Pitchford pointed out that his flirtation with Gool started months before November 1933 when she became his patient. He reiterated that throughout the period of her treatment he never took advantage of his professional position to further the flirtation:

> *"Nothing approaching the improper took place between us either in word or deed while she was under my treatment. A few weeks later, I found that a member of a family with whom my wife and I had been acquainted for some considerable time was attending the same school as Miss Talati and, taking advantage of this, I sent the latter a message and, subsequently some notes. By means of notes and messages, we attempted to arrange a meeting, but Miss Talati's daily routine did not allow of such meetings coming about. My desire*

508	PRO CO 850/42/2 Minutes of the proceedings of Committee of the Executive Council, dated 31ˢᵗ March, 1934.
509	Ibid.
510	PRO CO 850/42/2 Exhibit "E", "Statement of Dr. Henry Otley Watkins-Pitchford," Signed A. N. D. and dated 31ˢᵗ March, 1934.

to meet her alone was slowly taking the form of an obsession and I began to idealise the girl. About this time I became aware that she was said to be only fourteen years of age but as I never had any intention whatever of harming her in any way, I did not drop the affair. . .

"Eventually an assignation in a most unpropitious place (the beach) was made which failed, and another one was arranged and was kept. It is my letter to Miss Talati concerning this latter meeting which is attached to the charges against me. The meeting was hurried, and took place in a room which does not lend itself in any way to the enactment of anything more than what actually occurred, i.e., a hurried kiss and a whispered word. This meeting which lasted a maximum of ten minutes and was not behind closed doors was the only occasion on which Miss Talati and I have ever met alone. Nothing of any improper or indecent nature took place at that meeting nor were any suggestive words spoken."[511]

The remainder of Dr. Pitchford's exculpating statement singles out specific charges for refutation. Denying the charge of immoral intentions, he said: "I respected the girl, her age, family and community far too much to have attempted to seduce her. I therefore deny entirely and absolutely any charges of immoral intentions, any conduct in breach of good morals and decency and any impropriety of correspondence."[512] In his mind, Dr. Pitchford was only "stupidly fascinated" with Gool but did not have immoral designs toward her.

Being the only eye doctor at the time, Dr. Pitchford acknowledged in his exculpating statement that everyone in Zanzibar was his potential patient. He however denied the charge that he made Gool's acquaintance in his professional capacity:

"When I first started a mild flirtation with Miss Talati I did not know that she would one day come to me as a patient. Her coming to me as a patient was entirely incidental to the flirtation which was in no way enhanced or furthered by it. It was not until she had for some time temporarily ceased to attend as a patient that I chanced to find a means of communicating with her."[513]

Dr. Pitchford strongly denied the charge that his conduct was likely to bring into disrepute the public service of the Zanzibar Protectorate. He reiterated that his purposes and motives in flirting with Gool were not immoral as to be guilty of conduct likely to bring into disrepute the service of the Zanzibar Protectorate:

"In conclusion, the case may truly be summed up as a foolish, reckless, but not really harmful indiscretion on the part of one temporarily deprived of his normal powers of discrimination by an almost morbid and quite unreasonable obsession. The beginning was insidious and the increasing danger was not realized or admitted until the shock of discovery and all it might entail if my conduct was misunderstood, revealed to me the unfortunate position in which I had placed myself."[514]

---

511   Ibid.
512   Ibid.
513   Ibid.
514   Ibid.

On the one hand, the Executive Council Committee charged with investigating Dr. Pitchford's misconduct was convinced that throughout this intrigue Dr. Pitchford had no deliberate intention of seducing Miss Talati. The committee believed that the girl had not suffered any physical or moral damage from her communications or from being kissed by Dr. Pitchford: "It appears that the girl's ignorance of sexual matters remains as complete as it was before her meeting with Dr. Pitchford took place."[515] However, the committee found Dr. Pitchford guilty of conduct which was likely to bring into disrepute the public service:

"In our opinion this affair has been in the nature of a flirtation such as might take place between a schoolboy and a schoolgirl. The situation is, however, rendered serious by the fact that Dr. Pitchford, so far from being a schoolboy, is a married man of 33 years of age, a medical practitioner and a Government officer holding a responsible position. . .

"In some extenuation of Dr. Pitchford's conduct, the Committee desires to place on record its own knowledge that in some respects Dr. Pitchford deviates from the normal. While being efficient and capable in professional matters, he yet shows signs of not always being capable in private life of making a just judgment. He appears not to possess that sense of responsibility which is usual in normal adults. He is of a dreamy and artistic temperament, and is not in our opinion well fitted to discharge the full responsibilities of a medical officer in the service of the Government.

"We do not however consider that a medical examination of Dr. Pitchford in Zanzibar would serve any useful purpose. Such an examination would be in the main psychological and could only be conducted satisfactorily by a specialist in psychological medicine."[516]

On the other hand, the Attorney-General who chaired the committee could not regard the affair as a mere thoughtless and harmless flirtation. He considered it most probable that, "whatever Dr. Pitchford's intentions may have been, that seduction would have been the ultimate result had not, fortunately, the letter been found and the affair stopped in time."[517]

Finally, Zanzibar's Acting Chief Secretary weighed in on the matter and was of the opinion that the penalty of dismissal would not be justified in this case. His views are worth quoting at length because of the policy issues that they raise. He said:

"It is, I think, relevant to take note of the fact that when the matter came to the notice of the Government Dr. Pitchford was given the opportunity of tendering his resignation coupled with an admission of guilt, or alternatively of submitting to an Executive Council enquiry under the Colonial Office Regulations. He chose the latter alternative and has succeeded in exculpating himself from the more serious implications originally drawn from the

515   PRO CO 850/42/2 "Report," dated 4th April, 1934.

516   Ibid.

517   PRO CO 850/42/2 Acting British Resident, Zanzibar, to Secretary of State for the Colonies, Confidential Dispatch dated 12th April, 1934.

evidence then available. Dismissal would constitute a heavier punishment than that which would have been involved had Dr. Pitchford accepted the former alternative and its infliction now could not, in my opinion, be justified having regard to the result of the Executive Council Committee's enquiry. I consider that note should be taken of the fact that Dr. Pitchford's conduct was not criminal.

"While in my opinion the gravity of his misconduct was aggravated by his professional position in so far as his having been brought into professional contact with the girl imposed on him an added obligation to terminate the intrigue, I think it is also fair to take note of the fact that the penalty of dismissal might go beyond removal from the Colonial Service by leading to penalties of a professional character.

"I suggest that an assessment of the gravity of Dr. Pitchford's misbehavior must be made in relation to the general standard of conduct imposed on members of the public service, rather than in relation to the higher standard of conduct that might be expected of them. I consider that, measured by the general standard of conduct exacted from members of the public service in the past, Dr. Pitchford's conduct calls for severe punishment but that according to that standard dismissal would be an excessive punishment. While it might be in the interests of the service to make an example of Dr. Pitchford, I think that the main consideration must be to meet (sic) out a just punishment according to accepted standards of behaviour.

"I would also refer to the fact that while I have been in the Protectorate service two officers have been permitted to resign from the service under the charge of sodomy. If the punishment fitted the crime in these cases, dismissal in Dr. Pitchford's case would be clearly excessive."[518]

According to the Acting Chief Secretary, sodomy was a more serious offense than child molestation; in his view the later did not warrant resignation or dismissal from public service.

How the Colonial Office handled Dr. Pitchford's misconduct

On the 8th of April, 1934 Dr. Pitchford and his family left Zanzibar for Surrey, England, onboard the S.S. "Madura". Soon upon arrival in England Dr. Pitchford wrote to the Colonial Office to request an interview regarding his case; the interview was granted. Prior to the interview senior official in the Colonial Office expressed their views about the case. A. B. Acheson noted that he seemed to be a man of none too stable character. In Acheson's view it was a wise decision that Dr. Pitchford declined the alternative of instant resignation and instead chose to go through an enquiry. Acheson noted:

"Without subscribing to the view that the affair, had it not been discovered, would have ended with the seduction of the girl, I agree that serious notice

---

518   PRO CO 850/42/2 Note of the views expressed by the Acting Chief Secretary at the meeting of the Executive Council held in the Council Chamber, Beit-el-Ajaib, on Friday, the 6th of April, 1934.

must be taken of the matter, and I would accept the OAG's recommendation in principle. Dr W. P.'s conduct throughout the enquiry has been frank and straight forward; he must have felt his (ineligible) keenly, and his experience should have cured him of what may well have been nothing more than a temporary and rather ridiculous mental aberration.

"As regards transfer – an excellent opportunity for a fair exchange arises with Kenya, from which I understand Dr. Robertson, who has recently been the subject of a 'scandal' of a somewhat different character, is to be transferred to Zanzibar.

"Finally I hope that no question will arise of saying anything to the G.M.C. (General Medical Council). There is no suggestion that Dr W.P. took advantage or had any opportunity of taking advantage of his position as the girl's medical attendant in this matter."[519]

J. E. W. Hood observed that this was a curious case. "I remember a somewhat similar case many years ago in Cyprus where a Commissioner wrote letters to a school-girl (There was no doubt however in that case seduction had taken place) but got off with a reprimand. However fifty years ago different views were taken."[520] He agreed with the recommendation to transfer Dr. Pitchford to Kenya. He further noted: "I would not, however, go quite as far as to make him lose seniority or remain on 840 pounds for three years. It is never satisfactory to take away seniority. I think the S. of S.'s displeasure will be sufficiently marked if Dr. Pitchford is transferred to Kenya and has his salary reduced to 840 pounds, increments to run from the date of his leaving for Kenya, and no question of probation need be raised. We shall have to explain to Kenya."[521]

The interview was conducted by Mr. Hood, Dr. O'Brien and Mr. Acheson. During the interview Dr. Pitchford made three points:

(a) He alleged that the view of the Executive Council had been prejudiced by the line taken by the O.A.G. against him. The O.A.G. had practically told him before he elected to submit to disciplinary proceedings that, if he did not resign, he would probably be reported to the General Medical Council and his name struck off the Register. The O.A.G.'s attitude was well-known and Dr. Pitchford alleged that the members of the Executive Committee were influenced thereby.

He was advised not to pursue this line. An allegation of that kind is easy to make, it cannot be proved and there is no reason to suppose that members of the Executive Committee would not in a case of this kind exercise their own judgments. Dr. Pitchford was told that he had a fair and impartial enquiry and that he had no ground for thinking that his case had not been fairly dealt with locally.

(b) He urged that he should be permitted to return to Zanzibar, mainly because he was anxious to continue his eye work in which he had specialized and

519   PRO CO 850/42/2 Acheson's minute dated 21/4/1934.

520   PRO CO 850/42/2 Flood's minute dated 28/4/1934.

521   Ibid.

built up a very considerable and useful practice (not private practice); the closing down of this work would be contrary to the interests of the local people and he doubted whether he would have any similar opportunity for making use of his special qualifications in Kenya.

He was informed that he could make representations on this point if he liked, but that, in view of the circumstances of the case and particularly of the local scandal to which it gave rise, it was thought that very little hope could be held out of acceding to his request.

(c) He represented that the penalty was out of proportion to the seriousness of the offence. Admitting that he had been extremely foolish and lacking in discretion, he suggested that his misconduct ended there and that for such indiscretion a loss of salary of 260 pounds a year was excessive.

He was informed that he might make representations on this point also if he wished, but it was pointed out that the penalty recommended by the O.A.G. of which he was aware had already been mitigated in two respects, and he was not led to expect that he could be granted any concession at this stage. Dr. Pitchford indicated that he would probably write in on the second and third points but that, in view of what was said to him, he would drop the first.[522]

Although Dr. Pitchford made further representations to the Secretary of State for Colonies his plea to be allowed to return to Zanzibar was denied. The Colonial Office offered him the alternatives of resigning with a reduced gratuity or being transferred to Kenya with a reduced salary of 840 pounds a year rising by annual increments of 40 pounds to 1,000 pounds, without loss of seniority. There is no further correspondence on file but there is reason to believe he took the latter alternative.

Curious facts about this case include the following: (a) the complete absence of remorse on the part of Dr. Pitchford, (b) the inability of officials in Zanzibar and London to view the case as involving child abuse and endangering the welfare of a minor, (c) the reluctance of the Colonial Office to report the case to the United Kingdom General Medical Council, (d) the Executive Council Committee's inability to question the involvement of Eva Deacon, a mixed-race minor, as the go-between who allegedly wrote the replies to Dr. Pitchford's letters, and, (e) the sudden departure of Gool Talati's family from Zanzibar and never to return.

Dr. Pitchford did not see himself as personally responsible for initiating an erotic relationship with an underage school girl. How truthful were his descriptions of their relationship? Is it possible that he really did not know how old Miss Talati was? Why did he have to guess her age from how she looked or dressed? He could have asked his go-between, Eva, what grade Miss Talati was in from which he would have been able to surmise her age. Regardless, Dr. Pitchford justified himself by feigning ignorance of Miss Talati's age even after he was told her real age.

Dr. Pitchford's lack of moral remorse about his infatuation with an underage girl is puzzling. In a petition that he wrote to the Secretary of State for Colonies to request a reduction of his monetary punishment he notes:

---

522   PRO CO 850/42/2 Minutes of interview, signed by A. B. Acheson, dated 28/5/1934.

"Although I am admittedly guilty of having acted very foolishly and indiscreetly, yet the Executive Council did not find me guilty of the major part of the serious charges with which I was confronted. My wife and I have already suffered very great mental stress and considerable financial embarrassment on account of the circumstances attendant on the ordeal of standing my trial, and leaving Zanzibar unprepared for leave and at very short notice. I have apologized officially both to His Excellency the Acting British Resident, and to the Zanzibar Government, and am in fact very sorry for my foolishness and anxious to atone for it."

As far as he was concerned, harboring erotic fantasies about an underage girl was mere "foolishness." However, the fact that he did not see anything wrong with fantasying and erotically obsessing about a child becomes less puzzling when viewed in the context of Victorian culture and what being "a child" meant. According to James Kincaid, the question "What is a child?" is at the heart of the world the Victorians made. Throughout the nineteenth century, there developed an image of the child as a symbol of purity, innocence and asexuality. Yet at the same time, the child could be a figure of fantasy, obsession, and suppressed desires. This image of the child, as both pure and strangely erotic, is part of the mythology of Victorian culture.

Likewise, the inability of officials in Zanzibar and at the Colonial Office in London to consider the relationship as a case of child abuse and endangering the welfare of a minor has to do with Victorian culture. The Victorian conspiracy of silence about sex in general blocked any serious consideration of child sexual abuse in this case and possibly many others. It is of significance that Victorians used a wide range of euphemisms for child sexual abuse, such as "moral corruption", "ruining", "tampering", and "molestation". Acheson at the Colonial Office referred to Dr. Pitchford's behavior by none of these terms but rather as a "ridiculous mental aberration" and did not think it warranted serious punishment such as resignation or demotion with loss of seniority. In this regard, it is also important to note that although cases of child sexual abuses increased significantly between 1830 and 1914, only a small proportion of reported cases resulted in conviction.[523] Thus the leniency of the Colonial Office officials in the case of Dr. Pitchford was matched by the leniency of British magistrates and judges.

Although Miss Talati testified via a questionnaire submitted to her in comfort of her home, it never occurred to the Executive Committee Council to inquire from Miss Eva Deacon, the go-between, who facilitated the correspondence between Dr. Pitchford and Miss Talati. She is mentioned in the inquiry as being of mixed race but we do not know her age, school grade or if she was in the same class with Miss Talati. According to Dr. Pitchford, Eva was a member of a family with whom he and his wife had been acquainted for some considerable time. He found out, by what means we do not know, that Eva was going to the same school as Miss Talati and, "taking advantage of this, I sent the latter a message and, subsequently some notes."[524] Eva was privy to these messages and knew everything that was going on. What impact the affair may have had on her morals was apparently of no consequence to the Committee.

---

523   Jackson, Louise A. *Child Sexual Abuse in Victorian England* (London and New York: Routledge, 2000): 3.

524   PRO CO 850/42/2 Exhibit "E", Statement of Dr. Henry Otley Watkins-Pitchford, dated 31/3/34.

Finally, it is perplexing that following the conclusion of the enquiry Gool's family left Zanzibar and never returned. According to Asad Talati, the son of Shavakshaw, his uncle's family left Zanzibar because of his failing eyesight. Also, Asad informed the author that Gool Talati made at least one visit to Zanzibar after the family left. In 1947, Gool got married in Bombay to Adi Dubash.[525] Be that as it may, circumstances related to the case suggest the family may have left for other reasons. The Parsee community in Zanzibar at the time was very small. There is reason to believe what happened became public knowledge and the family left to avoid scandal and to save face. It also appears that the incident was afterwards never spoken about in family circles. Asad, who was twelve when he attended his cousin's wedding in 1947, did not know anything about this incident.[526]

Was Dr. Pitchford's obsessive infatuation a medical condition?

We noted above that the Executive Council Committee that inquired into Dr. Pitchford's misconduct thought that his flirtation with Miss Talati was of the nature "as might take place between a schoolboy and a schoolgirl"; that Dr. Pitchford did not appear "to possess that sense of responsibility which is usual in normal adults"; and that he was "of a dreamy and artistic temperament." The Committee would have recommended psychological evaluation but did not because Zanzibar did not have a resident psychiatrist at the time.

Moreover, sometime during the fifteen months when Dr. Pitchford was obsessively infatuated with Miss Talati he wrote to his father about what was going on. His father wrote back and offered some interesting observations. He could not help him, as he put it, "out of a phase of your life which is so uneasy, so unprofitable and so disabling."[527] Although his father did not consider his obsessive infatuation with Miss Talati to be "abnormal", he felt it to be "a dangerous borderline state between the normal healthy mind and the mind which has allowed an obsession to become established." He further noted: "I have been through those phases of idolatry and woman worship and have survived to view my past state as one does the remembrance of a delirium with its distortions and convictions, all so unacceptable to the normal mentality. Of course, it passes but the danger is that it may work a mischief before it dies or becomes exorcised. And your phase of the malady is crammed with pitfalls."[528] Lastly, Dr. Pitchford's father suggested that he was in want of a long change – "both of climate and of mental environment. Your letter suggests a touch of *tropic neurasthenia* and I shall be glad when your time for leave rolls around."[529] (Emphasis added).

Before we consider whether or not Dr. Pitchford was a neurasthenic, let us first consider the nature of the flirtation itself. Here was a 33 three-year old married man who sexually idealized a young girl and behaved like he was in love for the first time. As Richard von Krafft-Ebing says,

---

525   Telephone conversation, July 19, 2009.

526   Telephone conversation, July 27, 2009.

527   PRO CO 850/42/2 Exhibit "J" signed A.N.D. and dated 3/4/34.

528   .Ibid.

529   Ibid.

*First love forever trends in a romantic idealizing direction. It wraps the
beloved object in the halo of perfection. In its incipient stages it is of a platonic
character. . . With the approach of puberty it runs the risk of transferring the
idealizing powers upon persons of the opposite sex, even though mentally,
physically and socially they be of an inferior station. To this may easily be
traced many cases of misalliance, abduction, elopement and errors of early
youth, and those sad tragedies of passionate love that are in conflict with the
principles of morality or social standing, and often terminate in murder, self-
destruction and double suicide.[530]*

What would have been the end result of this dalliance is a question that will
forever remain unanswered. However, according to von Krafft-Ebing, "Purely
sensual love is never true and lasting, for which reason first love is, as a rule, but a
passing infatuation, a fleeting passion."[531] Maybe the flirtation was harmless, as Dr.
Pitchford seems to have believed, and would have eventually come to pass. Still,
what does this make of Dr. Pitchford? Was he a neurasthenic as his father thought?

During the nineteenth century varied factors were invoked as causes of tropical
neurasthenia. Robert Mayne was the first to define the term neurasthenia in his
Lexicon of Terms in Medical and General Science.[532] He attributed the condition to
debility of nerves. Later, the conception of neurasthenia gave way to a psychological
etiology and classification. George Miller Beard, the American neurologist and
electrotherapist, popularized the term as an explanation of, and reaction to a
malaise of modernity. For Beard, neurasthenia was the result of stress brought
about by the fast pace of urban life. In 1894, Sigmund Freud separated what he
described as anxiety hysteria from anxiety neurosis. In the medical community of
the 1930s, Dr. Pitchford's obsessive infatuation with Miss Talati could have been
categorized as one of many examples of "obsessional states."[533] At the time, Dr.
Millais Culpin was of the opinion that anxiety and "obsessional states" rested on a
psychological basis, and were, with hysteria, grouped as psychoneuroses or minor
psychoses. Dr. Millais Culpin did not subscribe to the association of neurasthenia
with tropical conditions or physiological causes. Instead, he suggested that
European maladjustment in the tropics was caused by sociological factors.

However, as a part of colonial topographical nomenclature the belief in
"tropical neurasthenia" persisted. As one of those disabilities of Europeans in the
tropics, it appears to have affected some and not every European who ventured
there. It is pertinent to ask who were most susceptible, especially in matters
involving sex, and why. The sex question was one unspoken issue that always was
at the back of the minds of imperial proconsuls in London. They were not sure
how unmarried Englishmen would behave sexually under conditions of colonial
isolation and separation from their countrymen. They feared these men would
find themselves possessed of an almost unbearable nervous tension which would
find relief through sexual liaisons with native women.

---

530   Krafft-Ebing, Richard von, "From Psychopathia Sexualis: A Medico- Forensic Study," In Barreca, Regina
      (ed.), *Desire and Imagination: classic essays in sexuality (Harmondsworth, England: Meridian, 1995): 131.*

531   Ibid. 131.

532   Mayne, Robert Gray, *An Expository Lexicon of the Terms, Ancient and Modern, in Medical and General
      Science (London: John Churchill, 1860).*

533   Culpin, Millais, M.D, F.R.C.S., "An Examination of Tropical Neurasthenia," *Proceedings of the Royal
      Society of Medicine (February 2, 1933): 47-58: 47.*

It is of interest to note that although his father intimated that his infatuation with Miss Talati was a case of "tropical neurasthenia", Dr. Pitchford does not seem to have believed he was afflicted with neurasthenia. There is no indication that he sought treatment for it. Had he sought treatment it is likely that S. M. Vassallo, a medical doctor at Zanzibar Hospital, would have put him on a regimen of iodine before considering invaliding him. In an article he published in May 1934, Dr. Vassallo suggested that neurasthenia was possibly triggered off by thyroid hyperactivity and prescribed iodine to rest the thyroid gland. He noted that nearly all his neurasthenic patients responded satisfactorily to this treatment.[534] Besides the endeavor by doctors like Vassallo to diagnose and treat tropical neurasthenia as a medical condition, "tropical neurasthenia offered a respectable label for symptoms for the listless or deviant behaviors of middle and upper class white men."[535] Apparently Dr. Pitchford was a man of weak moral and mental character and of little will power; he was, as the Committee of Inquiry surmised, not fitted to discharge the responsibilities of a government medical officer.

If the lenient treatment of Dr. Pitchford did not fit his misconduct the handling of the case of Engineer Frank Ingham five years later for cruelty to a horse was likewise questionable. Ingham was a thirty-six year old employee of the Posts and Telegraphs Department in Nairobi. Sometime in May 1939 he was sent to Entebbe Airport in Uganda to repair the airport's aeradio transmitter. On the night of 20-21st May, 1939, between the hours of 1:30 to 2:00AM at the Veterinary Research Center, Old Entebbe, in the Township of Entebbe, Mengo District, Ingham was caught by one Joshwa Ndeshwa, a syce, beating a tethered thorough bred horse with a stock whip.[536] A scuffle ensued whereby Ingham beat Joshwa with fists to prevent the later from apprehending him. Ingham escaped but was later arrested. He was released on bail and told to appear in the District Magistrate's Court, Entebbe, on May 25, 1939. In court Ingham pleaded that he was suffering from malaria at the time of the incident, and that he had been drinking and got the idea he would like to ride. He was convicted on Plea Contra Section 3 (a) Prevention of Cruelty to Animals Ordinance and for assaulting Joshwa.[537] He was fined 100 Shillings or one month jail with hard labor. He chose to pay the fine.

Subsequently, M. Nurock wrote to the Postmaster General, Nairobi, on behalf of the Chief Secretary, Uganda, to inform him about what he called "a deplorable incident" involving Ingham. Nurock noted that Ingham was fortunate to have escaped a term of imprisonment; and that it was essential (as in fact was arranged) that he should at once cease to be employed in Uganda. He intimated that it remained for the Postmaster General to consider what disciplinary action should be advised to His Excellency the Governor of Kenya, in accordance with the terms of his Agreement; and to report the matter to the Secretary of State. Nurock further noted that in view of the nature of Ingham's behavior and the apparent

534   Vassallo, S. M. "Tropical Neurasthenia: Its possible relationship to hyperthyroidism," *Transactions of the Royal Society of Tropical Medicine and Hygiene, vol.* XXVII, no. 6 (May, 1934): 625-627: 625.

535   Crozier, Anna, "What is tropical about Tropical Neurasthenia? The utility of the diagnosis in the management of British East Africa," *Journal of the history of medicine and allied sciences,* Vol. 64, Issue 4 (2009): 518-548: 533.

536   PRO CO 850/147/7 Uganda Police Charge Sheet dated 22 May, 1939.

537   Medical examination showed that Joshwa suffered bruises to the neck and a sore larynx as a result of being choked by Ingham as he fought him to escape.

absence of adequate motive for it, there were perhaps grounds for inquiring into the question of pathological causes, or mental lapses.[538]

On the advice of the Post Master General the Deputy Governor of Kenya dismissed Ingham from Government service effective June 20th. Under the terms of his contract the Secretary of State's approval was not required and no action would have been taken except to acknowledge the dismissal. However, Ingham petitioned the Post Master General and subsequently the Colonial Office to protest against his dismissal. His petition was concerned mainly with the undue severity of the Government's action in terminating his appointment and endeavor to show that due to his past record he deserved some leniency. Ingham also pleaded that although his offence (beating a defenseless horse) was not in question his behavior was the result of a temporary lapse of sanity due to overwork and a bout of malaria.

Ingham's case presents several extraordinary features. Ingham was found guilty and did not object to his conviction on charges of assault and cruelty to animals. His only complaint was that he had been dismissed on these grounds and produced various reasons in his petition to the Post Master General and the Secretary of State why his punishment did not fit the crime. Furthermore, although the Government of Kenya might have made fuller inquiries as to the explanation of Ingham's incomprehensible behavior, on the lines suggested by the Government of Uganda, they chose not to. Finally, was Joshwa entitled to arrest, without warrant, someone whom he found committing the offence of cruelty to animals, and if he was not entitled to do so was Ingham within his rights in using reasonable force to avoid detention?

Several officials in the Colonial Office were of the opinion that there were no grounds for intervening. However, C. J. Jeffries believed that the Government of Kenya could have been better advised to terminate Ingham's contract instead of dismissing him.[539] When Ingham arrived in London he called the Colonial Office and asked to see Sir George Tomlinson, at whose request K. W. Blackburn gave Ingham an interview. During the interview Ingham supplemented his petition by noting that he had lived in an outstation for most of his time and was not known to his superiors; the wireless staff in East Africa had given a great deal of trouble to the authorities and he had been chosen as a scapegoat to be an example to the others; Mr. Willoughby, the Engineer-in-Chief, was a non-drinker whereas he liked a drink; he did not blame the Governor but the people who reported him to the Governor; he was not drunk on the night when the offence occurred rather he was ill – and had frequently been ill although he had continued to do his work and so there were no reports on his medical history sheet; that the punishment, which wrecked his future, was unduly harsh particularly in view of the sentences inflicted on him by the Magistrate – sentences which he admitted were deserved; that he had sent his resignation before the offence which had been accepted and, therefore, his only request was for a reinstatement in order that he could find a job in England.[540]

---

538   PRO CO 850/147/7 M. Nurock to the Postmaster General, Nairobi, dated 30 May, 1939.

539   PRO CO 850/147/7 C. J. Jeffries minute dated 10 August, 1939.

540   PRO CO 850/147/7 K. W. Blackburn minute dated 18 August, 1939.

In J. F. Pedler's view, Ingham's representations to Blackburn made odd reading. According to Pedler, if Ingham was not drunk on the night when the offence occurred then he was suffering from sadistic madness.[541] Pedler cautioned his colleagues to be wary of assisting Ingham to re-enter Government employment in England. However, Sir George Tomlinson, who admitted feeling very uneasy about this case, doubted whether the penalty was justified by the facts and expressed his concern that it would ruin Ingham's prospects of getting a job in England. His opinion is worth quoting at length:

> Consider the nature of his offence. The beating of the horse in the dead of the night was a most curious and unusual occurrence. I imagine that in most cases of cruelty to animals it is the owner of the animal who inflicts the ill-treatment, either as a result of losing his temper or of willful neglect. But for a man to go at night to his neighbour's stable and flog the horse tied up there, is so strange as to suggest some mental instability . . .

> I do not think that much importance need be attached to the assault on the African syce. A fight of the kind that occurred was an almost inevitable sequence to the entry into the stable and the beating of the horse. These two offences were punished by the Magistrate by fines [of 5 pound sterling each]. If these punishments in any way fitted the crime, they hardly point to the further and infinitely more serious penalty of dismissal. . . .

> On looking at the thing as a whole, I cannot believe that Mr. Ingham's offence merited the extreme penalty of dismissal which, as I have said, must spell complete ruin for his future career. I think, therefore, that the dismissal ought to be rescinded.[542]

Several colleagues of Sir George, including Dawe, Blackburn, Roberts-Wray and Jeffries, concurred with his conclusion that dismissal was excessive and that some less Draconian technique should be adopted for securing Ingham's departure from the Kenya government service. Consequently the Secretary of State, Malcolm MacDonald, after "full consideration of this case" came to the conclusion that a more appropriate method of dispensing with Ingham's services would be by the termination of his appointment, with the payment of one month's salary. The termination of his appointment would be regarded as having taken effect from 20 June, the original date of dismissal.[543]

---

541   PRO CO 850/147/7 F. J. Pedler minute dated 18 August, 1939.

542   PRO CO 850/147/7 Sir G. Tomlinson minute dated 19 August, 1939.

543   PRO CO 850/147/7 Draft of Secretary of State's telegram to Kenya Government, dated 1 November, 1939.

9

Seyyida Salme's love affair with Heinrich Ruete

Introduction

Sometime in 1877 Emily Ruete, whose maiden name was Seyyida Salme (1844-1924), decided to write down some sketches of her life for her German-born children who until that time knew little more than that she was an Arab woman and a native of Zanzibar. Her memoirs, therefore, were originally not intended for the general public. However, at the urgent request of many, she finally decided to have them published. The memoirs, first published in German in 1886 were titled Memoiren einer Arabischen Prinzessin. The first English translation titled Memoirs of an Arabian Princess from Zanzibar (hereafter Memoirs) was published in London in 1888. The same year another English edition was published in New York by D. Appleton. Since then there have been two other English editions published by Markus Wiener (1989) and E. J. Brill (1993).

Because of the foreign languages in which they were published, the *Memoirs* were certainly not intended for a Swahili or Arab-speaking audience. It is not clear how Emily Ruete's *Memoirs* were received in Britain and the United States of America. However, some readers in Germany doubted whether Emily Ruete actually wrote the memoirs herself or had used a ghostwriter. One of these readers was Vice-Admiral Karl August Deinhardt (1842-1892) who opined that the *Memoirs* unfocused, and suggested that "the heart makes the author say more than what arrests the reader's attention."

Despite her detractors recent reviews of Emily Ruete's *Memoirs* (hereafter she is referred to by her maiden name Salme), edited and introduced by Emeri J. van Donzel, are favorable. One reviewer, Billie Melman, notes that van Donzel's "enlarged edition is useful to social historians of the Middle East, historians of colonialism and, because it is conveniently excerptable, suitable reading for students, particularly in that still thinly covered area of Middle Eastern women's history, where primary, inside sources by women are so scarce."[544] Melman further notes that the *Memoirs* are "a document about cultural difference, about cross-cultural representation, and comparison between cultures" which ought to be of great value to historians.[545]

Salme was the daughter of Seyyid Said bin Sultan Busaid, ruler of Oman and Zanzibar. Her father was born in 1791 and died in 1856. In various reports by Europeans who had the privilege of meeting Seyyid Said in person, he is described as a benevolent and venerable patriarch, a devoted ruler and parent, a sultan who lived an unpretentious lifestyle.[546] The later characteristic may be explained by the fact that he belonged to the Ibadhi *madhhab* (denomination) of Islam which discourages the display of royal pomp and magnificence especially in dress, residential houses, and even mosques.

Seyyid Said came to power in Oman after assassinating his cousin, Badr bin Seif Busaid, in 1806. Unlike previous rulers of Oman, Seyyid Said developed a keen interest on the African part of the "empire." His predecessors had first seized Zanzibar from the Portuguese in 1699, and the first Omani governor was installed there in Zanzibar 1700.[547] This was the beginning of a long and extended Omani colonialism that did not come to an end until 1964.

Seyyid Said first visited Zanzibar in 1828. It was probably on this visit that, as Coupland suggests, he realized that Zanzibar had the potential of raising his political prestige as well as improving his commercial and financial position.[548] Seyyid Said made a second visit to Zanzibar in 1830. According to Coupland, it was probably during this visit that he begun to build himself a sea-side palace a few miles from Zanzibar town,[549] which would come to be known as Beit el-Mtoni. At the time when he was establishing himself at Zanzibar his authority was being contested on the mainland especially by the Mazrui Arabs at Mombasa. Eventually he was able to defeat them. After prevailing over the Mazrui dynasty Seyyid Said felt that a permanent residence at Zanzibar would help to consolidate his political influence in East Africa.

Thus in 1840 Seyyid Said moved his family and court to Zanzibar, leaving his son Thuwein to administer Oman. Because very little is known about Seyyid Said's private life we do not know the size of his family at the time when he moved to Zanzibar. What we know is that he had at the time one legal wife, Azze, with whom he had no children. All his children, thirty six in number, were by his concubines.

---

544   Melman, (1994): 526

545   Ibid.

546   Said-Ruete, Rudolf, Said bin Sultan: Ruler of Oman and Zanzibar (London: Alexander-Ouseley Ltd., 1929): See Appendix A.

547   Kusimba, Chapurukha M. The Rise and Fall of Swahili States (Walnut, CA.: Altamira Press, 1999): 171.

548   Coupland, Roland, East Africa and Its Invaders: From the earliest times to the death of Seyyid Said in 1856 (New York: Russell & Russell, Inc., 1965): 152.

549   It is also likely that he appropriated it from one of the wealthiest traders in town.

After relocating to Zanzibar, Seyyid Said endeavored to cultivate commercial relations with India, Europe and the United States of America. Soon a number of foreign trading firms were established at Zanzibar and a number of consuls were appointed to represent Western businesses at the Zanzibar Court. Among the European trading firms were a number of German trading houses. One of these firms was Hansing and Company whose agent, Heinrich Ruete, would become Salme's lover and future husband.

Trade between Zanzibar and the rest of the world brought Seyyid Said enormous wealth in the form of custom duty. Foreign merchants paid five per cent of the value of any merchandise imported into Zanzibar. Moreover, Seyyid Said had his own private fleet of merchant ships which plied the ocean routes between Zanzibar and India, Europe, and the United States of America. By the standards of the day Seyyid Said was a very wealthy man. Even though he is described as living an unpretentious lifestyle, his wealth was mostly spent in conspicuous consumption. Being a Muslim he was permitted to marry up to four wives as well as to keep as many concubines as he could afford. As we will see, his wealth enabled him to exercise this privilege. He married three times even though two of those marriages ended in divorce. He also possessed a lot of concubines. The result was that he raised many children on whom he spent a considerable fortune.

Salme was born at the Beit el Mtoni palace in Zanzibar on August 30, 1844. Her mother, named Jilfidan, was a Circassian and one of more than seventy concubines of Seyyid Said. Seyyid Said bought Jilfidan when she was still a small girl. Salme thinks when her mother was bought she was "probably at the tender age of seven or eight, as she cast her first tooth in our house."[550] We do not know if Seyyid Said bought Jilfidan in Muscat. However, it very likely that after she was abducted from her village in the Caucasus she like many other Circassian girls was taken to Istanbul; from there she could have been bought by Egyptian slave dealers who conducted long-distance business with India, the Hejaz, and East African ports.[551] As a virgin her market value was automatically higher than that of older and non-virgins.

It is interesting to note that Salme does not express any feelings about her mother being bought, raised and turned into a concubine by Seyyid Said. Instead, she speaks approvingly about the fact that her mother had succeeded to endear herself to her father. She writes: "She was in great favour with my father, who never refused her anything, though she interceded mostly for others, and, when she came to see him, he always rose to meet her half-way – a distinction he conferred but very rarely."[552] Salme also mentions that her mother had many friends at Beit el Mtoni, "a circumstance rarely to be met with in an Arab harem."[553]

Salme's childhood years appear to have been happy ones. Unfortunately her childhood happiness was cut short by the deaths of both her parents. She was twelve years old when she lost her father in 1856, and she was fifteen when her mother died of cholera in 1859. Despite the common Arab practice of arranged

---

550 Ruete, Salme, Memoirs of an Arabian princess from Zanzibar (New York: Markus Wiener Publishing: 1989): 6.

551 Toledano, Ehud R. "Shemsigul: A Circassian Slave in Mid-Nineteenth-Century Cairo," in Edmund Burke, III, Ed. (Berkeley and Los Angeles: University of California Press, 1993): 66.

552 Ibid. 7.

553 . Ibid. 7.

cousin marriages, Salme appears not to have attracted the attention of any cousin before her father died. The lack of suitors at age twelve may not have caused Salme any concern. She, in fact, notes that her father was not in favor of betrothal at such an early age.

However, after she turned twenty one Salme may have become worried that she would not get married even though she does not say so in the *Memoirs*. Was it desperation that drove her into Heinrich's arms? Did she fully understand the consequences of fornication or such a relationship between an Arab Muslim woman and a European Christian man? This chapter attempts in part to piece together the facts as are available in order to explain the implications of Salme's love affair with Heinrich.

Before Salme met Heinrich she had to leave town following the debacle of the failed coup by Barghash to seize power from his brother Majid. Salme fled Zanzibar because she had supported Barghash. She first lived on her plantation at Kizimbani before renting a house at Bububu on the seashore. When this residence was desired by Dr. George Edwin Seward, surgeon and British Acting Consul (July 1865 to June 1867), Salme gave it up at the request of her brother Majid. Salme prepared to return to Kizimbani but her half-brothers Jamshid, Hamdan and Abd el Wehab prevailed over her to return and live in Zanzibar town.

The house that Salme returned to in Zanzibar happened to be adjacent to the house that Heinrich lived in. According to Salme, the three brothers mentioned above chose this residence for her. Seyyid Majid, who was then the Sultan, had nothing to do with the decision.[554] It is very likely that had Salme moved to the Beit el Tani contact with Heinrich may have been very difficult. Salme describes conditions at Beit el Tani as overcrowded. Moreover, the residence was connected to another palace, Beit el Sahel, by a suspension bridge such that there was constant movement between the two residences. Therefore, Salme's goings and comings would have been easily noticed or suspected.

By and large, it is reasonable to assume that after they became acquainted it was Salme who visited Heinrich because she was under minimal restriction in her new residence. In regard to her visitations, Salme could only have visited Heinrich at night because elite Arab women in her time rarely walked abroad during the day.[555] Moreover, night time was very conducive for such clandestine liaisons because at the time the streets of Zanzibar were not lighted. Besides, the proximity of the two residences likely enabled Salme to easily sneak into Heinrich's residence without having to travel a great distance and risking discovery.

Heinrich Ruete was born in Hamburg on March 10, 1839. In 1855, at the age of sixteen, he was sent by Hansing and Company as their representative in Zanzibar. For a while the young Rudolph appears to have led what Dr. Seward characterized as "a very blameless life".[556] According to Richard Burton when he arrived in Zanzibar toward the end of 1856 he found the tiny Caucasian community stationed there living a miserable life. The Europeans were forever quarreling among themselves: "All is wearisome monotony: there is no society,

554 Ruete, Memoirs, 258.

555 Ibid. 168.

556 Van Donzel, E. An Arabian princess between Two Worlds: Memoirs, letters home, sequels to memoirs, Syrian customs and usages by Seyyida Salme/Emily Ruete (Leiden: E. J. Brill, 1993): 12.

no pleasure, no excitement . . ."[557] Apparently European social life was curtailed by the limited number of single Caucasian women in Zanzibar. As Burton notes, the dearth of white females caused the European residents to be contented with Abyssinian or Somali girls.[558] Burton does not say whether these girls were taken as concubines or not.

Salme's love affair with Heinrich probably started sometime after July 1865 when she returned to Zanzibar town from Bububu. As already noted above, had Salme moved to Bet el Tani the chances of her meeting Heinrich would have been minimal if not impossible because of the seclusion she would have been subjected to. Yet, as Salme herself points out, even with such seclusion a meeting with men could not always be prevented.[559] So it appears that somehow Salme and Heinrich met and began their clandestine sexual liaison which eventually resulted in a pregnancy.

Their sexual liaison was not only illicit because it involved premarital sex but also because the two lovers belonged to different religions. In her *Memoirs* Salme is not forthcoming about the affair and whether or not she realized she was engaging in something not permissible by Islam. Instead, Salme devotes a very short chapter, amounting to only four pages, to dispel what she calls a good many untrue reports about her affair with Heinrich. She writes: "During the reign of my brother Madjid the Europeans enjoyed a very (sic) respected position; they were often and gladly received as guests at his house and on his estates, and were always treated with marked attention on such occasions. My step-sister Khole and myself were on most friendly terms with all foreigners in Zanzibar, <u>which led to various courtesies, such as the custom of the country admitted</u>."[560] (Emphasis added).

However, it is hard to believe that Seyyid Majid permitted his sisters to socialize with strange European men. The only European visitors they would have met would have been ladies who were not allowed into the inner chambers of the royal palaces. Suggestions that Salme used some of these visitors to deliver messages to Heinrich are at best preposterous. Be that as it may, Salme's relationship with Heinrich from which in time sprang love was soon the subject of rumor in Zanzibar town."[561] Soon there were rumors that she was pregnant. Although we have no information about whether Salme or Heinrich attempted to avoid pregnancy, we do know that methods of contraception were known and practiced at the time; one of these was coitus interruptus.

Rumor that Salme was pregnant caused Seyyid Majid, her legal guardian, to send his sister Khaduj to investigate the matter. We do not know what exactly the investigation involved. We have no information whether Seyyid Majid asked Khaduj to employ a midwife to perform a virginity or pregnancy test.[562] Be that as it may, Khaduj conspired with Salme and withheld the truth from Majid. Still, the suspicious Majid invited Salme to go on a pilgrimage to Mecca onboard a boat that belonged to his chief eunuch. Salme declined the offer knowing very well that

---

557   Quoted by Moorehead, Alan, The White Nile (New York: Harper & Brothers Publishers, 1960): 16.

558   Ibid. 16.

559   Ruete, Memoirs, 159.

560   Ibid. 263.

561   Ibid. 264.

562   In Zanzibar and elsewhere in the Middle East midwives performed a major gynecological and social role during pregnancy, birth, and early maternity.

"girls in a similar condition as her had been sent on similar voyages, but none of them had ever reached their destination."[563]

Had Salme accepted Majid's offer to go on a pilgrimage to Mecca she would have been killed and her death would have been Zanzibar's first royal "honor killing." To understand Majid's intention requires a closer scrutiny of Arab culture and mores. The family constitutes the fundamental social unit in Arabian society. Among the Arabs family status is largely dependent upon its honor, "much of which is determined by the respectability of its daughters, who can damage it irreparably by the perceived misuse of their sexuality."[564] Therefore, an Arab woman's virginity at marriage is highly valued because it is proof of her modesty and her 'ard (honor). It is the ultimate shame to the bride and her family if she is not found a virgin on her wedding night.

Thus "honor killing" is deeply rooted in the history of Arab society. In this regard, the practice predates Islam. It is argued that the practice stemmed from Arab patriarchal and patrilocal interest in maintaining strict control over designated familial power and gender structures. As Ruggi notes: "What the men of the family, clan, or tribe seek control of in a patrilineal society is reproductive power. Women for the tribe were considered a factory for making men. Thus honor killing is not a means to control sexual power or behavior. What's behind it is the issue of fertility, or reproductive power."[565]

Although the family (by means of the father or older brother) is directly responsible for defending its honor, the community through public opinion (including rumor mongering) can put pressure on the family to act. This seems to have been the case with Salme's affair. Rumor about what was going on including the possibility of Salme being pregnant caused Majid to want to verify the truth of the matter. Such a rumor not only scandalized the royal household but also threatened to undermine its prestige in the eyes of the Arab public. Therefore, the conspiracy to hide Salme's condition from Majid is evidence that Salme would indeed have been the victim of an "honor killing" had Majid ascertained the truth.

Today most "honor killings" occur in Muslim societies where much of a family's honor is still determined by the respectability of its women. In such societies men continue to fear that a family's honor can be irreparably damaged by its women's actual or suspected premarital and/or extramarital sexual intercourse. However, the commission of these killings in the name of Islam has been vehemently criticized. Most critics point out that in an Islamic context, punishment for sexual intercourse out of wedlock is supposed to be either indoor banishment or scourging if the woman is single, or if married, death by stoning. In either case, there must be four adult male witnesses willing to testify that the sexual act took place.

Given the dire consequences of her fornication why did Salme not consider abortion? The question brings us to the medical, social and legal issue of abortion in mid-nineteenth-century Zanzibari society. On the one hand, we can deduce why she did not consider abortion from what she says about medical services in Zanzibar at the time. She writes: "In all cases of sickness and disease we are

---

563   Gray, John M. "Memoirs of an Arabian Princess," Tanganyika Notes and Records, vol. 37 (1955): 49-70.

564   Ruiggi, Suzanne, "Commodifying Honor in Female Sexuality: Honor killings in Palestine," Middle East Report, no. 206, Power and Sexuality in the Middle East (Spring, 1998): 12-15: 13.

565   Ibid.

unfortunately exposed to the most ignorant quacks and mountebanks . . . our dead have not succumbed to their disease, but have been sacrificed to the barbarous treatment to which they were subjected."[566] She further notes that remedies used for severe sickness were, as a rule, more than useless. Cupping was considered the universal remedy for all kinds of maladies including cholera and smallpox; emetics, prepared of the most nauseous herbs, were frequently taken.[567] The best cure was believed to be Qur'anic inscriptions dissolved in water and the whole mixture swallowed. Salme herself had resorted to this remedy once when she had a violent attack of fever.[568]

On the other hand, Salme may not have chosen to abort her pregnancy for religious reasons. Termination of pregnancy by human intervention is forbidden under the rubric of Chapter 17, verse 33 of the Qur'an. However, renowned jurists of all four schools of Islamic jurisprudence made allowance for abortion for married women for just cause and only within the first four months, or 120 days, of pregnancy.[569] Salme's pregnancy due to illegitimate sexual intercourse cannot be considered a valid excuse for carrying out an abortion regardless of how many days had elapsed in the pregnancy.[570] A narrative by one of the Companions of the Prophet Muhammad, Abdullah bin Burayda, sheds light on the Islamic viewpoint in this regard:

> A woman came to the Messenger of Allah from Ghamid and said, "O Messenger of Allah! I have committed adultery, so purify me." He turned her away. On the following day she said, "O Messenger of Allah! Why do you turn me away? Perhaps, you turn me away as you turned away Ma'iz. By Allah, I have become pregnant." He said, "Well, if you insist upon it, then go until you give birth [to the child]." When she delivered, she came to the Messenger of Allah with the child wrapped in a piece of cloth and said, "Here is the child to whom I have given birth." He said, "Go suckle him until you wean him." When she had weaned him, she came to him with the child, who was holding a piece of bread in his hand and said, "O Prophet of Allah! Here is the child, as I have weaned him and he eats food." The Messenger of Allah entrusted the child to one of the Muslims and then ordered the punishment. She was put in a ditch up to her chest. He commanded the people to stone her and they did. . . .[571]

Burayda's narrative illustrates that a pregnancy due to illegitimate sexual intercourse is expected to be carried to its full term.

Because of Majid's intent to have Salme killed she was forced to flee Zanzibar. Under cover of darkness on the night of August 24, 1866, Salme was smuggled onboard the *HMS Highflyer* by Captain Malcolm S. Pasley. The same night the ship set sail without giving the usual notice as to her departure either to the

---

566   Ruete, Memoirs, 38.

567   Ibid. 205-206.

568   Ibid. 206.

569   Hewitt, Ibrahim, What does Islam say? (Wiltshire, England: The Cromwell Press Ltd., 1998):8; Al-Kawthari, Muhammad Adam, Birth Control and Abortion in Islam (Santa Barbara, CA: White Thread Press, 2006): 49-69.

570   Al-Kawthari, Abortion in Islam, 63.

571   Quoted by Al-Kawthari, Abortion in Islam, 64.

British Consul or to the Arab authorities.[572] The *Highflyer* was headed for the port city of Aden. Once in Aden Salme waited for nine months before Heinrich was able to join her.

In the meantime, Heinrich, who had remained in Zanzibar, went about unmolested as he wound up his business before departing for Aden. Likewise, when Captain Pasley returned a few months later to Zanzibar people were somewhat astonished to see that the Sultan gave him a most friendly reception. Gray gives a plausible explanation for Majid's paradoxical behavior. He personally wished Salme no harm and was most profoundly relieved by her departure.[573] However, his attitude toward Salme changed drastically when he later learnt that his sister had converted to Christianity in order to marry Heinrich. By converting to Christianity Salme committed the ultimate sin of apostasy and, as we will see below, paid dearly for it.

After Salme fled to Aden Seyyid Majid wrote to her to invite her to return to Zanzibar. The reasons for this invitation are not altogether clear, and it is not known whether Salme answered Majid's letter. Perhaps Majid invited Salme back because he learnt she was no longer pregnant, having lost the baby she was carrying when she fled Zanzibar. Meanwhile, Majid had also written to the Political Resident at Aden to ask for his help in facilitating Salme's return as well as to help her to live a decent life in Aden before she returned to Zanzibar. The response from Aden was discouraging. The Resident wrote: "Every effort has been made to induce Bibi Suleyma to quit her present quarters and adopt a more secluded life. But I regret without avail: indeed I have endeavoured to work upon the lady's feelings through the most respectable Arab families residing in Aden (that of the Aidroos and others) and have offered her a private apartment and establishment, but the Bibi seems determined to adhere to the step she has taken and to renounce her former life entirely and become Europeanized. To use her own words, she cannot, she says, after wearing the dress of Europeans revert to Arab dress. . . . Under the circumstances further attempts would be useless."[574]

Salme spent nine months in Aden patiently waiting for Heinrich. In the meantime she gave birth but the child died. While waiting for Heinrich she was instructed in the Christian religion. Salme does not offer any details about what she learnt about Christianity. Whatever it was it must have been very little. Salme's baptismal, with the name of Emily, took place in the English Church at Aden. Her baptismal was immediately followed by the wedding ceremony according to the English rite.[575] For reasons expressed in her letters home her "conversion" appears to have been superficial such that many years later she still regarded herself to be "an undeserving Christian."[576] Her "conversion" raises interesting questions about Muslim conversion to Christianity in general, and how she, as a former Muslim, experienced Christianity in particular.

To begin with, although Zanzibar was the first place that Christian missionaries came in contact with in East Africa, Zanzibar remained then, as it is now, virtually

---

572   Gray, "Memoirs," 52.

573   Ibid. 53.

574   Gray, "Memoirs," 53.

575   Ruete, Memoirs, 264.

576   Ibid. 281.

impervious to Christianity. The failure to win Muslims over to Christianity in Zanzibar was not so much due to lack of preaching, but because Islam had already cultivated among its followers a strong sense of community and common values. Thus, conversion to Christianity was considered to be a betrayal of one's community and religion in preference for Christianity and western culture. Therefore, conversion was a threat to the bonds of family and resulted in the persecution as well as the social ostracism of the convert. For most Muslims the price of conversion was too high to pay.

Salme accepted to be baptized because she wanted to be married to Heinrich. Both her baptism and Christian marriage were outward and visible signs of her new life as she endeavored to become Europeanized. Thereafter, Salme outwardly adhered to Christianity and inwardly struggled with her Islamic faith. It was not to be an easy struggle as one of her letters home indicates. In this letter Salme mentions one of her first "discomforts" following her baptism, namely answering to her Christian name. She says that she could not answer to her Christian name because she still felt she was "a good Muslim woman: "I appeared to myself so utterly despicable for posing differently from what I in reality was."[577]

Salme attributed her initial ambivalence toward Christianity to her lack of true conviction. She writes: "Conviction? Indeed, from whom and from where should I have gained the conviction? For nobody had taken any further notice of what I really believed. . . For the pastor it was apparently sufficient to hear me pronounce 'Yes' to everything he said to me at the baptism and the following marriage ceremony, in a language which was completely incomprehensible to me; nothing else was required. From that moment onwards I belonged to Christianity; all the rest I should in any case manage all by myself. . . Separated from my former religion, and knowing the new one by name only, there began for me a period which cannot be described by words. Never in my whole life – neither before nor after – have I, morally speaking, felt so miserable and deprived of every support as immediately after my baptism."[578]

Following her baptism Salme had expected that every Christian would have adopted, guided, and taught her what she needed to know about how to live a Christian life. She was shocked to find out that no such Christian fellowship existed. To compound matters further when she got to Hamburg she encountered Christians who dealt so disdainfully with their religion.[579] How, she asked herself, was their behavior supposed to make her attracted to her new religion?

Needless to say, she learnt German and desired to become as fully acquainted as she could "with the way in which Christians pray to their God."[580] When she was confident she learnt enough she asked her husband to take her to church. She writes: "One Sunday we indeed went, but when I stood at the door to enter, I had the feeling that I was about to do something wrong. . . The fact that the devout did not show any visible humility before the Almighty, I mean that they did not prostrate themselves, I found very curious and haughty, and this affected me as

---

577   Van Donzel, Arabian Princess, 411.

578   Ibid.

579   Ibid. 427.

580   Ibid. 431.

extremely distasteful."[581] Thus Salme found that her new Christian faith was not a good replacement of her old religion of Islam. Nowhere was this evident than in the performance of the physical acts of worship. This realization, as we will see in the next section, became a source of great anxiety for the remainder of her life.

Moreover, the absence of any sense of belonging to a Christian community must have weakened any resolve Salme had to try and be a good Christian. There were many occasions when Salme could have benefited from Christian fellowship. Salme's loss of her husband after only three years of stay in Hamburg must have been very traumatic. She describes how deeply worried she was when Heinrich was late coming home on the day he was run-over by a tram. When she was told what had happened she rushed to the hospital to see him, only to be rudely made to wait for a doctor's permission to do so! Heinrich died after three days of extreme pain and suffering. Salme had to arrange for the funeral. She does not mention getting help or even consolation from either the church or Heinrich's family.

Salme's apostasy and its consequences

Apostasy implies a rejection of one's religious identity as well as religious values. Historically, Judaism, Christianity and Islam have taken a very dim view of apostates. As we noted above, when Paul apostatized the Jews of Damascus wanted to kill him. After he returned to Jerusalem a similar threat to his life was made by the Hellenistic Jews. The Jews did not take kindly to Paul's apostasy because his ministry was suspected to be a heretical form of Judaism (Segal 1990: xii). More specifically, Paul was hated because he questioned the Judaic interpretation of salvation, namely that one can get salvation only by obeying Mosaic Law. Instead, Paul taught that salvation is achieved by faith and by the grace of God.

From a Christian viewpoint, the peril of apostasy, or falling away, which is mentioned in Hebrews Chapter 6, verse 6, is equated with "crucifying again the Son of God" and holding him up to public contempt. However, it is not up to Christians to pass judgment on sinners including apostates. The Bible says: "Do not judge, so that you may not be judged."[582] Instead, the punishing of apostates, like that of all other sinners, is the prerogative of God.

The Qur'an refers to apostasy and apostates in several verses from various chapters. The most important reference is probably chapter 4: 88-89, which read as follows: "Then what is the matter with you that you are divided into two parties about the hypocrites? Allah has cast them back (to disbelief) because of what they have earned. . . They wish that you reject Faith, as they have rejected (Faith), and thus that you all become equal (like one another). So take not *Auliya'* (protectors or friends) from them, till they emigrate in the way of Allah (to Muhammad). But if they turn back (from Islam), take (hold of) them and kill them whenever you find them. . ."

Many things can cause a Muslim to apostate. These include blasphemy (such as ascribing human qualities to Allah), burning or handling the Qur'an in a contemptuous manner, engaging in *shirk* (i.e., associating Allah with other gods), defaming a prophet's character, believing in reincarnation, and entering a church for purposes of worship. A person born of a Muslim parent who commits apostasy

---

581   Ibid.

582   The Holy Bible, Matthew 7: 1.

is called a *murtad fitri*, and his or her apostasy is considered to be treason against Allah. A person who converts to Islam and then apostatizes is called *Kafir al-Asli*[583] and his or her apostasy is considered to be treason against the *ummah* (community). Salme was therefore a *murtad fitri*.

Muslim jurists are not agreed whether or not apostasy ought to be punished by death. They are also not agreed whether apostasy is a crime or a sin. Those who think it is a crime maintain that it is punishable by death. The principal *hadith* on which the case for the death sentence for apostasy is built up is the one narrated by Ibn Abbas as follows: "Whosoever changes his religion, slay him."[584] Those opposed to the death sentence consider apostasy to be a sin and therefore not punishable by death. They have also questioned the authenticity of the above *hadith* because of the nature of its transmission (attributed to only one source). According to Rahman, the *hadith* is *mujmal* – a summary statement – and calls for further elucidation.[585]

Other opponents of the death sentence for apostasy have argued that since the Qur'an itself does not prescribe death as punishment for apostasy the above *hadith* cannot abrogate the Qur'an in this matter. Moreover, on the basis of the Qur'an's Chapter 4, verse137, which evidently implies that multiple, sequential apostasies are possible; death cannot be the punishment of apostasy. Otherwise, there would be no survivors to repeat the offense. In any case, there is no historical evidence which indicates that the Prophet Muhammad or any of his companions ever sentenced anyone to death for apostasy.

Moreover, those in favor of the penalty have tended to distinguish between peaceable apostasy and hostile apostasy; and whether or not female apostates may be killed. The distinction between peaceable and hostile apostates is made on the grounds that the former mean no harm to Islam and therefore can be spared their lives. However, the combination of apostasy and active hostility against Islam is said to warrant the killing of such hostile apostates. In regard to female apostates some exegetes have opined that since by their physical nature they cannot fight they pose no danger to Islam. Hence they should not be killed. Shafi`ite jurisprudence (which Omani Arabs in Zanzibar subscribed to) demands that both male and female apostates must be killed regardless of whether they are peaceable or hostile.

The main reason for punishing an apostate is expressed by al-Samarai as follows: ". . . Islam is not merely a religion but also a "nationality" and rebellion against it would mean treason. For such an act would be treachery and change from co-citizenship to enmity. . . The apostate causes others to imagine that Islam is lacking in goodness and thus prevents them from (accepting) it. Consequently he commits an offence not only against his own person but against others also…"[586] In this regard, the apostate is punished for the integrity of Islam just as the punishment for murder is for the security of life or the punishment for theft is for the protection of property.

It remains to be considered whether, short of the death penalty, an apostate can be subjected to any pressure, physical or otherwise, to recant his/her apostasy.

583   Rahman, S. A. Punishment of Apostasy in Islam (Lahore: Institute of Islamic Culture, 1972): 107.

584   Quoted by Rahman, Apostasy, 59.

585   Ibid. 61.

586   Ibid. 115.

According to Rahman, goodly exhortation may be utilized to persuade the apostate to change his/her belief. This is because an apostate may have been assailed by genuine doubts and, unless he or she herself is persuaded to see the error of her thinking, how is she to be convinced where the truth lies?[587] As we will see, some of the pressures facing apostates (especially non-militant ones) have involved changes in their civil status as to rights of property or marital status, etc.

The doubts that Salme exhibited about her conversion suggest that she may have been burdened with guilt. Other evidence that she was struggling with a guilty consciousness is to be found in the *Memoirs* and the letters that she wrote to her siblings in Zanzibar. In a letter to Seyyid Barghash dated 1883, she laments and pleads: "O God, God, my brother, and again God, God, do not harden your feelings against me any longer. The misfortune and hardship which have hit me in this world weigh down on me. If you forgive me, the Lord of the Worlds will be pleased with you. God says: 'On us our actions, and on you your actions.'" It is unlikely that Barghash replied to this letter.

Salme's anguish about her apostasy was not made any easier because some of her relatives (most likely her half-sisters) time and again tried to convince her to return to Islam. She notes in her memoirs that during her second trip to Zanzibar in 1888 she learnt that all of her surviving siblings wished urgently that she become a Muslim again. In a conversation she had at the time with Colonel C. B. Euan-Smith, the British consul-general, Salme told the Colonel that nothing would induce her to enter a harem again.[588]

In a letter that Salme had written to Emperor Wilhelm II she indicates that having once recognized the truth of the Christian religion, it was impossible for her to return to Islam. However, the distance that Salme had moved away from Islam cannot be determined by her recognition of the truth of Christianity because that is not easy to determine. Rather the distance can be determined by acts that she did that were very un-Islamic. For instance, during her second visit to Zanzibar onboard the *Adler* the commander celebrated her birthday by serving pork. Salme writes: ". . . in honour of a woman born a Muslim, the amiable commander of the *Adler* had a pig killed in my native country, which is faithfully adherent to Islam. If this had been predicated (sic) to me nineteen years ago by the most trustworthy of our fortune-tellers, I would have laughed in their faces, in spite of all superstition. What an un-intentional humour is often revealed in the heaviest fates of our life."[589]

What a difference nineteen years had made in Salme's life! Nineteen years previous when sailing from Aden to Marseilles she had struggled against all sorts of un-Islamic mores. One of her unhappiest moments was during mealtime when she had to eat in the company of people unknown to her. Moreover, as she notes in one of her letters, "I was always happy when these sessions came to an end, the more so because I suspected pork and lard in every dish. So it was that I declined everything which my senses considered not to be free of pork. Therefore I lived in the beginning mostly on biscuits, boiled eggs, tea and fruits alone."[590]

587   Rahman, Apostasy, 121.

588   Van Donzel, Arabian Princess, 87.

589   Ibid. 393.

590   Ibid. 408.

Furthermore, the voyage over the Red Sea turned out to be too hot so that all first class passengers were forced to sleep on deck. The sleeping arrangements contravened the seclusion of the sexes that Salme was used to. She writes: "If there was anything that seemed to mock my former seclusion from the world of men, it was these few nights here on board the ship. For during the last few nights all the first class passengers – man, woman and child – slept together on their mattresses in the saloon. . . Most amusing was the sight next morning when waking up! All the gentlemen in nightshirts and thin, white underpants, but nothing else. The ladies all in long, English nightgowns with a thin, white skirt over it."[591]

Other rude awakenings awaited Salme in Hamburg. As time went on she came to realize that a lot of German Christians did not trust in God and many did not even know what the Scriptures say about trusting in God. The reasons for their behavior eluded Salme. However, it must be noted that the general social climate in Germany at the time was not very religion-friendly. Industrial capitalism, nationalism and science, in its multiplying ramifications and amazing discoveries, were making Christianity untenable to the honest and informed mind.[592] Darwin's evolutionary thesis seemed to render obsolete the story of creation in the first chapter of Genesis. However, even though nominal Christianity was a part of general etiquette over 95 per cent of the Germans received Christian baptism and marriage.[593]

Yet, despite of the prevalence of nominal Christianity in Germany Salme says that it was her faith in God that kept her going especially after her husband's death. Salme does not say which God she placed her faith into. Was it the triune God or Allah? It is probable that she may have alluded to the former. After all, God says in the Bible to those in trouble "Come to me. . . and I will give you rest."[594] But again, as a former Muslim, she may very well have believed that whatever had happened to her was the will of Allah.

However, what is perplexing is the lack of Christian fellowship from which Salme may have drawn strength to persevere. There is no indication that Salme was embraced by the church both before and after her husband's death. One would think that the church would have considered the conversion of an Arab Muslim princess an important triumph for Christianity. That she was not warmly embraced or supported after the demise of her husband may have been due to a number of factors, one being that she was an Arab woman.

Salme's apostate experience was made the worse by the reduced circumstances she was forced to live under in Germany especially after the death of her husband. Before she fled Zanzibar onboard the *Highflyer* she is reported to have attempted to sell some of her property. However, there is reason to believe that she was not able to sell much without raising the suspicion of her brother Majid. She therefore must have left with little money instead of the boxes of dollars she is reported to have taken onboard the *Highflyer*.

Due to pressing financial needs Salme made several attempts to get her brother Seyyid Barghash to release her inheritance. One such attempt involved a trip from Hamburg to London in 1875 when she learnt that Seyyid Barghash would be

---

591   Van Donzel, *Arabian Princess*, 408.

592   . LaTourette, Kenneth S. *A History of Christianity* (New York: Harper & Row, Publishers, 1953): 1070.

593   Nicholls, James H. *History of Christianity, 1650-1950: Secularization of the West* (New York: The Ronald Press Co., 1956): 245.

594   *The Holy Bible*, Matthew 11: 28.

visiting. She was unable to meet her brother because British officials did all they could to block her access to Seyyid Barghash. In August 1885 Salme made her first trip to Zanzibar to try and secure her inheritance from her late father as well as what she considered was due to her from the estates of twenty-one brothers and sisters who had passed away since she left Zanzibar in August 1866. Salme calculated that she was entitled to about one hundred thousand dollars or twenty thousand pound sterling.

Salme's petitions to Seyyid Barghash for her inheritance proved futile. Her brother would not grant her a penny because, as far as he was concerned, she deserved none. Seyyid Barghash is reported to have told Salme's mediator Admiral von Knorr: "She asks for her inheritance according to Islamic law. This law allows her nothing because she has abandoned her religion and has separated herself from us. And thus, according to Muslim law, she has no right whatsoever."[595] Thus, according to Seyyid Barghash his sister had not only apostatized but had separated herself from her Muslim relatives. By opting to live in Germany, which being Christian belonged to *Dar al-Harb* (enemy territory), Salme had become a religious enemy. It was on this basis that Seyyid Barghash disinherited his sister. However, it appears that Salme believed that although she had apostatized she had not lost her legal entitlement to her inheritance. In this regard she may have been right because Muslim exegetes are in agreement that apostates remain legally entitled to their property; only their rights to dispose of it are in abeyance pending their repentance.[596]

Following the death of her husband Salme was for a while tempted to go back to Zanzibar. The temptation was, however, outweighed by two considerations. First, much as she herself remained (as she believed) an Arab woman to the core, she felt morally obligated to raise her children to become fully German. Second, she believed that her late husband would not have wanted his children to be raised in a culture other than German, especially in regard to their education. What Salme must have had in mind was her children acquiring western secular rather than religious education. This is because she had a very low opinion of Christian religious education which in her memoirs she compares unfavorably to Islamic religious education.

According to Salme, Islamic religious instruction has a longer lasting impact than Christian religious instruction. In one of the letters to an unnamed sister in Zanzibar she notes: "Muslims in general are but little instructed in their religion and yet they manifest such a firmness in their belief. On the other side there are the Christian children, painstakingly instructed in school. It seemed to me that religion is taught here as a mere science, and that at the first occasion it is forgotten again and even often criticized. . ."[597] Again, the real reasons for the Germans' shallow religiosity eluded Salme. It was not how Christianity was taught that caused limited adherence to it. Rather, it was the combination of the Church's legitimating of the status quo with all its injustices and Marxist critique of Christianity which caused general disrespect for religion.

In addition, the endeavor to separate church and state was detrimental to

---

595   Van Donzel, Arabian Princess, 79.

596   Peters, Rudolf and Geert J. J. de Vries, "Apostasy in Islam," Die Welt des Islams, vol. XVII, no. 1-4 (1976-77): 1-25: 7.

597   Van Donzel, Arabian Princess, 460.

Christianity in ways that Salme could not have fathomed. As LaTourette notes, "Education, for centuries under the auspices and control of the Church, now was being made a function of the state. That meant that youth was being trained primarily for the service of the state and was being indoctrinated with the ideology to which the state was committed rather than reared in the Christian faith."[598] Moreover, the inability of different denominations to agree on the form and content prevented any religious instruction from being given in German schools at the time.

The above combination of factors against Christianity in Germany and other parts of Europe constituted a test of the vitality of Christianity. These factors caused the propagators of Christianity to look outside of Europe for its renewal. It is not by accident that the nineteenth century witnessed for the first time the rise of a world-wide missionary enterprise with Africa as one of the targets. If, as Salme alluded, Christianity in Germany was taught as a science it was not so taught in Africa. In Africa the insistence of Christian proselytizers on the fear of hell and the beauty of heaven probably had the same impact as that intended by similar Islamic eschatological symbolism.

---

598   LaTourette, Christianity, 1075.

PART FOUR

Slavery and Politics in Colonial Zanzibar

10

The Slave Trade and Slavery in Zanzibar:
Opposing Views

Introduction

The origins of the slave trade in East Africa remain shrouded in the mists of history. Likewise, precisely when and why slavery started in Zanzibar remains unclear. According to Ibrahim Shao, slavery predated the arrival of Arabs in Zanzibar. Shao suggests that the traditional ruler of the Hadimu, the *Mwinyi Mkuu*, and his subordinates "appropriated surplus labour or value products through slavery and tenancy" even though both forms of bondage were not very pronounced.[599] Studies by Edward A. Alpers,[600] Frederick Cooper[601] and Abdul Sheriff,[602] emphasize the significance and connections between a new form of slavery and the rise of the Zanzibar Sultanate and the latter's place in the global capitalist system. This chapter departs from these studies in its emphasis on hitherto neglected aspects of the slave trade and slavery in Zanzibar. The chapter

599   Shao, Ibrahim F. *The Political Economy of land Reform in Zanzibar: Before and After the Revolution* (Dare-es-Salaam: Dar-es-Salaam University Press, 1992): x.

600   Alpers, Edward A. *Ivory and slaves: changing pattern of international trade in East central Africa to the later nineteenth century* (Berkeley: University of California Press, 1975).

601   Cooper, Frederick, *Plantation slavery on the east coast of Africa* (Portsmouth, N.H.: Heinemann, 1977, 1997).

602   Sheriff, Abdul, *Slaves, spices, & ivory in Zanzibar: integration of an East African commercial empire into the world economy, 1770-1873* (London: J. Currey; Athens: Ohio University Press, 1987).

examines the consequences of the slave trade and slavery on the slaves themselves rather than on their societies or on Zanzibar's economy.

By the early 1870s there were two categories of slaves on Zanzibar Island, namely, those that were domiciled in Zanzibar Town and those who resided in the rural areas. Slaves in Zanzibar Town could be divided into several sub-categories according to their occupations. There were domestic slaves who were mainly women (who worked as cooks, ayahs and concubines), children and eunuchs as well as slaves who were employed in unskilled labor such as porters (popularly known as *hamalis*) and artisans.

Slaves in the rural areas were mainly used in agriculture, especially on large-scale clove plantations. The areas where clove production predominated were formerly forested lands which the indigenous Hadimu and Tumbatu people mainly used as common hunting grounds and a source of building materials, and at times to open a new farm locally known as *konde*. How the Hadimu and Tumbatu ceded these lands to Arab immigrants remains unclear. However, according to Colette Le Cour Grandmaison the Arabs brought with them a sense of private property which was new to the Hadimu and Tumbatu people. Back in Oman permanent rights to water, large estates and substantial homes were incontestable signs of wealth. Therefore, those who had settled in Zanzibar had put to good use the capital accumulated in commerce and the slave trade to build residences and to buy land.[603] John Middleton suggests that in some cases the Arabs took plantation lands by superior force, and in others they acquired them by some form of purchase.[604] Whatever the facts historically, until the late 1950s the original Arab owners' rights were accepted as valid. As we shall see in chapter ten, when the Arab landlords began to evict their squatters these rights were questioned by the Afro-Shirazi Party (ASP) leadership who claimed that the Arabs only owned the clove trees but not the land on which they were grown.

In the meantime, the lucrative profits from cloves and the need for abundant labor at harvest time caused the plantation owners to accumulate slaves and land.[605] However, before we examine the opposing views about the slave trade and slavery in Zanzibar, we must consider what the attitudes of Arab slave masters, plantation managers and overseers in Zanzibar were toward black Africans in general and slaves in particular.

Although the Qur'an enjoins Arab Muslims to disregard color in their dealings with other peoples, Arabs were socialized and made color-conscious especially in their dealings with black Africans. Arab folklore denigrated blacks and especially censured interracial sexual liaisons between black men and Arab women. Arab exotic *mirabilia* is part of the popular ethnology that we find in the collection of stories known in Arabic as *Alf Laylah Wa Laylah*.[606] The ideas and emotions displayed in *Alf Laylah Wa Laylah* are elemental ones and concern life's

---

603   Grandmaison, Colette Le Cour, "Rich Cousins, Poor Cousins: Hidden Stratification among Omani
        Arabs in   Eastern Africa," *Africa: Journal of the International African Institute*, vol. 59, no. 2, Social
        Stratification in Swahili Society (1989): 176-184: 178.

604   Middleton, John, *Land Tenure in Zanzibar* (London: Her Majesty's Stationery Office, 1961): 42.

605   Ibid. 179.

606   Sir Richard F. Burton's English translation was titled *The Book of a Thousand Nights and a Night*.
        It was first translated into Kiswahili in 1929 by Edwin W. Brenn and Frederick Johnson and titled
        Mazungumzo ya Alfu-lela-ulela (London, New York: Longmans, Green and Co.)

fundamentals: death, old age, marriage, anger, revenge, fear, pain, love, regret, loyalty, beauty, religious faith, temptation, sickness, delight, luck – the gamut of life's experiences and feelings.[607]

However, it is the libidinous portrayal of black men in *Alf Laylah Wa Laylah* which is of particular interest if we are to understand Arab anxieties about possibilities of Arab women to engage in sexual liaisons with black men and the need to discourage them. In *Alf Laylah Wa Laylah*, black men are presented not only as libidinous but brutes that only a whore would prefer;[608] "the good woman will welcome death rather than be touched by a black man."[609] There are no stories in *Alf Laylah Wa Laylah* about Arab men consorting with black/African women. Yet many black women were purchased by Arab slave traders in order to be sold as concubines.[610]

Arab men who migrated to East Africa took concubines or married local women out of necessity. It appears that both religious and economic reasons made it difficult for Arab women to migrate to East Africa in great numbers. Strict separation of the sexes made it difficult for dhow captains to accommodate female passengers and when they did they charged higher fares for women than for men. In the 1930s dhow captains charged 8 rupees per male passenger and 12 rupees per female passenger on a single trip.[611]

Although Arab men consorted with African women they considered Africans in general to be racially and culturally inferior. According to Al-Azmeh, Arab exotic *mirabilia* (accounts of the fantastic) originating in travel literature and sailors' tales, primarily of the ninth and tenth centuries, subscribed to the "congenital deficiency of the minds of negroes" and other signifiers which indicated the Africans' lack of civilization such as being pingscent, malodorous, kinky of hair, and ugly of appearance.[612]

African cultural and racial inferiority was in the eyes of Arabs also a badge of their barbarism and savagery. They were culturally denigrated as *washenzi* (barbaric savages) who lacked any trace of *ustaarabu* (Arab gentility): they dressed differently, spoke differently, and behaved differently. African slaves in Zanzibar were forced or on their own endeavored to acculturate and adopt as much as they could the ways of their masters. First and foremost they converted to Islam. As we shall see conversion to Islam did little to ameliorate their status as slaves, however. Equally significant, the extent to which they could redeem or redefine their humanity was for the longest deterred by what Etienne Balibar calls "a racism

---

607   Farwell, Byron, *Burton: A biography of Sir Richard Francis Burton* (New York: Holt, Rinehart and Winston, 1963): 366.

608   Richard Burton himself harbored racist attitudes in regard to African sexuality. In a footnote in the opening episode of the *Nights* suggests that he himself shared the sexual anxieties reflected in its stories. He writes: "Debauched women prefer negroes on account of the size of their parts. I measured one man in Somali-land who, when quiescent, numbered nearly six inches. This is characteristic of the negro race . . . whereas the pure Arab . . . is below the average of Europe . . . Moreover, the imposing parts do not increase proportionally during erection; consequently, the deed of kind takes a much longer time and adds greatly to the woman's enjoyment. In my time no honest Hindi Moslem would take his woman-folk to Zanzibar on account of the huge attractions there and thereby offered to them." See: Southgate, "Images of Blacks," endnote # 77.

609   Southgate, "Images of Blacks," 25.

610   Ibid. 25.

611   Villiers, Alan, *Sons of Sinbad* (New York: Scribner, 1969): 76.

612   Al-Azmeh, Aziz, "Barbarians in Arab Eyes," *Past & Present*, No. 134 (Feb., 1992): 3-18: 4.

whose dominant theme is not biological heredity but the insurmountability of cultural differences."[613]

Opposing views about the slave trade and slavery in Zanzibar

Students of Africa history in general and of Zanzibar history in particular have given opposing views about the slave trade and slavery. The debates between John D. Fage and Walter Rodney and their supporters are representative of the former. Rodney's research for his doctoral dissertation on the Upper Guinea coast led him to conclude that Africans did not practice slavery until Europeans arrived in the late 1400s with the concept of slavery. Fage rejected the idea that slavery in West Africa was purely exogenously imposed. Likewise, whereas Rodney argued that the slave trade in West Africa had a disastrous effect on its population Fage rejected the idea that it did have any negative impact.[614]

European critics of the slave trade and slavery in Zanzibar used an anti-Arab propaganda in their endeavor to have both abolished.[615] Britain in particular was against the slave trade, especially the seizure and transport of captives from the African mainland to the Middle East, and, later endeavored to bring an end to slavery in Zanzibar itself.[616] To prevent human trafficking between East Africa and the Middle East Britain employed its navy to blockade the East African coast and to intercept Arab dhows that carried captives to the Middle East. As we shall see, the exercise revealed some of the horrors of the slave trade.

William Wilberforce (1759 – 1833) was a Tory evangelical who was very influential in the abolition of the slave trade and eventually slavery itself in the British Empire. It was under the influence of Thomas Clarkson that he became seriously absorbed with the issue of slavery. He later reflected: "So enormous, so dreadful, so irremediable did the trade's wickedness appear that my own mind was completely made up for abolition. Let the consequences be what they would: I from this time determined that I would never rest until I had effected its abolition." However, the slave trade that so engrossed Wilberforce's attention was the trans-Atlantic slave trade. We do not know if he was aware that human trafficking was also taking place on the eastern side of the African continent.

William Gladstone, one of the leading British politicians of the Victorian era, was also a Tory evangelical although later he abandoned it for the High church. Gladstone devoted most of his parliamentary time and attention from 1833 until 1841 to matters related with slavery and the slave trade. Influenced by his father's ownership of plantations and slaves in Demerara and Jamaica, Gladstone initially did not believe that slavery was an evil. When he accepted that slavery should be abolished he proposed that emancipation ought to be preceded by the slaves'

---

613   Balibar, Etienne, "Is There a 'Neo-Racism'?" in Etienne Balibar and Immanuel Wallerstein, *Race, Nation, Class* (London; New York: Verso, 1991): 20.

614   For a summary of Rodney's and Fage's arguments see: Immanuel Wallerstein, "Africa in a Capitalist World," *Issue: A Journal of Opinion*, vol. 10, no. ½, Tenth Anniversary Number (Spring-Summer, 1980): 24-25.

615   Berlioux, Etienne F. *The Slave Trade in Africa in 1872: Principally carried on for the supply of Turkey, Egypt, Persia and Zanzibar* (London: Frank Cass & Co. Ltd., 1971); for Zanzibar, 49-68.

616   Cave, Basil S. "The End of Slavery in Zanzibar and British East Africa," *Journal of the Royal African Society*, vol. 9, no. 33 (Oct., 1909): 20-33.

moral emancipation.[617] He would not free the slaves without assurance of their disposition to industry.[618] This view was shared by the missionaries in Zanzibar, especially Bishop Tozer.

In East Africa, scholarly debate about the nature of slavery in Zanzibar first occurred in the pages of the Makerere College Magazine of 1937 between Ali Muhsin and a person who signed himself as Sceptic. The significance of the views expressed in each letter calls for their quotation in extensor. Ali Muhsin's letter was entitled "Slavery as it used to be practiced in Zanzibar."[619] He wrote:

> At a time when thralldom was thought to be one of the inexorable laws of nature the island metropolis of East Africa also took an active part in that abominable human traffic. Slaves imported from the neighbouring territories were used to do predial as well as household work. This went on until the abolition of slavery when the Arabs underwent a great loss, being deprived of their labour.

> It was the slave who, under his master's supervision, planted the cocoanut and the clove for which that otherwise unimportant island is now so famous. However it must be observed that although slavery flourished in Zanzibar it was entirely devoid of the cruelties that were its usual concomitants in the other parts of the world. I cannot excuse the few isolated cases of atrocities perpetrated against humble bondsmen, but I can positively declare that these were rare exceptions that went to prove the rule.

> "As to your slaves – male and female – feed them with that you eat. If you cannot keep them, or they commit any fault, discharge them. They are God's people like unto you, and you are to be kind to them." These were among the ameliorative principles inculcated by the Prophet Muhammad for the mitigation of this evil that was a blot to civilisation. It is remarkable to note how almost to the letter these injunctions were carried out in Zanzibar.

> It was a very ordinary thing for a rich Arab to marry his slave, so much so that the intermingling of blood between them has caused a friendly and brotherly feeling between Arabs and Africans, two ethnologically different peoples. Manumission was a thing of almost everyday occurrence, and such was the happy state of slaves that they loathed freedom, in spite of their being, as a rule given by their masters pieces of land for their maintenance during their free life. They realized that so long as they remained in thralldom their masters were by duty bound to look after them, although in return they had to work for them.

> Such current stories as those about the practice of burying slaves under house foundations as sacrifices are simply groundless myths. Were there any scrap of truth in these fabrications, instead of the good feeling and mutual

617   Quinault, Roland, "Gladstone and Slavery," *The Historical Journal*, vol. 52, no. 2 (2009): 383-383: 366.

618   Ibid. 368.

619   *Makerere College Magazine*, Vol. 1, No. 4 (August, 1937): 111. I am very grateful to Jonathon Glassman for availing me photocopies of the letters by Ali Muhsin and "Sceptic" as I was unable to get a copy of the *Makerere College Magazine* by interlibrary loan in the USA.

*understanding that now prevail between the master and the freedman, there
would be nothing but bitter animosity.*

*When the British Government wanted to put a stop to slavery in Zanzibar, it
found in the then Sultan a ready and ardent supporter. Various treaties were
entered into, until finally the institution was abolished for good, thus bringing
all to an equal footing. Cooper's Naval Institute of Zanzibar stands as an
undying monument of the heroic and noble part played by the British Navy
in chasing down slavers who were illicitly trying to smuggle their fellowmen
to the Island Protectorate."*

Sceptic's rebuttal was published four months after Ali Mahsin's letter appeared.
It was entitled "Slavery in Zanzibar."[620] He wrote:

*"Permit me please to submit my few comments on "Slavery as it used to
be practiced in Zanzibar" in your last number. The harrowing atrocities
attending slavery in Zanzibar cannot be winked at, they are notorious. The
U.M.C.A. Cathedral at Zanzibar stands on the site of the old slave market and
its altar above the remains of a tree to which slaves were tethered and flogged:
those who did not flinch fetched highest bids; what an excellent test of quality!*

*The Arab lords as a safeguard against perfidy emasculated the slaves who
attended their ladies while at baths; they also perforated the ears of most to
prevent truancy. In the former case maids, without having to be mutilated,
would have done quite well, in the latter no excuses justify the act.*

*More than condign punishments were inflicted upon defaulting slaves, some
resulting in physical incapacities. If my friend champions the Arabs in this
and other respects and tries to exonerate them from such gross enormities
his judgment is ex parte and the dicta he employed to extol them constitute
but a threadbare falsity. When the Arabs raided the mainland and abducted
women, what was the excuse? The desire evinced by some to marry their
slaves, though in most cases these unions relapsed to concubinage, was
a cloak to conceal their lust and a subterfuge to legalize their abductions;
any reluctance on the slave's part was met with coercion. The blacks in no
instance married Arab women; it was the most unspeakable derogation. This
cannot be rightly termed "intermarriage." The Arabs in these marriages often
contracted incestuous bonds: two or more women of propinquity, in some
cases so marked as to render connivance impossible, would go to the same
harem. Slavery was at its acme in Zanzibar at the coming of the British; if
there was understanding between lord and slave, as asserted by my friend, the
latter would have opposed any schemes of manumission.*

*The contrary happened; cruisers and destroyers participated in the social task of
raising man from the substratum of indignity; slavers were chased and reduced
to comparatively nothing. Cooper's Royal Institute truly stands as an undying
monument to Cooper for the life he gave to fight recalcitrant Arabs who
continued buying and selling man despite British decrees against the practice.*

---

620   *Makerere College Magazine*, Vol. 1, No. 5 (December, 1937): 144.

To enumerate all the monstrosities committed by the Zanzibar slave dealers would take ages; the sensibilities of the Arabs were abnormally obtuse for they knew no compassion. If the truth were told we should no longer find people to cram our heads with feeble apologies; the Zanzibar Arabs were exacerbated at parting with unpaid and forced labour no less than were their more considerate congeners in America. Slavery and its inhumanities are a stain on the name and honour of Zanzibar to-day and very likely for ages to come."

Which of the above two viewpoints about Zanzibar slavery is credible? Was slavery in Zanzibar as humane as Ali Muhsin alleges it to have been? Was manumission an everyday occurrence? Which of the Sultans was a ready and ardent supporter of the abolition of slavery? Was slavery the ultimate evil that Sceptic makes it to be? Were male slaves emasculated so they could be employed to safeguard the chastity of Arab ladies? How perverse was concubinage in Zanzibar and what was its impact on the slave-concubines? These are the questions that are explored and answered in the remainder of this chapter.

First and foremost, not one Sultan but several were involved in the process of abolishing the slave trade and legal slavery in Zanzibar. Britain's initial endeavors to end human trafficking on the waters of East Africa started during the reign of Seyyid Said. In 1847 Seyyid Said was induced by the British to sign a treaty banning the export of slaves beyond his domains within East Africa.[621] Other treaties had to be signed with his successors.

In 1873 Sultan Barghash signed a Treaty with Britain to suppress the sea-borne traffic of slaves, and to close all public markets for imported slaves. In 1876 he prohibited by Proclamation the fitting out and dispatch of slave caravans from the interior; and decreed that slaves so arriving at the coast should be confiscated; and that slaves should no longer be moved by land along the coast, any so found being confiscated, and their owners punished. In 1889 Sultan Khalifa concluded an Agreement with the British Consul-General, to the effect that all slaves who should be brought into his domains after 1 November, 1889, and all children born in his dominions after 1 January, 1890, should be free. In 1890 Sultan Ali prohibited by Proclamation all exchange, sale, or purchase of slaves, and made provisions limiting the rights of inheritance and ownership.[622]

Seyyid Majid, who succeeded Seyyid Said in 1856, was far from being an enthusiastic supporter of any interference in the slave trade on his own behalf and in the behalf of the leaders of the Arab tribes who constituted his council of chiefs. As far back as 1864, Earl Russell's correspondence with Colonel R. L. Playfair indicates that the British believed any suggestions to prohibit the transport of slaves from port to port were not likely to be received favorably; in fact, Earl Russell cautioned Colonel Playfair against insisting on Seyyid Majid entering into a treaty with Her Majesty's Government at the time to prohibit the export of slaves from one frontier of his domains to another.[623]

In the early 1860s the British were more concerned with stopping the export of slaves to Arabia and other parts of the Middle East rather than with interfering

621   Cooper, Frederick, *Plantation Slavery*, 45.

622   Great Britain. Africa No. 1, Marquess of Salisbury, Instructions to Mr. A. Hardinge respecting the Abolition of the Legal Status of Slavery in the Islands of Zanzibar and Pemba, 10 February, 1897: 1.

623   PRO, FO 84/1279 Henry A. Churchill, Her Majesty's Political Agent and Consul at Zanzibar, to the Chief Secretary to Government, Bombay dated 14 August, 1867.

in what they referred to as "domestic slavery" in Zanzibar. This was despite the facts that at the time it was well known that from 20 to 30 thousand slaves were annually being imported into the island of Zanzibar and that this number by far exceeded the agricultural requirements of the island.

In 1867 Seyyid Majid agreed to prohibit the transport of slaves out of East Africa to Arabia and limited domestic slave trafficking to between Latitude 9 degrees South (at Kilwa) and Latitude 4 degrees South (at Lamu). However, this came about due to some arm-twisting by the British and a bit of diplomatic bargaining. To begin with, the then Political Agent, Churchill, threatened him that if Seyyid Majid did not go along he would be thwarted in everything he did and the British would avail themselves of the first opportunity to put an end to his reign.[624] This approach, according to Seyyid Majid's secretary, Sheik Suleiman bin Hemed, was tantamount to a man bent on breaking a hard stone to pieces by a hard blow in the center instead of a succession of little blows on the edges. Churchill got the message and endeavored to proceed by degrees which opened the door for diplomatic bargaining.

Churchill knew at the time Seyyid Majid was very opposed to the payment of an annual subsidy to Muscat. It so happened that Seyyid Majid's brother, Thuwein, the ruler of Muscat, had just been murdered by his own son Salim. Seyyid Majid used the murder as bargaining chip. He asked Churchill if Her Majesty's government would allow him to go to Muscat to avenge his brother's murder. If this request was unacceptable, and it be decided, contrary to Arab custom that Salim should reign in peace in Muscat then all that Seyyid Majid would solicit of Her Majesty's Government was that he hears nothing more of Salim the murderer or of his claims of annual subsidy from Zanzibar.[625]

Churchill replied to Seyyid Majid with regard to his request to be allowed to avenge the murder of his brother that his vengeance in comparison with the punishment that God could award the murderer, if He so pleased, would be very small. That already Salim, from the accounts Churchill had received, was already feeling the effects of remorse; that he could neither eat nor sleep in peace fancying he saw his father's ghost in everything that surrounded him; that already his people were against him and that Seyyid Turki was up in arms against Muscat. Churchill suggested to Seyyid Majid that should Salim be killed it could become a matter for consideration by the British to allow Seyyid Majid to be the ruler of Muscat as well as Zanzibar. However, that would necessarily depend very much on the manner in which he governed Zanzibar.

In the meantime, Churchill assured Seyyid Majid that he was in favor of the latter's demand namely, that the state of Zanzibar should henceforth be totally separated from that of Muscat and that all claims between them should be disallowed Churchill. It was due to this assurance that Seyyid Majid sent Churchill a written statement proclaiming his concession to prohibit the export of slaves to the Middle East.[626] Likewise, Seyyid Barghash was not a willing "agent" of abolition. Rather, his willingness came about after a long confrontation with the British navy on East Africa's waters and much diplomatic arm twisting from

---

624   Ibid.

625   Ibid.

626   PRO, FO 84/1279 Translation of Seyyid Majid's letter to Churchill, dated August 1867.

Britain that Seyyid Barghash signed a treaty on June 5, 1873 that made the slave trade finally illegal in his dominions.[627]

Furthermore, historical evidence contradicts Ali Muhsin's viewpoint that manumission was a thing of almost daily occurrence and that slavery in Zanzibar was so benign to the extent that slaves loathed freedom. On the one hand, the profitability of slave labor preempted the willingness of slave masters to let go of their slaves. Other than directly being put to work for the master, say in producing cloves and coconuts, slaves in Zanzibar could be pawned for cash or to pays debts[628] or they could be hired out by their master for wages – the employer paying half the wage to the slave and half to the master.[629]

On the other hand, were manumission to have been prevalent there would not have been a problem of runaway slaves. According to Abdulaziz Y. Lodhi, running away was especially common among plantation slaves. The problem necessitated some safeguards which included masters reporting descriptions of runaways to Government officials at the harbor and the ferrymen.[630] Those who apprehended runaways returned them to their masters for a redemption fee of one dollar per slave.[631] On being returned to their masters runaways faced severe punishment. R. G. Edib who during the late 1890s worked as Customs Master, Treasurer, Port Officer and Her Majesty's Vice-Consul in Pemba intervened in many cases of cruelty and injustice against slaves that he was nicknamed "*Rafiki ya Mtumwa*" by Sir Lloyd Mathews, Zanzibar's First Minister in the Sultan's Administration.[632] According to Edib, in some cases punishment meted by slave masters resulted in grievous physical harm. Edib notes that one male and two female slaves whom his wife was caring for in their own house at Chake Chake died from injuries sustained at the hands of their masters.[633]

In Zanzibar, one of the notorious plantations was none other than that owned by Khole, a grand-daughter of Seyyid Said. Her estate at Bungi, a few miles south of Zanzibar town, had a splendid house with a large rear enclosure that extended to the beach. Here the spinster Khole lived with her retinue of slaves. She is said to have exacted hard work on her slaves especially during the harvesting of cloves. To measure the clove buds she used a container (*pishi*) that was unusually larger and therefore took longer to fill for a normal daily wage. Khole was also rumored to be a nymphomaniac; like King Shahrayar in the *A Thousand Nights and One Night*, Khole supposedly killed her lovers after she was done with them.[634]

Be that as it may, Khole was one of those slave owners who granted their slaves freedom upon their death. As Lodhi notes, slave masters like Khole who manumitted their slaves did so for ulterior motives: "A master would grant freedom to his slaves when he, the master, had grown old and wanted to thank God and get His reward. Some masters would grant freedom before going on the pilgrimage to Mecca, or when they returned from Mecca."[635]

---

627   Lodhi, Abdulaziz, "The Institution of Slavery in Zanzibar and Pemba," research Report No. 16, The Scandinavian Institute of African Studies, Uppsala, 1973: 18.

628   Ibid. 14.

629   Ibid. 15.

630   Lodhi, "Institution of Slavery," 15.

631   Ibid. 16.

632   PRO FO 107/108 Edib vs. Anti-Slavery Committee, letter dated 15 April 1899.

633   PRO FO 107/108 Edib vs. Anti-Slavery Committee, letter dated 18 April 1899.

634   Ibid. 41.

635   Lodhi, "Institution of Slavery," 19.

As we have already noted, the reluctance on the part of many slave masters to give freedom to their slaves was because they did not want to lose a lucrative source of revenue. Resistance to the loss of slave labor was made the more obvious after the abolition of legal slavery in Zanzibar in 1890. Many slave owners either deliberately withheld information about the Decree that freed their slaves or put conditions to their release. Others found ways of taking their former slaves out of Zanzibar to Muscat, Jeddah and Mecca where they sold them again into slavery.

As the Customs and Port Officer, Edib's purview included overseeing the movement of passenger traffic out of Chake Chake's harbor. On 2 April 1898, as consular official Archdeacon J. P. Farler gave permission to a wealthy Arab man to take thirty six men and women to Muscat in a dhow under the pretence that they were his house servants. Having reason to believe that these men and women were being taken to Muscat to be ultimately sold, Edib refused to issue the Passenger Manifest. He told Farler that it seemed rather incredible that one Arab should require thirty six men and women servants to attend to him on his voyage to Muscat.[636] When the later persisted Edib went and consulted with the Vice-Consul, Dr. O'Sullivan-Beare, about the matter. The latter immediately went to the Port Office and questioned the men and women individually and separately and found out that they had been bribed by their master to accompany him to Muscat on a short visit. They appeared not to suspect any ill intentions on his part.

Claims and counter-claims of latter-day apologists and critics of the slave trade and slavery in Zanzibar have followed the same binary delineated by Ali Muhsin and Skeptic in 1937. In 1999, Isa Nasser al-Ismaily, a contemporary of Ali Muhsin, published his recollections of Zanzibar history titled *Zanzibar: Kinyang'anyiro na Utumwa*.[637] Al-Ismaily was born of Arab parents in 1927. Because of his truancy he was not able to finish secondary school. However, he later took private studies from private tutors and was given a scholarship to Cambridge University (Trinity College) where he studied law. On returning to Zanzibar he worked as *mudir*, district officer and later was promoted to administrative officer in the British Resident's Office. He was laid off by the Afro-Shirazi government after the 1964 Revolution and went into self exile in 1965, first to mainland Tanzania and in 1976 he went to live and work in Oman.

Al-Ismaily's views about the slave trade and slavery in Zanzibar were probably influenced by his being of Arab descent. He dismisses the evils of the slave trade, slavery and the role of Arabs as mere fabrications of the missionaries and those in England who wanted to abolish the slave trade. According to al-Ismaily, Arabs played a very minimal part in the slave trade; he contends that most of the slaves were brought to the coast by African chiefs in caravans:

Hakwenda Mwarabu ndani ya bara kwa kununua watumwa. Na vile vile, jingine la muhimu linalopasa kufahamika ni kwamba hiyo biashara ya utumwa waliyofanya Waarabu ilikuwa ndogo sana ukilinganisha na ile waliyofanya Wazungu. Ni kama tone la maji katika ndoo ya maji.[638]

636 PRO FO 107/108 Edib vs. the Anti-Slavery Committee, letter dated 18 April 1899.

637 Al-Ismaily, Isa bin Nasser, *Zanzibar: Kinyang'anyiro na Utumwa* (Ruwi, 1999).

638 Al-Ismaily, *Kinyang'anyiro*, 203: "No Arab went into the interior to buy slaves. It is important to know that any trading in slaves that the Arabs did was very little compared to what Europeans did. It was like a drop of water in a bucket of water."

Al-Ismaily also exonerates Islam and argues that slavery in Islamic societies was not based on color or racial distinctions; all racial groups were enslaved. More importantly, he asserts that a black or "white" person could be a master and also a slave; it all depended on circumstances and the ability to own slaves.[639] As for the evils of slavery, al-Ismaily writes: "Utaratibu wote wa utumwa kama ulivyokuwa ukifanyika huko pwani ya Afrika Mashariki na Waarabu Waswahili haukuwa wa uovu na ukhabithi katika kila mfano kama inavyodhaniwa kwa jumla."[640]

Critics of the slave trade and slavery in Zanzibar offer a different perspective. Lodhi notes that Arabs were deeply involved in the slave trade. He notes that even after the abolition of slavery Arab men in Zanzibar went to Mecca with large retinues of "servants" whom they sold in Jeddah. One informant, Sheik Ahmad Bukhari, told Lodhi that when he went to Mecca soon after World War I, more than 10 years after legal slavery had been abolished in Zanzibar, his companions on board the dhows had dozens of "servants" with them. These "servants", mostly young women, were sold secretly to merchants in Jeddah, Mecca and Medina. "It seems this was a common practice among wealthy former slave owners who, after 1897, employed their former slaves at minimal wages and continued to consider them as slaves, and the only way of selling them abroad appears to have been the pretext of going to Mecca where the "watumishi" (servants) were sold away as Khadims."[641]

Furthermore, recent research by the Zanzibar Department of Archives, Museums and Antiquities sheds more light on the cruelties perpetrated by slave masters in Zanzibar and Pemba. The Hinawy plantations in Mkoani District, Pemba, were until recently recalled as places where the mistreatment of slaves was the norm. The Hinawy family owned about 600 slaves who worked in plantations that stretched from Mgagadu to Jambangome on the western side of the island. The names of specific places on these plantations were associated with forms of punishment against runaway and unruly slaves. Ali and his son Abdulla sent runaway and unruly slaves to Mapinguni (the place of shackles), Mgononi (the fish trap) and Mashimoni (the pits) where they were subjected to horrendous forms of punishment. When their atrocious injustices came to light both were arrested and prosecuted. Ali Hinawy was deported, some of his properties were confiscated, and his victims compensated. His son Abdulla was sentenced to ten years in jail for emasculating two slaves and beating another to death.[642]

That being said, there are nineteenth century accounts by those who traded or owned slaves and Europeans who lived in Zanzibar during the slave trade which do shed light on the dynamics of slavery and what slaves went through. There are two autobiographies by persons closely involved with the slave trade and the ownership of slaves. One is by the legendary slave and ivory trader and plantation

---

639   Ibid. 257.

640   That slavery as practiced on the East African coast by the Arabs and Swahili was not evil and inhumane as is believed generally.

641   Lodhi, "Institution of Slavery," 35.

642   Zanzibar. Department of Archives, Museums and Antiquities, *Zanzibar Slave Memory* (Zanzibar: University College of Education Press, 2005): 35-37.

owner Hamed bin Muhammed al-Murjebi also known as Tippu Tip.[643] The other is by Seyyida (Princess) Salme the daughter of the founder of the Zanzibar Sultanate, Seyyid Said. It was written under her marital name, Emily Ruete.[644]

Hamed bin Muhammad al-Murjebi (hereafter referred to by his nickname Tippu Tip) was born in 1837 at Kwarara, a plantation that belonged to his mother's family, situated a few miles outside of Zanzibar town. According to Sir Charles Elliot, who was Her Majesty's Agent and Consul-General at Zanzibar from 1901 to 1902, he used to see Tippu Tip and describes him being of mixed Arab and African descent, although "the later strain showed itself markedly in his physiognomy."[645] Being darker in complexion not only made him sensitive to his appearance but, according to Leda Farrant, imbued in him an inferiority complex which made him to endeavor to distance himself from Africans: "In those days an Arab would consider it a great slight to be mistaken for an African."[646]

Melvin E. Page notes that Tippu Tip did not consider the slave trade of sufficient importance to develop a clear defense of his involvement.[647] However, Page suggests that Tippu Tip at times betrayed some uneasiness about his involvement in the slave trade because he believed it was contrary to the teachings of Islam:

> Both the Koran and hadith suggest only two ways in which an individual can become a slave: by birth in slavery or through capture in a war conducted for the furtherance of the faith. In East Africa, however, the law did not operate so strictly. As elsewhere, a liberal attitude toward commerce prevailed and some freedom of interpretation was permissible. But more importantly, local customs and contingencies were allowed to modify the law, permitting many more persons to become slaves; thus kidnapped Africans, as well as others captured in raids, were often enslaved. At the same time, more rigorous interpretations of the law applied in other spheres, especially in worship and family life.[648]

Despite the element of conflict between his involvement in the East African slave trade and the moral and spiritual teachings of his faith, Tippu Tip's deliberate amnesia about the illegality of the slave trade enabled him to harmonize the contradiction to his satisfaction.[649]

Although Tippu Tip's autobiography is silent about his involvement in the slave trade his acknowledgement that the Congolese warlord Ngongo Lutete was his slave[650] reveals his indirect involvement in the Congo and by this acknowledgement he is answerable to Lutete's slave raiding activities both before

643   Murjebi, Hamed bin Muhammed, *Maisha ya Hamed bin Muhammed El-Murjebi yaani Tippu Tip kwa maneno yake mwenyewe*, kimefasiriwa na W. H. Whitely (Kampala, Nairobi, Dar-es- Salaam: East African Literature Bureau, 1974): 21.

644   Ruete, Emily, *Memoirs of an Arabian Princess from Zanzibar* (Trenton: Markus Wiener, 1989).

645   *Preface* by Sir Charles Elliot, Heinrich Brode, *Tippu Tip: The story of his career in Zanzibar and Central Africa*, translated from the Arabic by H. Havelock (Zanzibar: Gallery Publications, 2000).

646   Farrant, Leda, *Tippu Tip and the East African Slave Trade* (London: Hamish Hamilton, 1975): xi.

647   Page, Melvin E. "Tippu Tip and the Arab 'Defense' of the East African Slave Trade," *Etudes d'Histoire africaine*, VI (1974): 105-117: 106.

648   Ibid. 107-108.

649   Page, "Tippu Tip," 108.

650   Murjebi, *Maisha ya Hamed*, 117.

and after Lutete became his own man. Lutete was acquired by Tippu Tip as a little boy. He was from the Batetela people that lived where the Lomami plunges from the high savanna plateau into the Congo equatorial forest. Before Tippu Tip freed him at the age of twenty five Lutete rose and became Tippu Tip's leading raiders who brought the most ivory and slaves back to his master. Tippu Tip was so pleased with him that he freed him and sent him home to the Lomami on condition that Lutete was to direct all the ivory and captives from the Lomami and Tshuapa basins to his strongholds at Kasongo and Nyangwe.

In the end Lutete and Tippu Tip and the Arabs at Kasongo and Nyangwe came to loggerheads. When the Belgians appeared on the scene Lutete realized he could make more profit trading ivory to them than to his former master and other Arabs at Nyangwe. When the Belgian-Arab wars started in 1892 Lutete chose to fight on the side of the Belgians and the Congo Free State. Commander Francis Dhamis' forces were reinforced by Lutete and 10,000 of his men, and together they marched on to attack the Arab stronghold at Nyangwe and prevailed over the Arabs. However, the victory closed one chapter of Tippu Tip's life and opened another. The Belgians offered him a governorship of Stanleyville which he accepted. After two years he retired to Zanzibar. By then, according to Abdul Sheriff, Tippu Tip was a man of substantial means; he had several plantations and thousands of slaves."[651]

Seyyida Salme's autobiography is a unique insider's view of life in Zanzibar in the last half of the nineteenth century, especially life in the royal palaces and relations between slaves and slave owners. She mentions two characteristics of royal palace life that are of particular interest namely, the presence of concubine-slaves and the eunuchs. Salme gives the impression that the royal concubine-slaves were a happy lot. However, as John Hunwick and Eve T. Powell aptly note it is a curious irony that the best path to an easier life for female slaves was to have their sexuality exploited and for male slaves to be deprived of their sexuality.[652]

Salme's mother, a Circassian named Jilfidan, was abducted as a little girl in the Caucasus region and was sold into slavery. She may have been about nine or ten when Seyyid Said acquired her. Subsequently Seyyid Said acquired other Circassian concubines whom Seyyida Salme mentions by name in her *Memoirs*. Their arch-rivals were the Abyssinians. In the Middle East as well as in Zanzibar the prized African concubine was the "Abyssinian" woman, because she was light-skinned, and perhaps viewed as more "Arab" than "African."[653] By the time of his death Seyyid Said had seventy five concubines!

Salme's attitude to concubinage, polygamy and the seclusion of women would have been very much unacceptable to modern-day feminists. She considered the seclusion of women an "inconvenience" that could be made bearable in time by habit.[654] More importantly, in her *Memoirs* she does not question whether an old man such as her father with so many concubines could adequately satisfy their sexual needs; instead she makes an indirect hint that he possibly did not. Salme mentions an incident whereby her father almost killed his second wife, a Persian

651   Sheriff, *Slaves, Spices & Ivory in Zanzibar*, 108.

652   Hunwick, John and Eve Trout Powell, *The African Diaspora in the Mediterranean Lands of Islam* (Princeton, NJ: Markus Wiener Publishers, 2002): 99.

653   Ibid. 114.

654   Ruete, *Memoirs*, 147.

princess named Shesade (Scheherazade). Although Salme does not explicitly say why her father almost committed murder, we can deduce that he found out he had been cuckolded.[655] We do not know whether after the incident Seyyid Said was wiser to heed the warning of the Iranian sage, Jami, who said the following about women married to older men:

> *Though her cheek be a tablet of purity, That tablet is utterly bare of the word fidelity. Who ever saw faithfulness in a woman in this world? Who ever saw anything but craftiness and treachery? ....If you are old, she must needs have another lover, A companion more vigorous than you. . . .*[656]

Seyyid Said's harem life was emulated by his affluent as well as not so affluent subjects in Zanzibar and on the mainland. Sheryl McCurdy notes that during the late 1880s, "the inner compounds of the Zanzibari traders' lodges in Ujiji [on Lake Tanganyika] housed wives, concubines, and female slaves of the domestic unit. In the lodges of Zanzibari trader Rumaliza (Mohamed bin Halfan al Barwani), the trading partner of Tippu Tip during 1889, some seventy women engaged in various domestic projects designed to keep the household running smoothly as well as to entertain guests and the wives and concubines themselves."[657] According to McCurdy, within this milieu these women had ample opportunity for the sharing of ritual practices including spirit possession, *unyago*, and dance performances.[658] What McCurdy did not consider is the possibility that they either cheated on Rumaliza or provided sexual satisfaction to one another because he was not able to. Be that as it may, before we consider tribadism between concubines let us consider sexual relations between slave masters and male slaves in nineteenth-century Zanzibar.

Although Sir Richard F. Burton's *Sotadic Zone*[659] excluded much of Africa south of the Sahara, in his book on Zanzibar which was published in 1872 he mentions that at Zanzibar the *liwat* (anal intercourse with another man) was considered a mere peccadillo despite the disapproval of the Qur'an and the displeasure of Seyyid Said.[660] Burton notes that Seyyid Said denied Muslim burial to a nephew who "died in agony after the bungling performance of an operation which his debaucheries rendered necessary, and the body was cast naked into the sea."[661] Christopher P. Rigby notes that after the death of Seyyid Said in 1856 the "vicious propensities of the Arabs" including *liwat* very much increased: "numbers of sodomites come from Muscat, and these degraded wretches openly walk about dressed in female attire, with veils on their faces."[662]

---

655   Ibid. 44.

656   Quoted by Minoo S. Southgate, "Men, Women, and Boys: Love and Sex in the Works of Sa'di," *Iranian Studies*, vol. 17, no. 4 (Autumn, 1984): 413-452: 419.

657   McCurdy, Sheryl, "Fashioning Sexuality: Desire, Manyema Ethnicity, and the Creation of the 'Kanga', ca. 1880- 1900," *The International Journal of African Historical Studies*, vol. 39, no. 3 (2006): 441-469: 461.

658   Ibid. 462.

659   Burton, Richard F. *Love, War and Fancy: The Customs and Manners of the East*, edited by Kenneth Walker (New York: Ballantine Books, 1964): 174.

660   Burton, Richard F. *Zanzibar: City, Island, and Coast*, in Two Volumes, Vol. I (London: Tinsley Brothers, 1872): 380. Burton visited Zanzibar in 1857. Besides taking note of male same-sex intercourse, Burton also noted that public prostitutes were few, and the profession ranked low because the classes upon which it depended could always afford to gratify their propensities in the slave-market.

661   Ibid. 381.

662   Rigby, Christopher P. *General Rigby, Zanzibar, and the slave trade, with journals of daughter, Mrs. E. B. Russell* (London: Allen & Unwin, 1935): 342.

If, according to Burton, *liwat* in Zanzibar was considered a mere peccadillo it means that it must have been in practice for a long time for it to be considered as such. This begs the question, was it homegrown or of alien origins?[663] According to Allen Edwardes and R. E. L. Masters, whether pederasty did or did not originate in the East is unimportant: "What the Orient did [was] to legitimatize and systematize man's other nature, which explains modern attitudes of tolerance and acceptance. . . ."[664] However, Gill Shepherd's research in Mombasa demonstrates the close connection between homosexuality and Arab immigration. Shepherd notes: "Significant for our understanding of the Swahili, homosexuality is common in the two original areas of the Arab immigrants to East Africa: Saudi Arabia and Oman. Their incorporation into Swahili life was often as superiors – traders, rulers, wealthy settlers – and their attitudes to homosexuality must have been influential."[665]

The connection between the slave trade and concubines, eunuchs and *liwat* in Zanzibar is particularly troubling because most of the victims were children who, according to Rigby, were increasingly targeted for capture. Rigby notes that although men and women continued to be captured, in some cases few but children were taken; "the reason given by the dealers being that children were driven more easily, like flocks of sheep. . . ."[666] The ages of the young captives, boys and girls, ranged from seven to eighteen years. In Zanzibar, the girls were sold at higher prices than the boys. In 1857, Burton noted that a small boy fresh from the mainland commanded $7 to $15; a girl under 7 or 8 years old, from $10 to $ 18.[667]

According to M. Haberlandt, the occurrence of what he calls contrary-sex among the African population of Zanzibar, inborn as well as acquired contrariness, was rare. It is unclear how Haberlandt was able to distinguish inborn from acquired contrariness. Be that as it may, the rarity of "congenital" homosexuality among the Central African peoples, from whom many Zanzibar slaves were drawn, was also mentioned by Dr. Oscar Baumann. In his travels he found only two cases – one in Unyamwezi (Tabora?), the other in Uganda.[668] By comparison, Haberlandt notes that the occurrence of contrary-sex was higher in other groups. He writes,

The rather high frequency in Zanzibar is doubtless attributable to the influence of Arabs, who together with Comorosans [immigrants from the Comoro Islands], and the prosperous Swahili mixed-breeds, account for the main contingent of acquired contraries. Typically engaging in sex at an early age, oversaturation soon occurs among these people, and they seek stimulation through contrary

---

663   Recent research suggests that in many parts of Africa the practice is of indigenous in origin. See, for example, Stephen O. Murray and Will Roscoe, eds. *Boy-wives and female husbands: studies in African homosexualties* (New York: St. Martin's Press, 1998).

664   Edwardes, Allen and R. E. L. Masters, *The Cradle of Erotica: A study of Afro-Asian sexual expression and analysis of erotic freedom in social relationships* (New York: The Julian Press, Inc., 1963): 206.

665   Shepherd, Gill, "Rank, gender, and homosexuality: Mombasa as a key to understanding sexual options," in Pat Caplan, ed. *The Cultural construction of sexuality* (London; New York: Tavistock Publications, 1987): 261.

666   Rigby, *General Rigby*, 130.

667   Burton, *Zanzibar*, 465.

668   Bloch, Iwan, *Anthropological Studies in the Strange Sexual Practices in all Races of the World*, translated by Keene Wallis (New York: Falstaff Press Inc., 1933): 18.

acts, in addition to normal acts. Later they lose desire for the female sex and become active pederasts... Their [love] objects belong almost exclusively to the black slave population... The adolescent slaves that are selected are kept away from any work, well pampered, and systematically effeminized (kulainishwa).[669]

Those systematically effeminized and used for too long became catamites who later turned into male prostitutes. Some of the later wore female clothing and others went about in male clothing but would wrap a cloth around the head in place of the skullcap. Many of the male prostitutes lived in Ng'ambo, a predominantly black slum area, and plied their trade very openly.[670]

Haberlandt's description of Zanzibar's male prostitutes - their mode of dress and their preference for female company - sounds akin to that of the male prostitutes of Oman known as *Xanith*. The likelihood of Arabs having introduced homosexuality in Zanzibar may be attributed to the fact that homosexuality in Middle Eastern societies by then had a longstanding tradition.[671] Joseph A. Massad notes that it was practiced in Medieval Arabia both before and after the advent of Islam.[672] One of Massad's sources, al-Munajjid's *Al-Hayah-al-Jinsiyyah*, indicates that the aristocratic and intellectual classes of the Abbasid Caliphate gained notoriety for pederasty and their preference for youthful boys. According to al-Munajjid, "Perhaps, the abundance of concubines [*jawari*] is what caused men to become averse to them, and to like youthful boys [instead]."[673]

In the Abbasid Caliphate the preference for boys had two consequences, one of which is of relevance to our discussion about sexuality and slavery in Zanzibar. On the one hand, in order for the Abbasid wives, concubines and singing girls to compete with boys for the favors of men they had to use every technique of pleasure to enchain the men. According to al-Munajjid, they perfected the art of love-making and performed sex in more than sixty different positions.[674] On the other hand, in competing with boys for the favors of men wives, concubines and singing girls were willing to offer that which men sought from boys. An anecdote cited by Khaled al-Rouayheb has it that a man who preferred *liwat* was chastised by his jealous wife who offered to give him what he liked in boys.[675] He declined on the excuse that although she had that which he wanted from boys it had an unpleasant neighbor (i.e. the vagina). Be that as it may, the willingness of the wife to engage in anal sex is known in Arabic as *istaneh* or heterosexual sodomy.

In the Middle East, the evidence of the practice of *istaneh* up to the end of the nineteenth century was the use of anal lubricants in order to render coitus easier. Arabian women commonly used olive oil as an anal lubricant. Coconut oil was also popular in some areas. To prevent anal looseness from constant sodomy Arab women anointed the anus with alum or some other astringent for the sake of tightness and tonicity.[676] We do not know how prevalent and popular *istaneh* was

669 Haberlandt Quoted by Murray, Stephen O. and Will Roscoe, eds., *Boy-wives and Female-Husbands: Studies in African Homosexualties* (New York: Palgrave, 1998): 63-64.

670 Haberlandt, 64.

671 Shepherd, Gill, "The Oman Xanith," *Man*. New Series, vol. 13, no. 4 (Dec., 1978): 663-671: 665.

672 Massad, Joseph A. *Desiring Arabs* (Chicago and London: The University of Chicago Press, 2007).

673 Quoted by Massad, *Desiring Arabs*, 108.

674 Ibid. 107.

675 El-Rouayheb, Khaled, *Before Homosexuality in the Arab-Islamic World, 1500-1800* (Chicago & London: The University of Chicago Press, 2005): 16.

676 Edwardes, *Erotica*, 220-221.

among the Arab slave owning elites in nineteenth century Zanzibar. Until further research is done we can only deduce from anecdotal evidence. During his visit to Zanzibar in 1857 Burton noticed that domestic slave girls rarely had issue. He attributed this characteristic to two factors, (a) their malignant unchastely nature, and (b) their unwillingness to become mothers.[677] According to Burton, fearing that her progeny by another slave could be sold away from her at any moment, a female slave obviated the pains and penalties of maternity by the easy process of procuring abortion.[678] Likewise, Sheryl McCurdy attributes the low fertility of Manyema slave-concubines in Ujiji and other interior Arab trade centers from the 1860s to the 1890s to abortion and infanticide as well as an anti-natal mentality caused by lack of security due to the slave trade.[679]

In the case of Zanzibar Burton did not consider other possible causes of low fertility especially anal intercourse as a means of contraception; the later was also considered by Arab men to be more pleasurable than vaginal intercourse. Our presumption about coitus interruptus is based on the following *hadith*. A man said: Apostle of Allah, I have a slave-girl and I withdraw from her (while having intercourse), and I dislike that she becomes pregnant. The Jews say that withdrawing the penis (*azl*) is burying the living girls on a small scale. He (the Prophet) said: The Jews told a lie. If Allah intends to create it, you cannot turn it away. Our presumption that Arab men in Zanzibar engaged in anal intercourse with their concubine-slaves as a means of pleasure is based on Middle Eastern literature which portrays Arabs to have been more erotophilic; their preference for anal intercourse being on account of the narrowness and greater contractile power of the sphincter compared to the vagina.

In Zanzibar, tribadism like *liwat* and *istaneh* was most likely introduced from the Middle East because it was more common there. According to al-Munajjid, during the pre-Islamic *jahiliyyah* the practice of sucking on the clitoris was common.[680] Likewise, Allen Edwardes notes, "in the restricted harem, *esh-sheykheh-el-bezzeh* (one who teaches the art of rubbing clitoris against clitoris) taught every girl in the sapphic sciences. To solace her in the long hours of desire for the male, nearly every concubine had her own private companion whom she styled *merseeneh* or *reehauneh* (myrtle) and with who she practices all the sapphic pleasures."[681] According to Haberlandt, female contrary-sex was common in nineteenth-century Zanzibar. Those so inclined either sought satisfaction with others contrarily disposed like them or sometimes with straight women who gave themselves over to it from coercion or greed. Haberlandt further explains:

> *The acts performed are: kulambana = to lick one another; kusagana = to rub the private parts up against each other; and kujitia mbo ya mpingo = to furnish oneself with an ebony penis. . . It is stick of ebony in the shape of a male member of considerable size, which is fashioned by black and Indian craftsmen for this purpose and is sold secretly. Sometimes it is made from*

---

677   Burton, *Zanzibar*, 464.

678   Ibid.

679   McCurdy, Sheryl, "Urban Threats: Manyema women, low fertility, and venereal diseases in Tanganyika, 1926-1936," in *"Wicked" women and the reconfiguration of gender in Africa*, ed. Dorothy I. Hodgson and Sheryl McCurdy (Portsmouth, NH: Heinemann, 2001): 216.

680   Quoted by Massad, *Desiring Arabs*, 106.

681   Edwardes, Allen, *The Jewel in the Lotus: A Historical Survey of the Sexual Culture of the East* (New York: The Julian Press, 1959): 255-6.

ivory. There exist two different forms. The first has below the end a nick where a cord is fastened, which one of the women ties around her middle in order to imitate the male act with the other. . . With the other form, the stick is sculpted with penis heads at both ends so that it can be inserted by both women into their vaginas, for which they assume a sitting position.[682]

Haberlandt further notes that the use of *mbo ya mpingo* was considered to be an Arabic invention.[683]

Dr. Iwan Bloch notes that sexual "aberrations" among Africans and between Africans and others in Zanzibar were not inborn but resulted from imitation and seduction. He writes:

That the tribadic practices of the Zanzibar negresses are not to be imputed to congenital homosexual predispositions is proved most strikingly by the circumstances that kulambana (cunnilingere) and kujitia mbo ya mpingo (apply the ebony penis to oneself) are mostly performed by both partners at the same time . . . If the psychology here were genuinely homosexual the 'masculine' partner would refuse this simultaneous passive role. So it is really just a matter of mutual masturbation, gratification sine vivo such as occurs in the Arabian harems where the unsatisfied women yearn in rigid seclusion.[684]

Besides using *mbo ya mpingo* and other means to satisfy their desires, a few harem residents were able to sneak out for clandestine liaisons with men like Salme did. However, this was made very difficult by the watchful presence of eunuchs. Salme mentions in her *Memoirs* that there were numerous eunuchs that attended her father's royal palaces. We learn that they provided riding lessons, served food, ran errands, accompanied the female occupants of the palaces wherever they went, and guarded the palaces. "Upper class" Arab households in Zanzibar emulated the Sultan's lifestyle and many had numerous concubines who were guarded by eunuchs. According to Farrant, an elderly eunuch was in charge of the Murjebi household when Tippu Tip was born: "He saw that everything ran smoothly and was responsible to the master for the protection of the women and punishment of the offending slaves."[685]

The presence of eunuchs in Zanzibar's "upper class" households was connected with the ongoing slave trade. Whereas young female slaves were bought and raised to be concubines, some of the young male slaves were turned into eunuchs. Farrant notes that Tippu Tip's father chose and took great care of slave boys to ensure that when he sold them they were healthy enough to survive castration. According to Farrant, the castration was done in Zanzibar or wherever the new owners took them: "The operation was not always successful and if the child did not die under the knife, he was abandoned to die crawling around the filthy streets begging for food and help."[686]

That being said, Salme's attitude and views about black Africans and their enslavement reflects the prejudices of her time, class, and cultural milieu. To

---

682   Haberlandt, 65.

683   Ibid. 65.

684   Bloch, *Anthropological Studies*, 44-45.

685   Farrant, *Tippu Tip*, 5.

686   Farrant, *Tippu Tip*, 7.

her African slaves were "great children" who needed the tutelage of their Arab masters. She also notes that slavery in Zanzibar and other Islamic countries was more benign than slavery in the New World:

One must . . . be careful not to judge slavery in the East by the same standard that is applied to slavery in the United States or in the Brazils. The slave of a Muslim is in quite a different and far superior position.

The worst features of this institution are the slave trade and the transport of these poor people from the interior of the continent to the coast. Great numbers perish of fatigue and of hunger and thirst, but all this is shared also by their leader. It is absurd to suppose that the slave traders cause these great hardships and privations on purpose; their own advantage requires to bring out the people in the best possible condition, as they have often invested their whole fortune in such an enterprise.[687]

Because she believed in the benign nature of Eastern slavery she criticized the freeing of the slaves that belonged to the British subjects who were resident in Zanzibar:

The apostles of the anti-slavery unions, after fighting hysterically for the liberty and rights of citizenship for the slave classes, disappeared on having gained their point, making no provision for their protégés than if they had been lilies of the field, except in so far – and probably to complete the grim farce – that their ladies at home sent woolen socks for the lilies on the burning soil of Africa.[688]

It is ironic that Salme criticized the British for not providing the freed slaves with the wherewithal to support them; she did not think that the plantation owners had any obligations to their freed slaves. Be that as it may, freedom without the means to support oneself was indeed tantamount to no freedom at all. This view was also aired by two Europeans who were resident in Zanzibar. These were Bishop William George Tozer and Dr. James Christie. Bishop Tozer was Bishop of Zanzibar from 1863 to 1873, the year that Sultan Barghash abolished the slave trade in the Zanzibar Sultanate. In this period he witnessed firsthand and was also told about numerous evils especially pertaining to the slave trade. What follows is gleaned from Bishop Tozer's response to the recommendations of a Commission which had been appointed in 1870 by the British Foreign Office to consider the whole question of the East African Slave Trade.

To begin with, Bishop Tozer notes that since the British commenced intercepting Arab dhows along the East African coast British men-of-war had been landing "their prize cargoes of slaves" either at Aden, Bombay, Mauritius, or Seychelles, with Aden receiving the larger number of freed slaves than either of the other depots. Bishop Tozer was alarmed at the great number of casualties at these depots. On inquiry, he found that out of 2,297 slaves landed at Aden between January, 1865, and January, 1869, the "casualties" amounted to no less than 1,046.[689] He found out that the mortality rate at Bombay was also exceptionally high while conditions at Mauritius and Seychelles left a lot to be desired. At the later places Bishop Tozer was also dismayed by the social and moral condition of

687   Ruete, *Memoirs*, 216-217.

688   Ruete, *Memoirs*, 216.

689   According to Lt. Col. Playfair, formerly Assistant Political Resident at Aden, the main cause of death was tuberculosis.

the released slaves which he describes as "very deplorable."[690]

Bishop Tozer expressed his displeasure with the rescue operation as something that could not be tolerated because it undermined the very reasons why abolition was pursued. He wrote:

> The plan of repressing the Slave Trade by capturing slaves involves some of the gravest responsibilities imaginable. I offer no opinion of my own as to whether our policy in this respect be right or wrong, but I maintain that we are bound by every principle of honour to do the best that we can for the slaves whom we separate from their Arab masters on the plea of humanity.

> ... and it is because a great nation like England cannot escape her responsibility to these people by simply shunting them out of sight at the least possible cost and trouble, and because such a policy is both short-sighted and delusive, that I feel compelled as a Christian Missionary, to enter my protest against it.[691]

Another European resident of Zanzibar who like Bishop Tozer felt compelled to enlighten the British public about the slave trade and slavery in Zanzibar was James Christie, a medical doctor by profession. Dr. Christie, by means of his very extensive medical practice among people of all classes, enjoyed rare opportunities, of which he fully availed himself, of acquiring an insight into the modes of life and prevailing ideas of all ranks from the Sultan to the slave. According to Dr. Christie, the slaves in Zanzibar had many peculiar privileges and the Arabs were by no means hard taskmasters; the slaves as a class were not exposed to wanton cruelty.[692]

Dr. Christie was ambivalent about the abolition of slave ownership by British subjects in Zanzibar. Although the 1833 Abolition of Slavery Act endeavored to free and thereby raise the slaves from the substratum of indignity, Dr. Christie notes that in Zanzibar there was no distinction between those freed by British subjects and the Arab-owned slaves. He writes:

> There should not be less than from four to five thousand negroes under the direct and immediate protection of the British Government in Zanzibar; but they do not appear as a distinct class amongst the negro population. . . . In appearance, mode of work and living, and also in regard to pay, there is no distinction whatever, and even amongst the domestic servants of Europeans, it cannot be known, except in case of special enquiry, who are slaves and who are free. . . . The slaves on an estate may be emancipated, and in the event of such an estate being transferred to another owner, who may be legally entitled to hold slaves, the freed men generally remain if they are allowed to do so under their former privileges."[693]

According to Dr. Christie, the most important privilege was the protection provided by the Arab masters.[694]

---

690   Tozer, William G. "On the Treatment of Freed Slaves," in Capt. H. A. Fraser, the Rt. Rev. Bishop Tozer and James Christie, *The East African Slave Trade and the Measures Proposed for Its Extinction, As Viewed by Residents in Zanzibar* (London: Harrison, 1871): 21.

691   Tozer, "Treatment of Freed Slaves," 26.

692   Christie, James, M.D. "Slavery in Zanzibar as it is," 47.

693   Ibid. 50-51.

694   Ibid. 52.

Dr. Christie considered the suppression of the slave trade to be a mockery if those taken off the Arab dhows were to be settled in Zanzibar; to do so was tantamount to landing the freed slaves at the very doors of their former owners.[695] The majority of the slaves rescued by the British Navy were either formerly owned by Arabs resident in Zanzibar or the mainland or had been kidnapped by northern Arabs from the same class of people.[696] However, Dr. Christie reserved his severest criticism about the abolition and rescuing of slaves from Arab dhows on the Commission's assertion that once rescued the freed slaves ought not to be a financial burden on the British Government. What he wrote is worth quoting at length:

> A few years ago, out of about seven hundred freed slaves, recently brought from the mainland, one hundred and forty-three were on my hospital list. These were all severe cases, and trifling ailments were not taken into account. Every means available were placed at my disposal for the treatment of these cases, and no expense was spared to promote the recovery of these people. They suffered from dysentery, syphilis, primary, secondary, and tertiary; malignant ulcerations of the most severe form, generally ending in death or necessitating amputation. . . . During the whole of my experience as a medical man, as house surgeon in a large general hospital and in visiting hospitals in Great Britain and the Continent, I have never seen such revolting cases of disease.

> Even to a medical man, who had gone through the routine of the dissecting-room, and as dresser in the surgical wards of an hospital, such sights were sickening. Three days ago one of the liberated slaves landed from HMS Dryad, was placed under my professional care suffering from a sloughing ulcer over the head of the femur, and nearly exposing the bone, and yet in apparently utter ignorance of the subject on which they report, the Commission say in regard to these people "that no charge for their maintenance is likely to be thrown upon the Imperial Government."[697]

"A more reckless statement was never penned," Dr. Christie concluded.[698]

Dr. Christie's description of the bodily condition of the rescued captives raises other important issues. The condition of those rescued is indicative of the newly imported slaves purchased by the Arabs for work in their houses or estates who were generally in very poor health conditions and unfit for any kind of work for months. Were they already diseased before their capture? Were they infected as they journeyed to the coast or did they get infected onboard the dhows? How were the sick and emaciated treated by the slave dealers? What happened to the captives on arrival in Zanzibar?

We still have very limited knowledge about diseases in the East African interior in the pre-colonial period. Juhani Koponen notes that no disease was reported in the first known caravan of porters from the coast to Lake Tanganyika although he cites one source which claims that out of one hundred men sent annually into the

---

695   Christie, "Slavery in Zanzibar," 54.

696   Ibid. 54.

697   Christie, "Slavery in Zanzibar," 59-60.

698   Ibid. 60.

interior in the early 1840s seldom more than twenty or thirty returned.[699] Be that as it may, the journeys to and from the interior of East and central Africa were long and hard. Food and water were barely sufficient for sustenance because on some stretches of the caravan routes they were very scarce. Likewise, starvation onboard the dhows was likely to ensue if fair winds did not prevail, especially for the slaves purchased at Kilwa for shipment to Zanzibar. It is not surprising, as Capt. H. A. Fraser noted that live skeletons in hundreds could consequently be seen landed at the Zanzibar Custom-house, "exciting neither pity nor comment among the accustomed and unsympathetic spectators."[700] According to Bishop Tozer, the British Consulate was unable to check and punish such flagrant acts of brutality as too often attended the arrival in harbor of slave dhows from Kilwa.[701]One of these brutalities was the abandonment on the waterfront of those who were too emaciated and sickly. All slave traders had to account for their human cargoes to the custom-house master commissioned by His Majesty the Sultan. The slaves were counted like cattle, and the tax was paid for each head. Instead of paying taxes for captives who arrived in a feeble state that to all appearances they had only a few days to live, the slave traders had them either thrown into the waters of the harbor or abandoned and left to die at the custom-house.[702]

Upon arrival in Zanzibar the captives went through a series of ritualized experiences. First, newly arrived captives were herded into holding pens or barracoons and fattened. Second, before they were auctioned their hair was inspected for lice and treated if necessary; they were also washed and groomed and their skin oiled. Third, they were auctioned to the highest bidder: "Savvy buyers inspected the captives for skin diseases such as yaws and leprosy. . . They examined the women for pregnancy, and fingered their vaginas to check for an abnormal discharge or to see if any were still virgins. Pregnant women and virgins cost more, as did comely women who were sold as concubines . . ."[703]

Once sold the rituals and experiences of enslavement varied according to the occupations of the slaves. In her *Memoirs* Salme notes that there were slave owners who had their young female slaves instructed in different branches of trade, such as dressmaking, embroidering, and lace-making, while the boys were employed in saddlery, carpentering, and so on: "The owners of such slaves managed thus to greatly reduce their expenditure, whilst those who were less provident gave their work out to be done, and paid heavily in proportion. . . . The slaves who had been brought up to some kind of trade were more highly valued than those who had not had this advantage. . . ."[704] For this reason, slaves were frequently sent from Zanzibar to Oman for a practical education.[705]

However, we do not know how those intended to be concubines were socialized into their role. According to Salme, those bought for the royal harem were somehow expected to simply "fit into" the harem's social milieu; those who did not

699   Koponen, Juhani, "War, Famine, and Pestilence in Late Pre-colonial Tanzania: A Case for a Heightened Mortality," *The International Journal of African Historical Studies*, vol. 21, no. 4 (1988): 637-676: 656.

700   Capt. Fraser, H. A. "Zanzibar and the Slave Trade," 10.

701   Tozer, "Treatment of Freed Slaves," 26.

702   Berlioux, Etienne F. *The Slave Trade in Africa in 1872: Principally Carried on for the Supply of Turkey, Egypt, Persia and Zanzibar* (London: Frank Cass & Co. Ltd., 1971): 59.

703   Liebowitz, Daniel, *The Physician and the Slave Trade: John Kirk, the Livingstone Expeditions, and the Crusade Against the Slave Trade in East Africa* (New York: W. H. Freeman & Co., 1999): 28.

704   Ruete, *Memoirs*, 81.

705   Ibid. 82.

were liable to be treated with hostility.[706] Those who were younger were adopted as playmates by some of Seyyid Said's daughters. Together with them she was, in her young mind, brought up as a member of the family until she was mature enough to render sexual service to the Sultan whom they had grown looking up to as a father. It is not hard to imagine how traumatizing this transition must have been.

Those who ended on the plantations were usually handed over to older slaves to be taught the necessary skills to survive their new environment. They were also allocated a piece of land to raise their own food. Most if not all slaves eventually converted to Islam, a process that first and foremost involved changing their names after proclaiming the *shahada*. This experience was similar to that of slaves in the Americas where the slaves were given baptized and given Christian names. As Orlando Patterson aptly notes, the changing of a name was a symbolic act of stripping the slave of his former identity.[707] Today in Zanzibar, one's name indicates either their slave ancestry or their Arab descent.

By and large, although captivity and slavery involved a lot of physical suffering, castration and sexual abuse caused psychological trauma which was far worse than whipping or toiling on the plantation. It is unfortunate that those who directly experienced the slave trade and slavery in Zanzibar did not leave personal accounts of their experiences and feelings about being captured and sold into slavery. However, even without such firsthand narratives about slavery we can still deduce their feelings about being sexually abused, treated like animals and made to feel inferior vis-à-vis their slave masters. Anger and a sense of deep hopelessness are two examples that come to mind.

It is of great significance to underscore the fact that Zanzibar slavery was based on the twin pillars of African racial and cultural inferiority. As was the case in the trans-Atlantic slave trade, African racial and cultural inferiority were used by the Arabs in Zanzibar to rationalize and justify the enslavement of black Africans. Even after the slaves converted to Islam such conversion did not elevate them to equal status with their masters even though Islam enjoined such equally before Allah. Did this transgression weigh heavily on the slave masters? It must have if we assume most of them believed they were good folks or pretended to be good Muslims.

According to Joy DeGruy Leary, instances of particularly egregious negative acts like wars of aggression, enslavement and genocide produce deep seated feelings of guilt because the perpetrators believe they are good, decent folks. The feelings of guilt result in discomfort which she has labeled as cognitive dissonance.[708] Leary writes: "Humans do not particularly like this discomfort so whenever it occurs we almost immediately try to resolve it. And we can resolve it one of two ways. One way is to own up to the negative act and address the harm caused by it. The other way is to justify the negative act rather than admit any wrongdoing."[709]

It is difficult to determine whether descendants of slave owners in Oman and Zanzibar harbored deep seated feelings of guilt about the slave trade and slavery. What we know is that they endeavored to excuse Arab ownership of slaves and

706   Ibid. 36.

707   Patterson, Orlando, *Slavery and Social Death: A Comparative Study* (Cambridge, MA: Harvard University Press, 1982): 55.

708   Leary, Joy D. *Post Traumatic Slave Syndrome: America's Legacy of Enduring Injury and Healing* (Milwaukie, OR: Uptone Press, 2005): 54.

709   Leary, *Slave Syndrome*, 54.

the inequalities that slavery bequeathed to Zanzibar society. Be that as it may, the history of slavery and Arab dominance in Zanzibar is a tale of unrequited injustice; innocent Africans were enslaved, economically and sexually exploited, and some castrated, and no recompense was ever made to the victims or their descendants.

As they say, historical injustices cast a long shadow. From the abolition of slavery in 1890 until 1964 the victims of slavery and their descendants were subject to discrimination and second class citizenship. According to Ali Muhsin, mainlanders who failed to "acclimatize" to Zanzibari culture were considered foreigners even if they had lived in Zanzibar for 50 or more years.[710] As Glassman has noted, the insinuation that mainlanders were aliens was imbued with the old language of slavery and as such aroused deep resentments.[711] Slave-baiting by the Zanzibar Nationalist Party led by Ali Muhsin not only aroused deep resentments among Zanzibaris of African descent but created a fertile climate for violent vengeance as will be demonstrated in chapter eleven.

Finally, throughout the colonial period the discourse on slavery never shifted from the domain of rhetoric about emancipation to the domain of social, economic and human rights of the former slaves and their descendants. Land ownership remained in the hands of non-African landlords and as Zanzibar transitioned toward independence land ownership increasingly became a very brittle issue. One of the consequences of the 1964 Zanzibar Revolution was the expropriation of the minority landlords whose estates were redistributed to their former tenants. According to Salmin Amour, between 1964 and 1974 about seventy-two landowners were expropriated of their plantations and an estimated 66,753 acres of land distributed to about 22,251 families.[712]

---

710 Zanzibar Protectorate, Commission of Inquiry into the Civil Disturbances on 1 June, 1961 and Succeeding Days, vol. 11, Eleventh Day, Friday 6, October, 1961.

711   Glassman, Jonathon, *War of Words, War of Stones: Racial Thought and Violence in Colonial Zanzibar* (Bloomington and Indianapolis: Indiana University Press, 2011): 156.

712   Quoted by Tambila, K. I. "Aspects of the Political Economy of Unguja and Pemba," in T. L. Maliyamkono, Ed. *The Political Plight of Zanzibar* (Dar-es-Salaam: Tema Publishers Co. Ltd., 2000): 81.

11

The Pitfalls of a Nascent Democracy: Political agitation, violence and murder after the June 1961 election in Zanzibar

Introduction

On Thursday, 1 June 1961, voting took place to elect 23 members of the Legislative Council in the British Protectorate of Zanzibar. In the morning of that day, while voting was in progress, disturbances broke out in Zanzibar town, spread to the rural areas of the island on 2 June, and continued, mainly in the central and northern areas of Zanzibar, until the security forces gained control of the situation on 8 June. As a result of these disturbances sixty eight people were killed and 381 injured. Many of those killed were 'Manga' Arabs[713] living in rural areas of Zanzibar Island.

On 8 September, 1961, the British Resident, Sir George Mooring, appointed a Commission of Inquiry, with the following terms of reference: "To inquire into and report upon the civil disturbances which occurred in Zanzibar on the first day of June, 1961, and succeeding days, including their causes and development and the

---

713   There were three main groups of Arabs in Zanzibar namely those who had lived there for many generations (many of whom were big land-owners); those who came down with the monsoon each year from Oman, some of whom settled as traders (these were known as Wamanga, pl.); those who came from the Hadhramaut who usually became engaged in urban trades (these were known as Washihiri, pl.).

steps taken to deal with them."[714] The Commission of Inquiry was composed of Sir Stafford Foster-Sutton, legal counsel and chairman, Sir Vincent Tewson and Caryll Archibald Grossmith, Esquire, commissioners. Assisting the Commission were P. N. Dalton (Zanzibar Attorney General), B. A. G. Target and W. Dourado (Crown Counsels), Fraser-Murray and S. H. M. Kanji (Counsels for the Zanzibar Nationalist Party), K. S. Talati and B. E. Kwaw-Swanzy (Counsels for the Afro-Shirazi Party).

Political Background to the Disturbances of June 1961

The single most important feature of Zanzibar's struggle against British colonial rule was the failure of anti-colonial nationalism to unify the population. Despite widespread antipathy toward British rule and a common desire to attain self-government, the struggle for independence was not a unifying force but instead was accompanied by a radical breakdown of the social order.[715] The breakdown was the result of (a) suspicions and fears by both the African majority and the Arab minority in Zanzibar should full political power devolve to the other, and (b) politics of identity which pitted citizens versus foreigners.

The British policy in Zanzibar was to devolve full political power into local hands. The question was into whose hands would full political power eventually devolve? As we shall see later, this question was at the heart of colonial Zanzibar's fractious politics. As Michael Lofchie notes: "The presence of three rival nationalist parties, each drawing its support from different communal segments of the population dramatize[d] the fact that the nationalistic consensus [had] not served to forge the bonds of solidarity among Zanzibaris."[716]

Prior to 1961, there had been only two serious disturbances in Zanzibar. The first happened in 1936 when 'Manga' Arabs violently protested against the Government's regulation of copra prices. The second, popularly known as *Vita vya Ng'ombe*, happened in 1951 following the imprisonment of some African cattle owners who had refused to have their cattle inoculated against anthrax. The consequences of these earlier disturbances were not as serious as those that were triggered off by electoral politics beginning in 1957 when provision was made, for the first time, for elections to be held throughout Zanzibar and Pemba on a common roll. Six of the twelve seats in the Legislative Council previously held by nominated unofficial members were to be filled by elected members: two were to be elected for Zanzibar Town, two for the rural districts of Zanzibar, and two for Pemba.

The first elections took place in July 1957. Five seats were won by Afro-Shirazi candidates, and one by an Independent candidate who supported the Afro-Shirazi Party (hereafter ASP). The Zanzibar Nationalist Party (hereafter ZNP) candidates were resoundingly defeated. The leaders of the two parties, Ali Muhsin Barwani, ZNP, and Abeid Amani Karume, ASP, opposed each other in the Ng'ambo constituency of Zanzibar, and Barwani was defeated by 3,328 votes to 918.

The turnout in the 1957 election (87 per cent of the registered electors voted) and the fact that the voting was conducted peacefully was indicative of the people's

---

714   Great Britain, *Report of a Commission of Inquiry into the Disturbances in Zanzibar during June 1961* (London: Her Majesty's Stationery Office, 1961): 1.

715   Lofchie, Michael F. *Zanzibar: Background to Revolution* (Princeton, NJ.: Princeton University Press, 1965): 69.

716   Lofchie, Michael F. "Party Conflict in Zanzibar," *The Journal of Modern African Studies*, vol. 1, no. 2 (Jun., 1963): 185-207: 188.

interest in the democratic process initiated by the British Administration. However, the results of the elections triggered off acrimonious bickering between the two rival parties whose functionaries succeeded in working up the political temperature which, by August, 1958, reached such heights, and bitterness, that it was considered by the Administration that a mere spark would produce a conflagration.[717]

To reduce tension, the Civil Secretary, P. A. P. Robertson, arranged a series of meetings between the leaders of the opposing political parties, popularly known as the "Round Table Conference." Although there was a lessening of tension, albeit on the surface, deep in the fabric of Zanzibari society friction continued to exist. Other developments, especially the activities of the Youths' Own Union, the youth branch of the ZNP, raised the Administration's concerns. It was reported that members of the Youths' Own Union were drilling and training in political uniforms in what was described as a military manner. On occasions they were observed to be usurping the functions of the police. Likewise, the members of the ASP Youth League were said to be a constant source of trouble to the police.[718]

To reinforce security, the Administration amended the Penal Code making the carrying of offensive weapons, besettling and intimidation, offences, and in April 1959, the Public Order Decree was passed, making it an offence, inter alia, to usurp the functions of the police, and to enable the Resident in Council, by order, to prohibit the wearing of political uniforms.

However, party politics in Zanzibar took a sudden turn towards the end of 1959 when three of the elected members broke away from the Afro-Shirazi Party and formed the Zanzibar and Pemba Peoples' Party (hereafter ZPPP). The formation of the ZPPP triggered an increase in political activity. Public meetings were increasingly characterized by vitriolic speeches against opponents. The ZNP claimed that the ASP speeches were racial in character and expressed disloyalty to Zanzibar's Sultan. The ASP countered with allegations that the speeches by the ZNP leaders were abusive and insulting.

When the newly appointed Resident Sir George Mooring arrived in Zanzibar in January, 1960, he immediately endeavored to defuse the tension by initiating discussions about constitutional progress with the leaders of the political parties. His endeavor, for a time, had the desired effect of reducing the tension between political parties to the extent that a second election was scheduled to take place in July, 1960.

Moreover, the proposed July, 1960, election had to be postponed pending further discussions and recommendations by Sir Hilary Blood, who was appointed Constitutional Commissioner and arrived in Zanzibar in April, 1960. He immediately proceeded to his task, reporting on 28 May, 1960. His recommendations, known as the "Blood Report", were generally accepted as the basis for constitutional advance by the ASP, but were rejected, and publicly burnt, by the ZNP.

Furthermore, the political climate in Zanzibar took a turn for the worse. By July, 1960, the tone of the Press, and political speeches, was so vitriolic that the British Resident decided it was necessary to call together the party leaders to discuss the volatile situation and, after prolonged discussion, they all agreed to sign a joint declaration, calling upon their members to cool their tempers and to behave with

---

717   Great Britain, *Report of Commission of Inquiry*, 2.

718   Ibid. 3.

"traditional good humor and politeness." From then on the situation improved again and attention was focused on the next general election, which was proposed to take place in January 1961.

Before the January 1961 election the franchise was extended to women and the age limit was reduced from 25 years to 21 years. Consequently, the number of people entitled to register to vote almost trebled the number of registered voters for the 1957 election, from 39,833 to 94,310. The general election duly took place in January 1961. However, unlike in 1957 in the January 1961 election the fortunes of the ZNP changed to the extent that it won nine of the twenty-two seats. The ASP won ten seats and the remaining three seats went to the ZPPP.

Due to the virtual tie between the ASP and the ZNP, neither could form a government unless it could command a majority of the elected members. The two parties negotiated with the three ZPPP members to this end. However, after prolonged bargaining two members undertook to support the ZNP and one undertook to support the ASP. As both parties could not form a government agreement between them was reached to form a coalition to act as a caretaker Government with the Civil Secretary as Chief Minister, on the understanding that a further election would be held as early as possible.

The fact that the ZNP had increased its representation from nil in the 1957 election to nine elected members Party in the January, 1961, general election came as a considerable shock to the leaders of the ASP and its supporters. This shocking success led to a genuinely held belief that there must have been some fraud, such as double counting, impersonation, and other election offences. Being convinced of this the ASP determined to watch the situation very closely in the forthcoming June election, and to make it their business to ensure that no "cheating" took place.

As a means of reducing the possibility of the deadlock that occurred in January, the number of elected seats was increased to 23 by dividing the original two Southern Pemba constituencies of Kengeja and Mkoani into three, namely, Kengeja, Mkoani and Mtambile. The election duly took place on 1 June, 1961. The turnout was extremely high. Of the 94,218 registered voters, 90,595 recorded their votes, representing a poll of 96.15 per cent. Both the ZNP and the ASP won ten seats and the ZPPP won three seats. The ZNP and the ZPPP formed a coalition and were able to form a Government. Both the outcome of the election and the formation of a coalition Government were unacceptable to the ASP leadership and their supporters. The results of the election appeared to confirm the ASP suspicion of fraud which was the cause of the disturbances that erupted early in the morning on 1 June, as the voters in the Raha Leo constituency queued to vote.

The sequence of the events of 1 - 8 June, 1961[719]

Although Thursday 1 June, 1961, began with a reasonably tranquil atmosphere the day quickly turned into a nightmare that would last for eight days. By 7:45 a.m. trouble at Gulioni (Raha Leo constituency) was reported to the police. An Arab member of the ZNP was pulled out of the voting queue because he was allegedly not entitled to vote there. By 8:14 a.m. a disorderly crowd had gathered outside the

---

719   The sequence of events outlined in this section is summarized from: Great Britain, *Report of the Commission of Inquiry into Disturbances in Zanzibar during June 1961* (London: Her Majesty's Stationery Office, 1961): 8-13.

polling station and extra constables had to be sent. They were reinforced by a party of twenty-five other constables at 8:43 a.m. Within a very short time reports were received of disorders at the Civic Center Polling Station at Raha Leo, at Kisiwandui School in the Darajani constituency, and the Trade School and Holmwood School Polling Stations at Jang'ombe. In each of these cases the cause of the disturbance was similar, namely, the seizure, assault, and removal from the voting queue of individual members of the ZNP, by supporters of the ASP. This behavior derived from a suspicion, firmly held by members of the ASP, that the ZNP had prepared a campaign of "vote stealing" involving impersonation and double-voting.

Because of rumor that Arabs were being assaulted by Africans a party of Arabs armed with sticks was reported at about 10 a.m. to be headed towards Darajani, and that a truck full of "Manga" Arabs, armed with sticks, had been stopped in Hollis Road. Meanwhile at Darajani it had become necessary for the police to resort to tear-gas to disperse an unruly crowd, composed mainly of ASP supporters, from the precincts of the polling station.

The appearance of vehicles containing members of the militant ZNP Youths' Own Union in the vicinity of the trouble spots heightened suspicion among ASP supporters. Other developments exacerbated the situation. At 11 a.m. the ZNP decided to withdraw from the election at Raha Leo and Jang'ombe, on grounds that their supporters were being intimidated and prevented from voting. The ZNP leaders then instructed their supporters to rally to their party Headquarters at Darajani with the object, so it was alleged, of giving moral support to their members wishing to vote at the nearby Darajani Polling Stations. With the assembling of the crowd of ZNP supporters at their headquarters, some armed with sticks and some with knives or swords, the situation deteriorated.

When the ASP supporters at the Darajani polling stations saw the armed crowd of ZNP supporters they rushed to piles of firewood which were lying near at hand (in the adjoining market) and armed themselves with these, and also gathered up stones from the piles of coral which were lying nearby. Stoning from both parties ensued and the police took up a position between them in an endeavor to restore order. At the time the police at Darajani numbered fifty. At 12:34 p.m. the Superintendent of Police considered the situation so serious that he decided to read the Riot Act, and the police eventually succeeded in dispersing the crowds which numbered many hundreds.

The crowds moved away in the direction of Mtendeni, Msufini and Mwembeladu, and there is evidence that at this time ASP supporters were assaulted by ZNP supporters from neighborhood shops and offices; many were dragged off their bicycles and beaten up. Soon rumor spread about Africans being killed by Arabs, and was responsible for much of the violence in the next eight days.

On 2 June, reports of trouble in some rural areas such as Chwaka, Bambi, Ndagaa and Kitope Ndani were received. The extension of disorder to the rural areas called for the reinforcement of security. The British Resident arranged with the Chief of Staff, Nairobi, for the dispatch of a Company of the King's African Rifles to be sent. The troops arrived in Zanzibar at 7:30 a.m. on 3, June. Later in the day it was determined that further reinforcement was necessary. Another company of the King's African Rifles was sent from Nairobi and reached Zanzibar at 12:30 p.m. According to the Commission of Inquiry, 3 June was undoubtedly the worst day of the disturbances. Thirty-two persons were killed. Early in the day there was a report that Arabs were chasing Africans in the center of Ng'ambo, a predominantly African squatter community.

On the morning of 4 June, all was quiet in Zanzibar Town. However, looting and violence were reported in other areas such Mwembeladu, Kizimkazi, and at Mwembetanga. During the day nine Arabs were killed, and two Africans and five Arabs were admitted at hospital seriously injured. To further reinforce security two more companies of the African King's Rifles were sent from Kenya late on 4 June and early in the morning on 5, June. With the arrival of these further units it was considered that there were then enough troops in Zanzibar Island to regain control of the situation in the rural areas.

On 5 June, trouble involving armed Makonde, Africans originating from then Portuguese East Africa (Mozambique), in the area of Tunguu. At Kazole a crowd of 30 to 50 of Makonde men armed with spears, machetes, knobkerries and other weapons, was encountered by the Commissioner of Police. They were breaking into a shop. After shots were fired by the Commissioner the crowd dispersed. Some were subsequently taken prisoner by a patrol of the King's African Rifles. Murders were also committed in this area. The number killed and injured on 5 June, throughout the Island, was given as one African and five Arabs killed, two Africans and one Arab admitted to hospital seriously injured.

Although a further number of isolated incidents occurred between 6 and 8 June, the deployment of forces in the rural areas of Zanzibar appeared to have brought the situation under complete control. Altogether, the casualties between 1 and 8 June were 68 deaths (64 Arabs, 3 Africans and 1 other); 290 casualties treated as out-patients (144 Africans, 137 Arabs and 9 others); seriously injured and admitted to hospital were 91 persons (39 Africans, 51 Arabs and 1 other).

According to the Commission of Inquiry, the preponderance of Arabs killed was due to the fact that most of those killed were "Manga" Arabs who by virtue of their occupation as small traders lived in rural areas and among predominantly African communities. As the Commission put it:

Manga Arabs have inherited the reputation gained by their race (sic) in events of which the riot in Zanzibar in the year 1936 is not the only instance, and have consequently come to be regarded...as the 'bogeymen' of Zanzibar. The circumstances tended...to focus attention upon them when hysteria replaced reason. Moreover, the extent to which the element of, what many have regarded as an opportunity for, 'paying off old scores', should not be underestimated.[720]

Be that as it may, the Commission of Inquiry concluded that the number of "Manga" Arabs who lost their lives should not be interpreted as necessarily indicating the extent of racial antagonism between "Africans" and "Arabs". Neither was the Commission of Inquiry convinced that the disturbances were in any sense the result of any premeditated plot by any person, group of persons, or political party. These conclusions require further examination especially in the context of the economic, political and racial dynamics of Zanzibar as a multi-racial society whose majority of the people (Africans) until 1963 lived under the double-yoke of Arab and British imperialism. The African sense of experiencing a double-yoke of Arab and British imperialism is explored in detail below.

720   Great Britain, *Report of Commission of Inquiry*, 13.

Factors Contributing to Tension in Zanzibar

The violence and the murders of 1 – 8 June, 1961, were the result of short-term as well as long-term dynamics of a unique colonial state. By 1961 people of Arab descent still constituted a very small minority of Zanzibar's population. Besides the Busaid royal family, Arab immigrants from Oman, Yemen and Hadhramaut had preserved for themselves a privileged position by monopolizing access to the institutions of the Sultanate Government, especially the judiciary and civil service. Of particular significance, as Lofchie aptly points out, the descendants of the early Arab migrants formed a self-regenerating elite group:

> *Their decisive advantages in wealth and style of life enable[d] the younger generation to achieve superior education and thereby to qualify more easily for the highest positions in government and commerce . . . In this way, and through nepotism, favoritism, and other forms of preferential treatment, they monopolize[d] the strategic sectors of the administration and retain[ed] firm control over the entire state apparatus, the educational system and the clove industry.[721]*

This privileged position enabled them to enjoy a larger representation in the Legislative Council and other governing bodies until the election of 1957.

Before 1957 members of the Zanzibar Legislative Council were nominated by the British Resident. However, Britain's decision to grant its African colonies independence entailed the need to also introduce their colonial subjects to some elements of democracy, including the election of representatives in colonial legislatures. Early in 1957 provision was made, for the first time, for elections to be held throughout Zanzibar and Pemba on a common roll. The franchise was then limited to males of not less than 25 years of age who were required to have certain other qualifications, the principal one being Zanzibar citizenship.[722]

In the meantime, the first political party in Zanzibar, Hizbu l'Watan l'Raia Sultan Zanzibar, was formed in 1955. Renamed Zanzibar Nationalist Party, it became the vanguard of nationalism led by Zanzibaris of Arab descent. At this juncture it is pertinent to consider why Zanzibaris of Arab descent seized the moment to be in the forefront of contemporary Zanzibar nationalism. According to Lofchie, Arabs in Zanzibar did not become nationalists because they were disenfranchised or discriminated against but rather because they realized that as a minority they were at risk of losing to the African majority in a democratically self-governing State.[723]

To pre-empt the risk of losing out to the African majority, the leadership of the ZNP endeavored to attract as many African supporters as they could and to divide the ranks of ASP which was formed only a few months before the 1957 elections. The ZNP main strategy was to (a) to pre-empt mainland African influences by appealing to Zanzibar citizenship and cultural "exceptionalism", (b) to use Islam and religious unity as rallying points, and (c) to oppose the politicization of racial

---

721   Lofchie, M. "Zanzibar," in Coleman, James S. and Carl G. Rosberg, eds. *Political Parties and National Integration in Tropical Africa* (Berkeley and Los Angeles: University of California Press, 1966): 482-3.

722   Great Britain, *Report of Commission of Inquiry*, 2.

723   Lofchie, "Zanzibar," 483.

identity.[724] The leader of the ZNP, Ali Muhsin, actually petitioned the British Resident to make it an election offence to campaign on racial grounds, and he later blamed the Government for having failed to do so.[725]

According to the Commission of Inquiry that investigated the disturbances of June 1961, the election of 1957 was the beginning of a social revolution in Zanzibar: "The fact that that election resulted in a resounding defeat of the ZNP, with the resultant disappointment to its supporters, no doubt contributed to the rise in the political temperature which from then onwards began to gain momentum."[726] From the beginning, the momentum of Zanzibar's nascent democracy spelt doom. The use of inflammatory and immoderate language at political rallies by the ZNP and ASP leaders obviously had a more direct impact on the raising of the political temperature in Zanzibar from 1957 to 1961 and beyond.

The first signs of trouble occurred soon after the 1957 election. In March 1958, there were cases of Arab landlords, supporters of the ZNP, who brought pressure to bear on their African squatters to support the ZNP. Those who declined to fall in with their landlords' wishes were turned off their land without compensation.[727] Another cause of these evictions was an irresponsible speech made by an ASP cadre sometime in or about March, 1958, that intimated that the land the squatters worked on did not belong to the landlords, that they only owned the trees. Evidently, the speech greatly angered the landlords. The situation became so serious that the Administration issued a communiqué setting out the legal position of squatters in relation to their landlords; numerous meetings in the rural areas were organized at which the position was explained, and arrangements for the assessment of compensation for evicted squatters were made.

Another incident which was politically motivated occurred in September, 1958. The incident involved an attempt to replace mainland African dock laborers with *Wachukuzi wa Kienyeji* or native-born casual laborers. The Commission of Inquiry which looked into the dispute determined that the "true predominant motive" of the captains and owners of the dhows and schooners was not the furtherance of their own genuine interests in a trade dispute, but sprang from a dislike of the political and alleged racial origins of the trade unionists and was intended by them as a mere demonstration of their power to prevent certain persons from the free and lawful exercise of their callings.[728]

Besides the above short-term causes of conflict, long term causes of tension in Zanzibar included differences in ideology and political agendas between the ASP and ZNP. The ZNP, asserted Karume, was capitalistic, wealthy and Arab; the ASP was for the working people, the Africans[729] From its very inception, the ZNP endeavored to portray itself as a loyalist party. The use by the ZNP of the Sultan's Flag at its meetings, and the fact that the band formed by its youth movement frequently

---

724   The opposition to racialized politics was obviously prompted by the name Afro-Shirazi Party. However, its Constitution permitted persons of any race to be members of the party.

725   Great Britain, *Report of Commission of Inquiry*, 16.

726   Great Britain, *Report of Commission of Inquiry*, 13.

727   The ASP organized a resettlement scheme with the object of helping some of their evicted supporters.

728   Zanzibar Protectorate, *Report of the Arbitrator to Enquire into the Trade Dispute at the Wharf area at Zanzibar*, by Sir John M. Gray (Zanzibar: Government Printer, 1959): 11.

729   Campbell, Jane, "Multiracialism and Politics in Zanzibar," *Political Science Quarterly*, vol. 77, no. 1 (Mar., 1962): 72-87: 80.

arranged to be present at functions attended by the Sultan, were intended to create the impression that the ZNP alone was the loyal party.

More importantly, the ZNP presented itself as a non-racial and purely nationalistic party. The leadership of the ZNP appealed to Zanzibar's cultural exceptionalism versus the dangers of foreign cultural influences. Of particular significance were concerns by the Arab minority that people who were not Zanzibar citizens would influence the outcome of the nationalist struggle against the British. Arab anxieties were succinctly expressed by Hamyan Khalfan Nassor, Secretary of the Arab Association in Pemba as follows:

> We in this country have our tradition that we cherish. Our loyalty to the throne [Sultan] is very great, and we have many other traditions which have been handed to us from generation to generation. To give a chance to half-baked immigrants [Africans] to have any say in our political life is only to disrupt our heritage.[730]

However, for Ali Muhsin unlimited immigration from the mainland was also unacceptable for economic reasons. When he was asked by the Commission of Inquiry about immigration, Ali Muhsin had this to say:

> You see, the difficulty is these are two islands with very limited potentialities. They can only absorb a certain number of people. At the same time we have been trying to rid this country, even in the past, with racial representation in the Legislative Council, of racial representation; but people have been living quite amicably. . . Now in order to maintain that, with the new feelings of racial hatred that have been engendered in other parts of Africa, I think it is imperative that Zanzibar should be safeguarded against that infiltration, the infiltration of disruptive elements; and this was the thing, or one of the things, which started this idea of the Nationalist Party being formed; that is to prevent ideas which started in South Africa, went to Kenya and might come to Zanzibar, which are becoming more or less universal in East and Central Africa – racial feelings, and so on. Another thing is, as I said at the beginning, our economic potentialities are limited: there has been here a good deal of under-employment, and the tendency has been for the rich people, the Indian merchants and the Arab landowners, building contractors and so on, to prefer cheap labour from the mainland, to bring it here to the detriment of the indigenous workers of Zanzibar. This has been the tendency. I am not quite sure, but I think the 1948 Census, which was on tribal lines, gave the number of mainland Africans in Zanzibar as over 40,000. That is a large number in relation to a total population of 300,000.[731]

As far as Ali Muhsin was concerned, it was fair to remove "foreigners" from jobs that Zanzibaris wanted; that this was the policy of both His Highness' Government and that of the ZNP.[732] As Ali Muhsin put it, this was not something out of the ordinary:

> It has happened in any country where the locals have to take jobs which have

---

730   Quoted by Campbell, "Multiracialism," 73.

731   Zanzibar Protectorate, *Commission of Inquiry into the Civil Disturbances on 1 June, 1961, and Succeeding Days*, vol. 10, Tenth Day, Thursday, 5 October, 1961: 105-6.

732   Zanzibar Protectorate, *Commission of Inquiry into the Civil Disturbances on 1 June, 1961, and Succeeding Days*, vol. 11, Eleventh Day, Friday, 6 October, 1961: 98.

been taken by others. The Government can press it within the Government service, but members of the public are justified in doing the same for other jobs where a local man of equal qualifications – or at least one who can cope with the work even if the qualifications are a bit lower – his duty is to take it.[733]

Ali Muhsin's position makes explicit the intent of his editorial in *Mwongozi* of 9 December, 1960, in which he made the clarion call, "Zanzibar for the Zanzibaris." According to Kwaw-Swanzy, such editorials and ZNP speeches which raised issues of immigration and unemployment contributed to the incitement of a segment of Zanzibar community who were led to believe mainland African immigrants were the cause of their unemployment.[734]

Ali Muhsin was not equally fearful about the influx of immigrants from the Comoro Islands, Hadhramaut or Oman. He did not think that immigrants from these places were susceptible to causing disturbances like the immigrants from the mainland. Yet there was incontrovertible evidence that "Manga" Arabs were the one group of immigrants that had caused more disturbances in Zanzibar than the others. Kwaw-Swanzy noted that "Manga" Arabs were involved in communal violence in 1928 and in 1936; the later riots led to the murder of a British officer.[735]

Furthermore, vitriolic speeches by ZNP leaders contributed to the incitement of their supporters. Not only were leaders of the ASP subjected to ridicule and name calling,[736] in some of their speeches the ZNP leaders called for violence. Abeid Karume testified before the Commission of Inquiry that at a ZNP rally which he attended sometime in May 1961, Ahmed Seif Kharusi exhorted ZNP supporters that as "respectable people" it would be a shame to be ruled by one from Wanyamwezi and Wandengereko. Kharusi further said: "We must do everything we can even by shedding blood; we must rule ourselves rather than be ruled by Wanyamwezi and others."[737] At the same rally, Ali Muhsin is said to have said: "We will not agree; we will not agree to be [738]under these mainlanders like, for example, this Manjo. It is better we should shed blood. I ask you members of the Nationalist Party, do you agree to be ruled by Manjo?" The audience answered, "No, we do not" three times. Ali Muhsin continued: "Are you ready to shed blood in order not to be ruled by Manjo?" and the audience replied that they agreed to shed blood.[739]

The ASP, on the other hand, used African identity as an ideological weapon against the threat of Arab domination posed by the ZNP.[740] As Lofchie notes, "The ASP's campaign was based largely upon establishing an identity between the ZNP and the Arab oligarchy. This idea appeared in one form or another in the great majority of ASP speeches, and there were very few ASP meetings at which the term ZNP was not used as a synonym for Arab political domination."[741]

The ASP's loyalty to the Sultan was questionable. According to Seif Sharif

---

733   Ibid.

734   Ibid. 101.

735   Zanzibar Protectorate, *Commission of Inquiry*, vol. 11, 6 October, 1961: 66.

736   Karume was referred to as "boat boy" "Mnyamwezi", and "Manjo".

737   Zanzibar Protectorate, *Commission of Inquiry into the Civil Disturbances on 1 June, 1961 and Succeeding Days*, vol. 12, Twelfth Day, Saturday, 7 October, 1961: 57.

738   Ibid.

739   Ibid.

740   Lofchie, *Zanzibar*, 169.

741   Ibid. 208.

Hamad, in the late 1950s Karume said in one of his public rallies that if the ASP won the elections, the party would make Zanzibar a republic.[742] When the Sultan heard this he invited Karume to his palace and entertained him and, in passing, asked him about his statement. Supposedly, Karume said, "My lord, what I meant was, in having a republic we should continue with the wise leadership of you, our sultan." Seyyid Khalifa answered, "Yes, I know. You are my son."[743] Whether Karume meant what he said and how he felt about the Sultan's paternalism only he knew.

Other long-term causes of tension in Zanzibar were the legacies of slavery, Arab racism, and miscegenation. According to Lofchie, the real emotional force which animated electoral politics in Zanzibar was not the mere possibility that a racial oligarchy would preserve itself but the historical association between Arab rule and slavery.[744] Likewise, Haroub Othman notes that behind the façade of Zanzibar as a place where different races lived together in peace and harmony was racial inequality and animosity based on a system of absolute Arab superiority and African inferiority.[745]

The ASP's resentment and fear of Arab domination was exacerbated by the unrepentant attitudes about slavery by Ali Muhsin and others who were of Arab-descent. They either endeavored to minimize Arab involvement in it or the numbers of African slaves that were exported to the Middle East. They also argued that slavery and the trade in slaves had nothing to do with Islam. However, while it may be true that Islam as religion had nothing to do with the origins of human trafficking in the region it did recognize the right of possessing slaves as well as taking into marriage or concubines those whose right hands possessed.[746]

Transition to independence and the position of the Sultan and his Dynasty

From the seventeenth century onwards, East Africa and especially Zanzibar was a terrain for Arab exploitation, control, and influence. Beginning with the Ya'ariba dynasty in the seventeenth century and the early years of the Busaid dynasty, Oman and Muscat rulers claimed that they were the rulers of the East African coast. According to Ross and Holtzappel, the Omanis actually conquered Zanzibar around 1700[747] and their conquest further opened Zanzibar to Arab immigration. By the end of the eighteenth century Zanzibar was inhabited by three ethnic groups, namely, the Arabs, the "Moors" and the "Swahili". The "Moors" and "Swahili" were considered to be in opposition to the ruling Arabs, "who possessed the force to control the island, but who were thought of as parasites, sucking out the wealth of the island and repatriating it to Muscat."[748]

The ascendancy of Arab dominance in Zanzibar coincided with the political

742   Burgess, G. Thomas, *Race, Revolution, and the Struggle for Human Rights in Zanzibar: The memoirs of Ali Sultan Issa and Seif Sharif Hamad* (Athens: Ohio University Press, 2009): 182.

743   Ibid. 183.

744   Lofchie, *Zanzibar*, 209.

745   Othman, Haroub, *Zanzibar's Political History: The past haunting the present?* Center for Development Research, Denmark, Working Paper No. 93.8, October 1993: 5.

746   See Qur'an chapters 2: 177, 178; 4: 25, 36; 8: 67 – 71; 24: 33; 33: 26.

747   Ross, Robert and Fk. G. Holtzappel, "The Dutch on the Swahili Coast, 1776-1778: Two Slaving Journals, Part I, *The International Journal of African Historical Studies*, vol. 19, no. 2 (1986): 305-360: 318.

748   Ibid. 322.

career of Seyyid Said bin Sultan. Seyyid Said, who came to power in Muscat in 1804, did not move his capital to Zanzibar until 1840. The transfer of his capital was, according to Calvin H. Allen, the result of Seyyid Said's reconsidering of his policies in the Arabian Gulf after experiencing setbacks in his endeavor to control the Straits of Hurmuz: "Obviously, Said felt that Muscat had few prospects without control of the Gulf, and given the absence of control, it was preferable to abandon the port in favor of East Africa."[749] Be that as it may, Seyyid Said's transfer of his capital was the beginning of an Arab dynasty at Zanzibar whose latest representative was still sitting on the throne as Zanzibar erupted in violence in June 1961.

Between 1840 and 1961, Zanzibar was ruled by ten sultans if we exclude Khalid bin Barghash who usurped the throne for three days in August 1896. Omani rule and the dominance of the Arab minority in Zanzibar affairs in this period can be compared to Dutch and British rule and the dominance of the European minority in South Africa especially during the years of apartheid. In both cases we have a minority wielding political power, exploiting the majority black population, and using racial or cultural ideology to justify their dominance and exploitation.

The extension of Dutch and later British power in South Africa began in 1652. By the 1950s the institutionalization of racism was further consolidated by the policies of apartheid. The African majority was by then not only racially discriminated but was politically marginalized. Hence for the African National Congress (ANC) the struggle for freedom was also a struggle against white racial discrimination. Likewise, by mid-1961 the result of many years of racial discrimination and political marginalization of the African majority in Zanzibar was a climate in which those of Arab descent were increasingly made to feel unwelcome in the adopted home.[750]

In Zanzibar, the period of one hundred and twenty-one years of rule Omani rule was not enough to make the occupant of the throne in 1961 feel that the monarchy was secure. Communication between the British Government and the Sultan, Abdulla bin Khalifa, about the possibility of the United Kingdom making financial provision for the Sultan in the event of his having to abdicate or being deposed suggests that there was unease regarding his future in an independent Zanzibar.

On the one hand, the British found themselves in a bind after encouraging the development of democracy in Zanzibar. Clause IV of the 1890 Agreement which turned Zanzibar into a British Protectorate guaranteed on behalf of the United Kingdom the maintenance of His Highness the Sultan of Zanzibar's throne to himself and also to his successors.[751] Clause IV was no doubt designed to meet the circumstances of some other person laying claim to, or attempting to seize, the throne. It goes without saying that in 1890 neither Seyyid Ali nor the United Kingdom visualized the possibility of Zanzibar emerging into independence as a democratic country.[752]

In international law there is an exception to the rule that treaties cannot be dissolved by the withdrawal of one of the parties without the consent of the other. This exception is that a vital change of circumstances may be of such a kind as to justify a party in demanding to be released from the obligations of a treaty. Had the

749   Allen, Calvin H. "The State of Masqat in the Gulf and East Africa, 1785-1829," *International Journal of Middle East Studies*, vol. 14, no. 2 (May, 1982): 117-127: 124.

750   Gilbert, Erik, "Coastal East Africa and the Western Indian Ocean: Long-Distance Trade, Empire, Migration, and Regional Unity, 1750-1970," *The History Teacher*, vol. 36, no. 1 (Nov., 2002): 7-34: 29.

751   PRO CO 822/1891 Position of the Sultan in an Independent Zanzibar, minute by Mr. Perrott dated 8 November 1962.

752   Ibid.

British made a case that there had indeed been such a vital change of circumstances since Clause IV of the 1890 Agreement was drawn up as to absolve the United Kingdom from the obligations imposed by Clause IV, a counter argument could have been made by the Sultan that Britain was responsible for making conditions so impossible for him that he had no option but to abdicate. Moreover, since there was no time limit to the treaty of 1890 the intervening event of independence did not affect British obligations under Clause IV. Therefore, it was in Britain's interest to ensure that the Sultan stayed on the throne after independence. Failure to do so would require the disbursement of substantial sums of money annually to support the Sultan and his family. The obligation would not continue beyond the lifetime of the incumbent Sultan.[753]

The view was expressed in some circles and was strongly supported by the British Resident that the Sultan, if presented with the alternatives of abdicating with an assured financial position or of staying on in Zanzibar with an uncertain future, would choose the former course. However, the terms of such financial support were not to be left open to misrepresentation by him or his family at a later stage. In short, the Sultan was to be given sufficient assurance for him to be able to continue as Sultan in Zanzibar confident in the knowledge that if things went seriously wrong in the islands his future was safeguarded.[754]

Meanwhile, British efforts to ensure the continuity of the monarchy in Zanzibar included their endeavor to secure the affirmation of the opposition parties at the 1962 Lancaster Conference of their loyalty to the Sultan and the continuity of the dynasty. In Zanzibar, the leadership of the ZNP turned out to be ardent campaigners in favor of the continuity of the Omani dynasty and champions of multiracialism; the later was intended to pre-empt interracial animosity which had led to bloodshed in neighboring Kenya during the Mau Mau Emergency.

Ali Muhsin's apprehension about racialism in Zanzibar was based on the same understanding as that of the British Resident, Sir George Mooring, which was that the divisions which led to the disturbances of June 1961 were racial, social and economic. Sir George Mooring for his part was convinced that the advance to early independence depended on the formation of a Coalition Government of the two major parties. In his view, if Zanzibar were to attain independence under the ZNP-ZPPP Government, or under a Government led by the ASP, disorders which would probably be accompanied by great loss of life would follow when British control over the internal security was relinquished.[755]

---

753   PRO CO 822/1891 Position of the Sultan in an Independent Zanzibar, J. C. Morgan to A. W. Taylor, Secret Memorandum dated 20 February, 1962.

754   Ibid.

755   PRO CO 822/1891, "Constitutional Development in Zanzibar."

Selected Bibliography

Al-Azmeh, Aziz, "Barbarians in Arab Eyes," Past & Present, No. 134 (Feb., 1992): 3-18.

Al-Ismaily, Isa bin Nasser, Zanzibar: Kinyang'anyiro na Utumwa (Ruwi, 1999).

Al-Kawthari, Muhammad Adam, Birth Control and Abortion in Islam (Santa Barbara, CA: White Thread Press, 2006).

Allen, Calvin H. "The State of Masqat in the Gulf and East Africa, 1785-1829," International Journal of Middle East Studies, vol. 14, no. 2 (May, 1982): 117-127.

Allott, Anthony, The Limits of Law (London: Butterworths, 1980).

Alpers, Edward A. Ivory and slaves: changing pattern of international trade in East central Africa to the late nineteenth century (Berkeley: University of California Press, 1975).

Arhem, Kaj, Maasai and the State: The Impact of Rural Development Policies on a Pastoral People in Tanzania, IWGIA Document (Copenhagen, 1985).

Armour, Charles, "The BBC and the Development of Broadcasting in British Colonial Africa 1946-1956", African Affairs, vol. 83, no. 332 (1984).

Balibar, Etienne, "Is There a 'Neo-Racism'?" in Etienne Balibar and Immanuel Wallerstein, Race, Nation, Class (London; New York: Verso, 1991).

Beachey, R.W. "The East African ivory trade in the nineteenth-century," Journal of African History, vol. VIII, 2 (1967): 269-290.

Beinart, William, "Empire, Hunting and Ecological Change in Southern and Central Africa," Past & Present, No. 128 (Aug., 1990): 162-186.

Berlioux, Etienne F. The Slave Trade in Africa in 1872: Principally carried on for the supply of Turkey, Egypt, Persia and Zanzibar (London: Frank Cass & Co. Ltd., 1971).

Bloch, Iwan, Anthropological Studies in the Strange Sexual Practices in all Races of the World, translated by Keene Wallis (New York: Falstaff Press Inc., 1933).

Brode, Heinrich, Tippu Tip: The story of his career in Zanzibar and Central Africa, Translated from the Arabic by H. Havelock (Zanzibar: Gallery Publications, 2000).

Bulpin, T. V. The Hunter is Death (Long Beach, CA: Safari Press, 1987).

Burgess, G. Thomas, Race, Revolution, and the Struggle for Human Rights in Zanzibar: The memoirs of Ali

Sultan Issa and Seif Sharif Hamad (Athens: Ohio University Press, 2009).

Burton, Richard F. Love, War and Fancy: The Customs and Manners of the East, edited by Kenneth Walker (New York: Ballantine Books, 1964): 174.

Burton, Richard F. Zanzibar: City, Island, and Coast, in 2 Volumes, Vol. I (London: Tinsley Brothers, 1872).

Campbell, Jane, "Multiracialism and Politics in Zanzibar," Political Science Quarterly, vol. 77, no. 1 (Mar., 1962): 72-87.

Carstairs, C. Y. "The Colonial Cinema," Corona, vol. 5, no. 2 (1953).

Cave, Basil S. "The End of Slavery in Zanzibar and British East Africa," Journal of the Royal African Society, vol. 9, no. 33 (Oct., 1909): 20-33.

Chafetz, Morris, Liquor: the servant of Man (Boston, Toronto: Little, Brown and Co., 1965).

Chipungu, S.N. ed. Guardians in Their Time: Experiences of Zambians under colonial rule (Macmillan, 1992).

Christopher, A.J. Colonial Africa (London: Croom Helm; Totowa, NJ: Barnes & Noble Books, 1984).

Clark, J. Desmond, Quoted by Doran H. Ross, "Elephant the Animal and its ivory in African culture," African Arts, vol. 25, no. 4 (Oct., 1992): 65-108.

Classen, Constance, Aroma: the cultural history of smell (London: Routledge, 1994).

Contini, Paolo, "The Evolution of Blood-Money for Homicide in Somalia," Journal of African Law, vol. 15, no. 1, (Spring 1971).

Cooper, Frederick, Plantation slavery on the east coast of Africa (Portsmouth, N.H.: Heinemann, 1977, 1997).

Coupland, Roland, East Africa and Its Invaders: From the earliest times to the death of Seyyid Said in 1856 (New York: Russell & Russell, Inc., 1965).

Cresswell- George, E. V. H. "The Truth about the Lupa: Reply to Geneva Criticisms," East Africa and Rhodesia, 7 October, 1937.

Crozier, Anna, "What is tropical about Tropical Neurasthenia? The utility of the diagnosis in the management of British East Africa," Journal of the history of medicine and allied sciences, vol. 64, issue 4 (2009): 518-548.

Culpin, Millais, "An Examination of Tropical Neurasthenia," Proceedings of the Royal Society of Medicine (February 2, 1933): 47-58: 47.

Davis, J. Merle, "The Cinema and Missions in Africa," International Review of Missions, vol. XXV, no. 99 (July, 1936).

Diawara, Manthia, African Cinema: Politics and culture (Bloomington, IN: Indiana University Press, 1992).

Edwardes, Allen, The Jewel in the Lotus: A Historical Survey of the Sexual Culture of the East (New York: The Julian Press, 1959): 255-6.

Edwardes, Allen and R. E. L. Masters, The Cradle of Erotica: A study of Afro-Asian sexual expression and analysis of erotic freedom in social relationships (New York: The Julian Press, Inc., 1963).

El-Rouayheb, Khaled, Before Homosexuality in the Arab-Islamic World, 1500-1800 (Chicago & London: The University of Chicago Press, 2005).

Farrant, Leda, Tippu Tip and the East African Slave Trade (London: Hamish Hamilton, 1975).

Farwell, Byron, Burton: A biography of Sir Richard Francis Burton (New York: Holt, Rinehart and Winston, 1963).

Feierman, Steven, Peasant Intellectuals: anthropology and history in Tanzania (Madison: The University of Wisconsin Press, 1990).

Ford, Dan, Pappy: The Life of John Ford (Englewood Cliffs, NJ: Prentice-Hall, Inc., 1979).

Fortie, Marius, Black and Beautiful: A life in Safari land (Indianapolis & New York: The Dobbs-Merrill Co. Publishers, 1938).

Gardner, Ava, Ava: My Story (New York/Toronto/London/Sydney/Auckland: Bantam Books, 1990).

Giblin, James L. The Politics of Environmental Control in Northeastern Tanzania, 1840-1940 (Philadelphia: University of Pennsylvania Press, 1992).

Giblin, James L. A history of the excluded: making family a refuge from state (Oxford: James Currey; Dar-es-Salaam: Mkuki na Nyota; Athens, OH: Ohio University Press, 2005).

Gilbert, Erik, "Coastal East Africa and the Western Indian Ocean: Long-Distance Trade, Empire, Migration, and Regional Unity, 1750-1970," The History Teacher, vol. 36, no. 1 (Nov., 2002): 7-34.

Glassman, Jonathon, War of Words, War of Stones: Racial Thought and Violence in Colonial Zanzibar (Bloomington and Indianapolis: Indiana University Press, 2011).

Grandmaison, Colette Le Cour, "Rich Cousins, Poor Cousins: Hidden Stratification among Omani Arabs in Eastern Africa," Africa: Journal of the International African Institute, vol. 59, no. 2, Social Stratification in Swahili Society (1989): 176-184.

Gray, John M. "Memoirs of an Arabian Princess," Tanganyika Notes and Records, vol. 37 (1955): 49-70.

Great Britain, Report of a Commission of Inquiry into the Disturbances in Zanzibar during June 1961 (London: Her Majesty's Stationery Office, 1961).

Harris, Tim, Donkey's Gratitude: twenty-years in the growth of a new African nation – Tanzania (Edinburgh: The Pentland Press Ltd., 1992).

Harris, Warren G. Clark Gable: A Biography (New York: Harmony Books, 2002).

Harrison, Brian H. Drink and the Victorians: the temperance question in England, 1815-1872 (Pittsburgh: University of Pittsburgh Press, 1971).

Homewood, K.M. and W. A. Rodgers, Maasailand Ecology (Cambridge: Cambridge University Press, 1991).

Huber, H. Marriage and the Family in rural Bukwaya, Tanzania (Frisbourg: The University Press, 1973).

Hungwe, Kedmon, "Southern Rhodesian Propaganda and educational Films for Peasant Farmers, 1948-1955," Historical Journal of Film, Radio and Television, vol. 11, no. 3 (1991).

Hunwick, John and Eve Trout Powell, The African Diaspora in the Mediterranean Lands of Islam (Princeton, NJ: Markus Wiener Publishers, 2002).

Iliffe, John, "The Age of Improvement and Differentiation," in Isaria N. Kimambo and A.J. Temu, eds. A History of Tanzania (Nairobi: East African Publishing House, 1969).

Iliffe, John, A Modern History of Tanganyika (Cambridge: Cambridge University Press, 1979).

Jackson, Louise A. Child Sexual Abuse in Victorian England (London and New York: Routledge, 2000).

Jacobus X, Untrodden fields of anthropology, 2 volumes, vol. 1 (New York: Falstaff Press Inc., 1937).

Jeffries, Charles, The Colonial Police (London: Max Parrish, 1952).

Johnston, Erika, The Other Side of Kilimanjaro (London: Johnson, 1971).

Kjekshus, Helge, Ecology Control and Economic Development in East African History: The case of Tanganyika, 1850-1950 (London: Heinemann, 1977).

Knowlton, Richard and Virginia Berridge, "Constructive imperialism and sobriety: Evidence of alcoholism among candidates for the British Colonial Service from 1898-1904," Drug: education, prevention and policy, vol. 15, no. 5 (October 2008): 439-450.

Koponen, Juhani, "War, Famine, and Pestilence in Late Pre-colonial Tanzania: A Case for a Heightened Mortality," The International Journal of African Historical Studies, vol. 21, no. 4 (1988): 637-676.

Krafft-Ebing, Richard von, "From Psychopathia Sexualis: A Medico- Forensic Study," In Regina Barreca, ed., Desire and Imagination: classic essays in sexuality (Harmondsworth, England: Meridian, 1995).

Kusimba, Chapurukha M. The Rise and Fall of Swahili States (Walnut, CA.: Altamira Press, 1999).

Lasswell, Harold D. "The Structure and Function of Communication in Society" in The Communication of Ideas: a series of addresses, edited by Lyman Bryson (New York, 1948).

Latham, Gwynneth and Michael Latham, Kilimanjaro Tales: The Saga of a Medical Family in Africa (London: New York: The Radcliffe Press, 1995).

Leary, Joy D. Post Traumatic Slave Syndrome: America's Legacy of Enduring Injury and Healing (Milwaukie, OR: Uptone Press, 2005).

Liebowitz, Daniel, The Physician and the Slave Trade: John Kirk, the Livingstone Expeditions, and the Crusade Against the Slave Trade in East Africa (New York: W. H. Freeman & Co., 1999).

Lodhi, Abdulaziz, "The Institution of Slavery in Zanzibar and Pemba," Research report No. 16, The Scandinavian Institute of African Studies, Uppsala, 1973.

Lofchie, Michael F. "Party Conflict in Zanzibar," The Journal of Modern African Studies, vol. 1, no. 2 (Jun., 1963): 185-207.

Lofchie, Michael F. Zanzibar: Background to Revolution (Princeton, NJ.: Princeton University Press, 1965).

Lofchie, M. "Zanzibar," in James S. Coleman and Carl G. Rosberg, eds., Political Parties and National

Integration in Tropical Africa (Berkeley and Los Angeles: University of California Press, 1966).

Lotz, Roy E. Crime and the American Press (Praeger, 1991).

Macoun, Michael J. Wrong place, right time: Policing the end of Empire (London; New York: The Radcliffe Press, 1996).

Maguire, R.A. "The Masai Penal Code", Journal of the Royal African Society (October 1928): 12-18.

Malkmus, Lizbeth and Roy Armes, Arab and African Film Making, (London: Zed Books Ltd., 1991).

Mamdani, M. Citizen and Subject: Contemporary Africa and the Legacy of late Colonialism (Princeton, NJ: Princeton University Press, 1996).

Marcus, Steven, The other Victorians: a study of sexuality and pornography in mid-nineteenth-century England (New York: Norton, 1985, 1966).

Marwa, Sebastiani M. Mashujaa wa Tanzania: Mtemi Makongoro wa Ikizu (Peramiho: Benedictine Publications, 1988).

Massad, Joseph A. Desiring Arabs (Chicago and London: The University of Chicago Press, 2007).

Mayne, Robert Gray, An Expository Lexicon of the Terms, Ancient and Modern, in Medical and General Science (London: John Churchill, 1860).

McCurdy, Sheryl, "Urban Threats: Manyema women, low fertility, and venereal diseases in Tanganyika, 1926-1936," in "Wicked" women and the reconfiguration of gender in Africa, ed. Dorothy l. Hodgson and Sheryl McCurdy (Portsmouth, NH: Heinemann, 2001).

McCurdy, Sheryl, "Fashioning Sexuality: Desire, Manyema Ethnicity, and the Creation of the 'Kanga', ca. 1880-1900," The International Journal of African Historical Studies, vol. 39, no. 3 (2006): 441-469.

McKinley, E. H. The Lure of Africa (Indianapolis: Indiana University Press, 1974).

Middleton, John, Land Tenure in Zanzibar (London: Her Majesty's Stationery Office, 1961).

Moggi, Franz, Jeannette Brodbeck and Hans-Peter Hirsbrunner, "Therapist-Patient Sexual Involvement: Risk Factors and Consequences," Clinical Psychology and Psychotherapy, 7 (2000): 54-60.

Morris, H.F. "The Award of Blood Money in East African Manslaughter Cases", Journal of African Law, vol. 18, no. 1 (Spring 1974).

Murjebi, Hamed bin Muhammed, Maisha ya Hamed bin Muhammed El-Murjebi yaani Tippu Tip kwa maneno yake mwenyewe, kimefasiriwa na W. H. Whitely (Kampala, Nairobi, Dar-es- Salaam: East African Literature Bureau, 1974).

Murray, Stephen O. and Will Roscoe, eds. Boy-wives and female husbands: studies in African homosexualties (New York: St. Martin's Press, 1998).

Mytton, Graham, Mass Communication in Africa (Edward Arnold, 1983).

Ndagala, Daniel K. Territory, Pastoralists, and Livestock: Resource Control among the Kisongo Maasai (Uppsala, 1992).

Notcutt, L. A. and G. C. Latham, The African and the Cinema: An account of the work of the Bantu Educational Cinema Experiment during the period March 1935 to May 1937 (London: The Edinburgh House Press, 1937).

Othman, Haroub, Zanzibar's Political History: The past haunting the present? Center for Development

Research, Denmark, Working Paper No. 93.8, October 1993.

Page, Melvin E. "Tippu Tip and the Arab 'Defense' of the East African Slave Trade," Etudes d'Histoire africaine, VI (1974): 105-117.

Paneth, Donald, "Sensationalism", Encyclopedia of American Journalism. New York: Facts on File, 1983.

Patterson, Orlando, Slavery and Social Death: A Comparative Study (Cambridge, MA: Harvard University Press, 1982).

Peters, Rudolf and Gert J. J. de Vries, "Apostasy in Islam," Die Welt des Islams, vol. XVII, no. 1-4 (1976-77): 1-25.

Pope-Hennessy, James, Lord Crewe (London: Constable, 1955).

Quinault, Roland, "Gladstone and Slavery," The Historical Journal, vol. 52, no. 2 (2009): 383-383.

Rahman, S. A. Punishment of Apostasy in Islam (Lahore: Institute of Islamic Culture, 1972).

Ranger, T. and O. Vaughan, eds. Legitimacy and the Twentieth-Century Africa: Essays in honor of A.H.M. Kirk-Greene (The Macmillan Press Ltd., 1993).

Rawnsley, Gary D. Radio Diplomacy and Propaganda: The BBC and VOA in International Politics, 1956-64 (Macmillan Press Ltd., 1996).

Read, David, Barefoot over the Serengeti (London: Cassell, 1979).

Rigby, Christopher P. General Rigby, Zanzibar, and the slave trade, with journals of daughter, Mrs. E. B. Russell (London: Allen & Unwin, 1935).

Rigby, P. Persistent Pastoralists (London: Zed, 1985).

Roberts, A. D. "The Gold Boom of the 1930s in Eastern Africa," African Affairs, vol. 85, no. 341 (Oct., 1986): 545 - 562.

Ross, Robert and Fk. G. Holtzappel, "The Dutch on the Swahili Coast, 1776-1778: Two Slaving Journals, Part I," The International Journal of African Historical Studies, vol. 19, no. 2 (1986): 305-360.

Ruete, Emily, Memoirs of an Arabian princess from Zanzibar (New York: Markus Wiener Publishing: 1989).

Ruiggi, Suzanne, "Commodifying Honor in Female Sexuality: Honor killings in Palestine," Middle East Report, no. 206, Power and Sexuality in the Middle East (Spring, 1998): 12-15.

Rushby, George G. No More the Tusker (London: W. H. Allen, 1965).

Said-Ruete, Rudolf, Said bin Sultan: Ruler of Oman and Zanzibar (London: Alexander-Ouseley Ltd., 1929).

Savage, Gail, "The willful communication of a loathsome disease: Marital conflict and venereal disease in Victorian England," Victorian Studies (Autumn, 1990): 35-54.

Schneider, Harold K. "Male-Female Conflict and Lion Men of Singida," in African Religious Groups and Beliefs: Papers in Honor of William R. Bascom, edited by Simon Ottenberg (Meerut, India: Archana Publications for Folklore Institute, 1982).

Scott, Ayman, "Print the Legend": The Life and Times of John Ford (New York: Simon & Schuster, 1999).

Shao, Ibrahim F. The Political Economy of land Reform in Zanzibar: Before and After the Revolution (Dare-es-Salaam: Dar-es-Salaam University Press, 1992).

Shepherd, Gill, "The Oman Xanith," Man. New Series, vol. 13, no. 4 (Dec., 1978): 663-671.

Shepherd, Gill, "Rank, gender, and homosexuality: Mombasa as a key to understanding sexual options," in Pat Caplan, ed. The cultural construction of sexuality (London; New York: Tavistock Publications, 1987).

Sheriff, Abdul, Slaves, spices, & ivory in Zanzibar: integration of an East African commercial empire into the world economy, 1770-1873 (London: J. Currey; Athens: Ohio University Press, 1987).

Shiman, Lillian L. Crusade against Drink in Victorian England (New York: St. Martin's Press, 1988).

Smith, Russell G. Medical Discipline: The professional conduct jurisdiction of the General Medical Council, 1858-1990 (Oxford: Clarendon Press, 1994).

Smyth, Rosaleen, "The Development of British Colonial Film Policy, 1927-1939, with special reference to East and Central Africa," Journal of African History, vol. 20, no. 3 (1979): 437-450.

Smyth, Rosaleen, "Movies and Mandarins: The Official Film and British Colonial Africa," in British Cinema History, James Curran and Vincent Porter, eds., (Totowa, NJ: Barnes and Noble Books, n.d.).

Smyth, Rosaleen, "The British Colonial Film Unit and Sub-Saharan Africa," Historical Journal of Film, Radio and Television, vol. 8 (1988).

Smyth, Rosaleen, "The Feature Film in Tanzania," African Affairs, vol. 88, no. 352 (July, 1989).

Smyth, Rosaleen, "The Post-War Career of the Colonial Film Unit in Africa," Historical Journal of Film, Radio and Television, vol. 12, no. 2 (1992): 163-177.

Southgate, Minoo S. "Men, Women, and Boys: Love and Sex in the Works of Sa'di," Iranian Studies, vol. 17, no. 4 (Autumn, 1984): 413-452: 419.

Ssali, Mike H. "The Development and Role of an African Film Industry in East Africa with special reference to Tanzania, 1922-1984," PhD dissertation, University of California at Los Angeles, 1988.

Steinhart, E. I. "Hunters, Poachers and Gamekeepers: Towards a Social History of Hunting in Colonial Kenya," The Journal of African History, vol. 30, no. 2 (1989): 247-264.

Tambila, K. I. "Aspects of the Political Economy of Unguja and Pemba," in T. L. Maliyamkono, ed. The

Political Plight of Zanzibar (Dar-es-Salaam: Tema Publishers Co. Ltd., 2000).

Taylor, Richard, Film Propaganda: Soviet Russia and Nazi Germany (London: Croom Helm, 1979).

Thompson, Dudley, From Kingston to Kenya: the making of a Pan-Africanist Lawyer (Dover, Massachusetts: The Majority Press, 1993).

Tidrick, Kathryn, "Masai and their Masters: A Psychological Study of District Administration," African Studies Review, vol. 23, no. 1 (April, 1980):

Tozer, William G. "On the Treatment of Freed Slaves," in Capt. H. A. Fraser, the Rt. Rev. Bishop Tozer and James Christie, The East African Slave Trade and the Measures Proposed for Its Extinction, As Viewed by Residents in Zanzibar (London: Harrison, 1871).

Ukadike, N. Frank, Black African Cinema (Berkeley: University of California Press, 1994).

Van Donzel, E. An Arabian princess between Two Worlds: Memoirs, letters home, sequels to memoirs, Syrian customs and usages by Seyyida Salme/Emily Ruete (Leiden: E. J. Brill, 1993).

Vassallo, S. M. "Tropical Neurasthenia: Its possible relationship to hyperthyroidism," Transactions of the Royal Society of Tropical Medicine and Hygiene, vol. XXVII, no. 6 (May, 1934): 625-627.

Vaughan, J. Koyinde, "Africa and the Cinema," in Langston Hughes, ed., An African Treasury (New York: Crown Publishers, Inc., 1960).

Wallerstein, Immanuel, "Africa in a Capitalist World," Issue: A Journal of Opinion, vol. 10, no. ½, Tenth Anniversary Number (Spring-Summer, 1980): 24-25.

Washburn, Philo C. Broadcasting Propaganda: International Radio Broadcasting and the Construction of Political Reality (Praeger: Westport, Connecticut, London, 1992).

Williams, J. Grenfell "Broadcasting in the African Colonies", BBC Quarterly, 6, 4 (Winter 1951-52).

Zaffiro, J. "Twin Births: African Nationalism and Government Information Management in The Bechuanaland Protectorate, 1957-1966", The International Journal of African Historical Studies, vol. 22, no. 1 (1989): 51-77.

Zanzibar Protectorate, Report of the Arbitrator to Enquire into the Trade Dispute at the Wharf area at Zanzibar, by Sir John M. Gray (Zanzibar: Government Printer, 1959).

Zanzibar Protectorate, Commission of Inquiry into the Civil Disturbances on 1 June, 1961, and Succeeding Days, vol. 10, Tenth Day, Thursday, 5 October, 1961.

Zanzibar Protectorate, Commission of Inquiry into the Civil Disturbances on 1 June, 1961, and Succeeding Days, vol. 11, Eleventh Day, Friday, 6 October, 1961.

Zanzibar Protectorate, Commission of Inquiry into the Civil Disturbances on 1 June, 1961 and Succeeding Days, vol. 12, Twelfth Day, Saturday, 7 October, 1961.

CPSIA information can be obtained at www.ICGtesting.com
Printed in the USA
BVOW01s0320301013

334962BV00002B/81/P